Creating Comics

BLOOMSBURY WRITERS' GUIDES AND ANTHOLOGIES

Bloomsbury Writers' Guides and Anthologies offer established and aspiring creative writers an introduction to the art and craft of writing in a variety of forms, from poetry to environmental and nature writing. Each books is part craft-guide with writing prompts and exercises, and part anthology, with relevant works by major authors.

Series Editors:

Sean Prentiss, Vermont College of Fine Arts, USA

Joe Wilkins, Linfield College, USA

Titles in the Series:

Environmental and Nature Writing, Sean Prentiss and Joe Wilkins

Poetry, Amorak Huey and W. Todd Kaneko

Short-Form Creative Writing, H. K. Hummel and Stephanie Lennox

Forthcoming Titles:

Advanced Creative Nonfiction, Sean Prentiss and Jessica Hendry Nelson

The Art and Craft of Stories from Asia, Xu Xi and Robin Hemley

Fantasy Fiction, Jennifer Pullen

Advanced Fiction, Amy E. Weldon

Creating Comics

A Writer's and Artist's Guide and Anthology

Chris Gavaler and Leigh Ann Beavers

BLOOMSBURY
NEW DELHI • LONDON • OXFORD • NEW YORK • SYDNEY

BLOOMSBURY INDIA
Bloomsbury Publishing India Pvt. Ltd
Second Floor, LSC Building No. 4, DDA Complex, Pocket C-6&7,
Vasant Kunj, New Delhi 110070

First published in India 2025
First published in Great Britain 2021

Cover design: Namkwan Cho
Cover image © Chris Gavaler

This edition published with permission from Bloomsbury Publishing Plc,
50 Bedford Square, London, WC1B3DP, UK

A catalogue record for this book is available from the British Library.
A catalog record for this book is available from the Library of Congress.

ISBN: 978-93-61316-64-7

Series: Bloomsbury Writer's Guides and Anthologies

Typeset by RefineCatch Ltd, Bungay, Suffolk
Printed in India by Manipal Technologies Limited, Manipal

To find out more about our authors and books
visit www.bloomsbury.com and sign up for our newsletters

CONTENTS

ILLUSTRATIONS

Please note that uncaptioned illustrations do not appear in this list.

ACKNOWLEDGEMENTS

Creating Comics grew from our Making Comics course at W&L University. It would not exist without our students:

Spring 2016: Anthonia Adams, Andrew Baca, William Chiropolos, Perry Clements, Lindsay George, MC Greenleaf, Rachel Hicks, Tan Hunjan, Emily Kochard, Iman Messado, Emma Nash, Brianna Osaseri, Brittany Osaseri, Abby Pannell, Iggy Plato, and Hayley Price.

Spring 2018: Hung Chu, Maddie Geno, Henry Luzzatto, Anna Nelson, Daisy Norwood-Kelly, Katie Paton, Mims Reynolds, Coleman Richard, Grace Roquemore, and Emily Tucker.

The student illustrations in *Creating Comics* come from the second class. Portions of chapters two, chapter four, and the introduction were originally published in different form as "Clarifying Closure" in the *Journal of Graphic Novels and Comics* in 2018, "Undemocratic Layout: Eight Methods of Accenting Images" in *The Comics Grid* in 2018, and as "Teaching the Art of Comics" translated into Italian in *Innovative Teaching Experiments: Sociology Through Pop Culture* in 2020.

We would also like to thank the W&L Lenfest Program and the Provost's office for their generous support.

Permissions

Street Ballet IV, New York, NY (2016) and *Street Ballet XIII, Houston, TX* (2018), copyright © Elizabeth Bick.

From *Winter Cosmos* by Michael Comeau, copyright © 2018 Michael Comeau, courtesy of Koyama Press.

Graphic Novel Excerpt from UNTERZAKHN by Leela Corman, copyright © 2012 Leela Corman. Used by permission of Schocken Books, an imprint of the Knopf Doubleday Publishing Group, a division of Penguin Random House LLC. All rights reserved.

Angola Janga by Marcelo D'Salete, copyright © 2019 Marcelo D'Salete. Courtesy of Fantagraphics Books (www.fantagraphics.com).

"Darling, I've Realized I Don't Love You" by Eleanor Davis, copyright © Eleanor Davis. Courtesy of Fantagraphics Books (www.fantagraphics.com).

From *Woman World* by Aminder Dhaliwal, copyright © 2018 Aminder Dhaliwal, Courtesy of Drawn & Quarterly

"Naji al-Ali" by Marguierite Dabaie, copyright © 2018 Marguerite Dabaie

From *Alienation* by Inés Estrada, copyright © Inés Estrada. Courtesy of Fantagraphics Books (www.fantagraphics.com).

Graphic Novel Excerpt from PASSING FOR HUMAN: A GRAPHIC MEMOIR by Liana Finck, copyright © 2018 Liana Finck. Used by permission of Random House, an imprint and division of Penguin Random House LLC. All rights reserved.

Micrographica © Renee French.

From *I'm Not Here* by GG, copyright © 2018 GG. Reproduced courtesy of Koyama Press.

"Lot C (Some Time Later)" by John Hankiewicz, copyright © 2006 John Hankiewicz.

"How to Kill a . . . by Isabel Ruebens" by Jaime Hernandez, copyright © Jaime Hernandez. Courtesy of Fantagraphics Books (www.fantagraphics.com).

From *Found Forest Floor* by Gareth A. Hopkins and Erik Blagsvedt, 2017.

From *Night Fisher* by R. Kikuo Johnson, copyright © R. Kikuo Johnson. Reproduced courtesy of Fantagraphics Books (www.fantagraphics.com).

From *We Are On Our Own* by Miriam Katin, copyright © 2006 Miriam Katin. Reproduced courtesy of Drawn & Quarterly.

March © John Lewis and Andrew Aydin

From *Jobnik!* by Miriam Libicki, copyright © 2008 Miriam Libicki

Images from *The Book of Sarah,* by Sarah Lightman, copyright © Sarah Lightman. Reproduced with permission from Myriad Editions (www.myriadeditions.com).

From *Leaf* from Daishu Ma, copyright © Daishu Ma. Reproduced courtesy of Fantagraphics Books (www.fantagraphics.com).

From *Alack Sinner* by José Muñoz and Carlos Sampayo, © CASTERMAN.

From *Creation* by Sylvia Nickerson, copyright © 2019 Sylvia Nickerson.

"The Hook" by Thomas Ott, copyright © Thomas Ott. Reproduced courtesy of Fantagraphics Books (www.fantagraphics.com).

Graphic novel excerpt from IMAGINE WANTING ONLY THIS by Kristen Radtke, copyright © 2017 Kristen Radtke. Used by permission of Pantheon Books, an imprint of the Knopf Doubleday Publishing Group, a division of Penguin Random House LLC. All rights reserved.

From *Chlorine Gardens* by Keiler Roberts, copyright © 2018 Keiler Roberts, Courtesy of Koyama Press

From *I Know What I Am: The Life and Times of Artemisia Gentileschi* by Gina Siciliano, copyright © Gina Siciliano. Courtesy of Fantagraphics Books (www.fantagraphics.com).

From *Somnambulance* by Fiona Smyth, copyright © Fiona Smyth. Reproduced courtesy of Koyama Press.

Graphic novel excerpt from PERSEPOLIS: THE STORY OF A CHILDHOOD by Marjane Satrapi, translation copyright © 2003 by L'Association, Paris, France. Used by permission of Pantheon Books, an imprint of the Knopf Doubleday Publishing Group, a division of Penguin Random House LLC. All rights reserved.

From *SuperMutant Magic Academy* by Jillian Tamaki, copyright © 2015 Jillian Tamaki. Reproduced courtesy of Drawn & Quarterly.

From *Blankets* by Craig Thompson, copyright © 2015 Craig Thompson. Reproduced courtesy of Drawn & Quarterly.

"The Paranoid Truth" by Seth Tobocman, copyright © Seth Tobocman.

"Drop" and "Unfaded" by Adrian Tomine, copyright © Adrian Tomine. Reproduced courtesy of Drawn & Quarterly.

From *The Way of Nature* by C. C. Tsai and Zhuangzi, Copyright 2019 Princeton University Press.

Introduction: An Art-Focused Approach to Creating Comics

"Comics," writes Bart Beaty, "have rarely been considered an art form akin to painting, sculpture, or photography," even though "comic book artists have long aspired to be treated with the seriousness that painters, sculptors, and even illustrators have been accorded" (2012: 18, 6). And yet comics in the twenty-first century have achieved serious treatment across a wide range of academic disciplines, most prominently English and the neighboring fields of American Studies, Communication, Comparative Literature, Composition, Media Studies, Philosophy, Popular Culture, Psychology, and Rhetoric. That seriousness has sometimes prompted a change in nomenclature. When designing W&L University's "Making Comics," we considered listing our hybrid creative-writing and studio-arts course as "Graphic Narratives," a title that would have further increased enrollment since two students reported not signing up because they or their parents considered "comics" insufficiently serious for a college class.

That attitude has a long history.

The term is a misnomer coined to describe the daily strips and full-page Sunday features of late nineteenth- and early twentieth-century newspapers. "Comic books" began as reprint collections, establishing formatting norms in 1934, before developing original content, most notably with *Action Comics*, the title that transformed a fledgling pulp niche into an international mass market in 1938. Although Sterling North soon told readers of *National Parent-Teacher* that comic books were "Badly drawn, badly written and badly printed—a strain on young eyes and young nervous systems," he did not judge the comics form itself as intrinsically bad, only the "poisonous mushroom growth" of "'comic' magazines," of which "at least 70 percent of the total were of a nature no respectable newspaper would think of accepting" (1941: 16). James Frank Vlamos did condemn the newspaper "funnies" the same year, but it was due to the "Murder and torture" of its superhero content, a departure from the "colorful and carefree world [readers] delighted in younger days" (1941: 411). Fredric Wertham nominally acknowledged the existence of "'good' comic books," but only in contrast to "those which glorify violence, crime and sadism," since "All comic books with their words and expletives in balloons are bad for reading" (1954: 10).

Wertham meant specifically children's reading, the audience that defined "comics" for decades. When writers Arnold Drake and Leslie Waller partnered with comics artists Matt Baker and Ray Osrin in 1950 to produce the book-length, adult-market noir work *It Rhymes With Lust*, their publisher advertised it as a "Picture Novel." Jack Katz preferred to call his 1974 *The First Kingdom* a "graphic novel," a term Will Eisner popularized with his 1978 *A Contract with God and Other Tenement Stories*. Though Eisner wished to differentiate his book from the comics of the superhero-dominated children's market, Marvel created the Marvel Graphic Novel imprint in 1982, with DC Graphic Novels following in 1983. Eisner next coined "sequential art" in 1985, but Pantheon Books still used "graphic novel" to market Art Spiegelman's *Maus* in 1986. When *Maus II* appeared on *The New York Times* best-seller list in 1991, Spiegelman wrote a letter, objecting to "a carefully researched work based closely on my father's memories of life in Hitler's Europe and the death camps classified as fiction" (1991). The *Times*, noting that Pantheon listed the work as "history, memoir" and Library of Congress as "nonfiction," moved the work to the hard-cover nonfiction list, where it premiered at No. 13 the following week. The collected volume won a Pulitzer Prize in 1992, under the hybrid category Special Awards and Citations. *Maus* is now most commonly called a "graphic memoir," the comics subgenre that has garnered the most literary acclaim.

Though still analyzing comics as a form of literature, Michael Dean acknowledged the formal potential of comics art in 2000: "The comic book image is potentially as varied as all of the visual arts, ranging from the psychedelic abstractions of some of the undergrounds to the photorealist style of recent artists such as Alex Ross or even the photorealist expressionism of Jon J. Muth's recent adaptation of Fritz Lang's *M*" (156). In 2001, Chris Ware's *Jimmy Corrigan: the Smartest Kid on Earth* became the first graphic work to win *The Guardian*'s prestigious First Book Award. Although Michael Chabon's *The Adventures of Kavalier and Clay* is not a comic, after the comics-focused novel won the even more prestigious Pulitzer for Fiction the same year, academia's attitude toward the form shifted. The University of Florida's Ph.D. program in Comics and Visual Rhetoric has hosted comics conferences since 2002, one of nearly a dozen academic conferences now held annually. *Modern Fiction Studies* devoted an issue to graphic narratives in 2006, "the first special issue in the broad field of modern and contemporary narrative devoted entirely to the form of graphic narrative," which the editors argued demonstrated "the viability of graphic narrative for serious academic inquiry" and ended the need "to prove the worthiness and literary potential of the medium of comics" (Chute & DeKoven 2006: 766–7). Over three dozen journals have since published special issues on comics. Emerson College launched a Graphic Novel Writing and Illustration summer program in 2008, converting it to an online certificate in 2011, the same year the University of Dundee's Scottish Centre for Comics Studies launched its Masters program in Comics and Graphic Novels. Undergraduates at the University of Oregon began minoring in Comics and Cartoon Studies in 2012, and West Virginia's West Liberty University introduced its Graphic Narrative major in 2013. Beginning in 2016, French scholar Benoît Peeters served as the first Visiting Professor in Graphic Fiction and Comic Art at Lancaster University, the first comics-defined position in the UK. Comics courses are now common in colleges and universities across North America and Europe, with individual graphic narratives appearing on literature syllabi ranging from Medieval to Modern and in departments as seemingly non-comics-oriented as Politics, Religion, and Classics.

Beaty, however, notes how "art departments, and in particular art history departments, lagged in the adoption of courses and research on comics" (2012: 18). Vermont's Center for Cartoon Studies, the California College of Arts, and the Pennsylvania Academy of the Fine Arts offer Masters in Fine Arts in comics, and Gainesville, Florida's Sequential Artists Workshop is a one-year, non-accredited program targeted at comics creators aware of the anti-comics attitude in arts. "For some reason drawing, painting, and literature are all legitimate art forms," a SAW student reported, "but there's still this idea that when you combine them some sort of dark magic happens and the end product is no longer art. So, I think the idea of a comics MFA program is great, but that there's still this silly prejudice against comics in the mainstream art world" (Illustration Class 2012). Silly or not, the prejudice encompasses not only comics but the larger category of "word and image" works that has produced what W. T. J. Mitchell describes as "invasions of the visual arts by literary theory," placing "the border police . . . on the alert to protect the territory of art history from colonization by literary imperialism" (1996: 48).

As a result, comics studies has evolved as a predominantly literary field. Oregon's minor has been dominated by English professors including the program director, West Liberty's major is one of four offered by its English department, and Florida's Ph.D. program is also through English. The most prestigious nominations and awards comics have received have been as literature too. In addition to Spiegelman and Ware mentioned above, David Small was a 2009 National Book Award finalist for his graphic memoir *Stitches*, Alan Moore and Dave Gibbon's mini-series *Watchmen* was included in *Time* magazine's 2010 list of the one hundred best English-language novels published since 1923, Lauren Redniss's graphic biography *Radioactive* was a National Book Award finalist in 2011, Nick Drnaso's graphic novel *Sabrina* was nominated for the Booker Prize in 2018, and Lynda Barry won a MacArthur "Genius" Award in 2019.

While literary approaches to comics are invaluable, the underdevelopment of artistic approaches is unfortunate for a visual form, one that need not include text at all. Though Scott McCloud, in his seminal *Understanding*

Comics, established that "it doesn't have to contain words to be comics" (1993: 8), his later *Making Comics* insists that even wordless comics is foremost about storytelling and so is an art form closer to literature than to fine arts. "You might be able to draw like Michelangelo," warns McCloud, "but if it doesn't communicate, it'll just die on the page—while a cruder but more communicative style will win fans by the hundreds of thousands. Question number one: will readers get the message?" (2006: 29). While artists in any medium are likely concerned with communicating, clarity of message is rarely considered a work of art's defining goal. Many artists also create series of connected images, but few are foremost concerned that "navigating through them is a simple, intuitive proccss," one that will "be transparent to the reader" so that "the reading flow can continue uninterrupted" (2006: 36). The "principles of pure, clear storytelling" are the "starting point" for no artist working outside the comics form (2006: 52). Ultimately McCloud's instructions unintentionally coincide with Karl E. Fortress' 1963 assessment of "the funnies" as "non-art": "The comic strip artist is not concerned with art problems, problems of form, spatial relationships, and the expressive movement of line. In fact, a concern with such problems would, in all probability, incapacitate the comic strip artist as such" (1963: 112). Marcos Mateu-Mestre is equally direct, warning prospective comics creators that "when we are drawing for a storyboard or a graphic novel, we are first of all doing an exercise in storytelling, as opposed to creating pieces of art for a show," and since "the image is the vehicle and the end in itself," we "cannot afford to get the audience stuck on a particular frame just because the drawing or the scene looks great" (2010: 14).

Mateu-Mestre, Fortress, and McCloud are wrong. Comics images are more than vehicles, comics can and should be concerned with so-called art problems, and storytelling clarity need not be its single driving principle. As Mitchell implores, art history "cannot treat the words that are so necessary to its work as mere instrumentalities in the service of the visual images or treat images as mere grist for the mill of textual decoding" (1996: 48). The same demand must be made of comics creators, especially when the mainstream industry has institutionalized Mitchell's grist mill mentality. Brian Michael Bendis warns writers drafting scripts for artists: "You don't want to get in the way of the artists and their choices. They are not your art monkeys" (2014: 37). Dennis O'Neil reveals a similar imbalance, warning writers that artists "sometimes forget to put in things," requiring the writer to add "captions that explain the motives of the characters or describe events that aren't in the story" (2001: 31, 28). Bendis and O'Neil detail the writer-driven creative process, beginning with a writer's pitch document and story outline that must be approved by editors and revised before expanded to a full or partial script and assigned to a penciller and later an inker, letterer, and colorist. Christy Mag Uidhir calls this the "assembly-line model" of "mass-art comics," before offering a means for differentiating which collaborators should be considered authors and which mere assistants (2012: 47–8). The concern coincides with what Uidir identifies as a recent and "largely heretofore absent visual, if not art historical, interest in comics" (48), evidence that the ambiguously collaborative nature of traditional comics may be another reason Art departments have been slow to embrace them.

The majority of a comics script also describes visual content that later replaces it, creating an even more peculiar relationship between word and image. In an attempt to distinguish comics from other image-text forms, Thomas E. Wartenberg explores the "asymmetry between text and image in an illustrated book" (2012: 89). "The most obvious feature of an illustration," he writes, "is that it is *directed*, that is, stands in necessary relation to some other thing that it is the illustration *of*. In most cases, what an illustration is an illustration of is a previously existing story" (89). Wartenberg argues that a successful illustration "must be a *faithful* representation of what the text says" (89) and that "illustrations are ontologically dependent upon the text that they illustrate" (90). In the case of a *Classics Illustrated* comics adaptation of *The Last of the Mohicans*, Wartenberg notes that the images illustrate "not the story derived from *the text that appears with it* but rather the story-world specified by the text of the novel" (95; Wartenberg's emphasis). He therefore concludes that standard comics are distinct from illustrated books because "the images of comics are not illustrations of a preexisting story specified by a written text" (93). But a comics script is "a previously existing story," and script-derived comics images illustrate the story-world specified by the text of its originating script. The citation format of the Modern Language Association makes this explicit: works cited entries are alphabetized by writers' last names, with artists included after the title's work and with the phrase "illustrated by." That imbalance between script and image is an institutionalized assumption of English departments and further explains the bias against the form.

Reliance on a scripter's visual descriptions is inherently limiting; as Matt Fraction said of *Hawkeye* artist David Aja: "he produces things I'd never think of, let alone know how to explain in a script for someone to draw" (Bendis 2014: 58). Not all comics, however, are entirely or primarily script-based. O'Neil acknowledges the benefits of less directed collaboration, allowing the "writer to be inspired by something in the art" that "suggest[s] clever lines, characterization, even plots twists that improve the final product" (2001: 31). Bendis argues that artists are "co-writing" and asks his collaborators to see a script as only a "guide": "If you agree with my choices, fine. If not, you do what you have to do" (2014: 36). Editor Mary Jo Duffy describes Frank Miller and Bill Sienkiewicz's even more balanced process for *Elektra: Assassin*:

> after Bill had finished painting the issue, and the pages were all assembled with whatever other photostats, Xeroxes, doilies, staples, or sewing

> thread Bill felt was needed to give them the right look, Frank would do a final draft, taking full advantage of whatever new and unexpected touches Bill had incorporated into the artwork. The story changed dramatically as Frank and Bill played off each other in ways that combined genius, lunacy, and magic. Certain scenes and characters were dropped entirely as others expanded.
>
> MILLER & SIENKIEWICZ 2012

The so-called Marvel Method employed by Stan Lee during his most prolific creative period in the early 60s also relied heavily on artists as co-writers—albeit uncredited ones. Jack Kirby and Steve Ditko developed stories either based on Lee's initial summaries or independently, submitting complete, penciled pages with empty speech, thought, and caption containers which Lee would then fill based on the pages' visual information.

When the writer and artist are the same person, the developmental relationship between story and image is inevitably more unified—an internal creative process that aligns with cultural assumptions about and preferences for works of art and literature created by single authors. It is not coincidental that the first *Atlantic Monthly* article lauding comics as having any, albeit "lowbrow," artistic or literary worth featured creators who combined the roles of writer and artist: Frank Miller, Dave Sim, and Howard Chaykin (Rose 1986: 80). That trend has continued and deepened with writer-artists consistently receiving highest acclaim. Writers Alan Moore, Neil Gaiman, and Kelly Sue DeConnick are notable exceptions, as are collaborative artists Bill Sienkiewicz, Dave McKean, and Emma Rios, but the individual creations of Jessica Abel, Lynda Barry, Alison Bechdel, Chester Brown, Charles Burns, Roz Chast, Daniel Clowes, Juliet Doucet, Carla Speed McNeil, Joe Saco, Marjane Satrapi, David Small, Jillian Tamaki, Craig Thompson, Adrian Tomine, Tillie Walden, and Chris Ware suit the expectations of a lone author controlling all aspects of a creative work.

Though collaborations can produce equally strong results, they require writers who write visually and artists who draw narratively. The current market for aspiring comics creators, however, offers mostly specialized textbooks that divide the field into discreet subareas. Writers may read O'Neil's *The DC Comics Guide to Writing Comics* or Bendis' *Words for Pictures: The Art and Business of Writing Comics and Graphic Novels*. While invaluable for understanding the mainstream industry, both focus on a narrow area of the larger form and the very specific subgenre of superhero comics. Artists might buy Stan Lee and John Buscema's *How to Draw the Marvel Way* or Christopher Hart's more recent *Simplified Anatomy for the Comic Book Artist*. While both are also useful for the specialized style of superhero art, both are as limiting in their approach to the general field, and neither are of use to non-artists. Will Eisner's *Comics and Sequential Art*, Scott McCloud's *Making Comics,* and Jessica Abel and Matt Madden's *Drawing Words and Writing Pictures* all present more holistic approaches, but they do so while largely conforming to conventional understandings of the form that inhibit creators from exploring beyond traditional panels, frames, and gutters and into the wider and less defined sequential image-texts. Lynda Barry's *Syllabus* and *Making Comics* avoid the pitfalls of commercial comics and are excellent at helping students overcome creative obstacles, but the approach does not emphasize revision and a continuing development of visual approaches.

None of these textbooks would lead to such works as artist Dianne Kornberg's collaborations with poet Elisabeth Frost on *Bindle* (2009) and poet Celia Bland on *Madonna Comix* (2014). Though both are "comics" in the broadest sense, both work significantly outside the creative approaches offered by Barry, Eisner, McCloud, and Abel and Madden, let alone by O'Neil, Bendis, Hart, and Buscema and Lee. It is equally difficult to imagine such image-text books as Bianca Stone's *Poetry Comics*, Richard McGuire's *Here*, or Lauren Redniss' *Radioactive* emerging from a traditional comics creative process. While mainstream comics prioritize script over image, comics as an art form should emphasize image. This is true even with Stone's image-text poetry, a hybrid form introduced in 1979 by David Morice as an outgrowth of concrete poetry and which has had the journal *Inkbrick* dedicated to it since 2014. While *The New York Times* recognized *Radioactive* as a "book-length comic," one of the few "knotty works of art" within the form (Garner), Redniss's website identifies her work as "visual non-fiction"—a term that technically includes graphic memoirs and graphic journalism, but distances itself from the comics tradition. Eisner adopted "graphic novel" when approaching publishers for the same reason, though *The New York Times* called McGuire's *Here* "brilliant and revolutionary . . . for which the term 'graphic novel' feels awfully small" (Sante 2015).

Whatever the terminology, if the form is no longer defined in opposition to fine art, then comics includes a range of twentieth-century and contemporary visual artists producing comics-like images, including Frans Masereel, Lynd Ward, Max Ernst, Max Klinger, Filippo Tommaso Marinetti, Cy Twombly, Matt Mullican, Carolee Schneemann, Russell Crotty, Adam Dant, Nancy Spero, Mark Titchner, Sam Durant, Aleksandra Mir, Donald Urquhart, Glenn Ligon, Jakob Kolding, Clair Fontaine, Howard Finster, Jonathan Monk, Olivia Plender, Keith Haring, Susan Hiller, Jean-Michel Basquiat, Carroll Dunham, and Guerrilla Girls. Kent Worcester, the "Words & Pictures" editor of *New Politics*, recognizes the same overlap: "While we tend to associate the phrase with comics and cartoons, fine art is also implicated in the interaction of words and pictures," naming Sue Coe, Raymond Pettibon, Jenny Holzer, Barbara Kruger, Christopher Wool, Mel Bochner, and Amy Pryor, who the magazine featured in a section typically devoted to "editorial cartooning, comic strips, comic books, and graphic novels" (Worcester 2016: 106–22). Mitchell also acknowledges the recent "emergence of comics as a newly 'serious' medium of art, collected and exhibited by major museums," one that rejects "the old boundaries between art and mass culture, juvenile and adult forms of expression, generic distinctions between satire and autobiography, fiction and nonfiction, poetry and philosophy and history" (2014: 255).

Since we are interested in expanding creative possibilities, we define comics as widely and inclusively as possible: the art of juxtaposed images. While the form can be traced back to at least eighteenth-century engravings and medieval illuminated manuscripts, the overtly "comics" portion of its history is centered in the twentieth century, and the majority of its works, with notable exceptions, are middling. Even one of its earliest advocates, Jules Feiffer, declared comic books "junk" and "a second-class citizen of the arts," acknowledging there were "a few exceptions" by 1965, "but nonjunk comic books don't, as a rule, last very long" (2003: 72). Two decades later, Lloyd Rose similarly half-praised comics for existing "in a subaesthetic area, with no redeeming intellectual or social qualities, only instinct and rude energy" (1986: 80). Even superhero comics writer Alan Moore argued in 1985 that "to move forward as a medium" comics required "a drastic improvement in the standard of comic writing" (2008: 6).

While comics have drastically improved, their continuing growth requires "writing" that is primarily visual and not linguistic. Moore points out that "in constructing a story, one doesn't always have to start with an idea. It's quite possible to be inspired toward a story by having thought of some purely abstract technical device or panel progression or something" (2008: 9). By "something," he means the image, and he provides two examples of his own stories that developed from visual thinking:

> One idea was that it would be nice to make something of Swamp Thing's capacity for camouflage . . . maybe have part of his leg or his body visible in the foreground of a panel somewhere with the reader and the other characters not realizing that they're looking at the swamp creature for a couple of seconds. This eventually became the first two pages of #22, "Swamped."
>
> 2008: 9

A car-crash scene in *Swamp Thing* #26 originated not from a plot point but Moore's desire to incorporate Burma Shave billboards in a progression of panels, an example of selecting story-world content not based on story needs but on its applicability to the comics form.

The change in approach may require yet another challenge to terminology, since "graphic novel" and "graphic narrative" may be inadequate and even misleading. Rather than "comics being a combination of drawings and literature, or film and literature," Seth argues that "comics are closer to a combination of poetry and design," because the "brevity, the rhythm, the breaks for silence . . . are elements that probably have more to do with free verse then they do with the traditional novel" (Seth 2004). The clearest difference between prose and poetry is poetry's use of line and stanza breaks, effects similar to the units produced by caption boxes and speech balloons. If panels are treated as semantic units, then their page arrangement resembles concrete poetry more than the arbitrary page-edge breaks of prose formatting. Might all comics actually be visual poetry? Narrative and poetry are sometimes regarded as opposing literary poles, yet narrative poetry is its own category. Would one-panel cartoons be more usefully understood as visual lyrics? If we accept Edgar Allan Poe's definition of a lyric as a poem that can be read in thirty minutes, should nearly every mainstream comic ever published be called a graphic lyric?

The editors of *Indiana Review* published works by comics poet Bianca Stone in a 2015 Special Folio titled "Graphic Memoir," further blurring terms. But rather than suggesting a definition for "comics poetry," Alexander Rothman instead hopes "to maintain as much expressive openness for the form as possible" by asking questions:

> What else can comics do? What untapped expressive power hides among those myriad elements of the comics page/spread/book/scroll? . . . What are the effects of these choices and their repetition? . . . What are the expressive differences between black-and-white and full color, or among various limited palettes? Why might we still describe an evocative image verbally when we could draw it. . .or vice versa? What are the effects of different visual approaches to lettering? Or the distribution of text across the field of the page? What changes when text is in a caption or a balloon, or simply floating on the page? And if it's in a balloon, what if the tail points to the speaker in one panel, and a potted plant in the next? What can we get from the strategic deployment of a visual motif throughout a work?
>
> 2015

These are the type of convention-challenging questions that all artists and writers should be asking themselves—whether they regard themselves as sequential artists, graphic novelists, graphic memoirists, visual nonfiction writers, visual narrative poets, comics poets, or simply comics creators.

While branching into art history, comics studies has expanded into creative writing and studio arts too. Our course, Making Comics, combined both, an approach we extend here. If you are a graduate, undergraduate, or independent student of comics, *Creating Comics* maps the fundamentals of the form to build a foundation that offers the widest creative freedom by defining the fullest range of possibilities. We will help you answer Rothman's questions and many more like them, through a sequence of instructional chapters that explores the craft of comics from angles that bridge the unnecessary divide between art and literature. If you are a writer with little art experience, you will learn how to develop engaging images. If you are an artist with little writing experience, you will learn how to develop engaging characters and stories. If you are new to both art and writing, you will learn both sets of skills in unison, creating stories through image-making. And even if you are a writer who wishes only to write scripts or an artist who wishes only to render scripts, this book will hone your skills while giving new insight into your collaborator.

The sequence of chapters builds a comprehensive overview of the comics craft. Chapter 1, "Images," explains why starting with a script might not be the best way of starting a comic and instead presents an image-first approach, covering the basics of media, sizing, line quality, drawing style, visual research, framing, and revision. It culminates in the creation of a specific character developed from your initial drawings and not from a preconceived script. Chapter 2, "Hinges," reveals the range of inferences that can connect two side-by-side images and leads you to discover and develop connections between images of your own characters. Chapter 3, "Sequences," approaches story from the internal angle of your characters' motivations and then as visual actions subdivided into basic units of plot that allow you to expand and compress sequences according to the needs and whims of your storytelling preference. Chapter 4, "Pages," tackles the relationships of images on the shared canvas of a single page, showing you creative options for layout, reading paths, visual phrases, image accents, and value balance. Chapter 5, "Words," explores the double nature of words as definitions that exist in readers' minds and images that exist on the page, revealing the complex relationships between meaning and rendering and how words and other images can combine for a range of effects. Finally, chapter 6, "Processes," pulls together the preceding lessons into four systematic approaches of image-first, story-first, layout-first, and canvas-first, as well as the book-length considerations of page schemes, allowing you to understand and select the approach that works best for your own creative process.

The last portion of the book is an anthology featuring excerpts from black and white comics by over three dozen artists. While we emphasize a diverse range of contemporary publications, we include a few historical examples too, as well as some works that aren't normally categorized as comics at all. We include a discussion of anthology selections at the end of each chapter, but we encourage you to study the excerpts on your own too, finding inspiration in all of the possibilities they suggest.

1

Images

CHAPTER OUTLINE

"So every once in a while I try to write a story," explains novelist Peter Cameron,

> and since the writer Iris Owens once told me that she didn't believe in writer's block because all you needed was *one* sentence, the first sentence, and there you go, I occasionally try to come up with opening sentences, this being easier than coming up with complete ideas for stories.
>
> 2010: 430

Cameron followed this open-ended opening-sentence creative process when writing his award-winning short story "The End of My Life in New York." It begins:

> When I come home from Paula's dinner party, Philip is still awake, sitting up in bed, contemplating a book.
>
> 2010: 266

The sentence is rich in cascading possibilities: Who is Philip? Who is the narrator? Who is Paula? Why didn't Philip go to Paula's dinner party too? Does Philip have a problem with Paula? Does she have a problem with him? How does Philip feel about the narrator going without him? Cameron didn't know the answer to any of these when he first wrote the sentence. Exploring these questions requires an author to develop details about the characters, their relationships, and the larger situation—and there you go, the short story starts writing itself.

But is this an effective process for starting a comic? That first sentence could appear in a caption box in a first panel—but then what image would accompany it? If it's a drawing of a man sitting in bed with a book, it will have to provide additional details (maybe Philip is a dark-skinned, prematurely balding athletic-looking man in floral pajamas reading a mangled paperback of *Pride and Prejudice*), but the words and images would still be largely redundant. Scott McCloud terms that word-picture relationship "duo-specific," and effective comics usually avoids it because the redundancy undermines what's most interesting about the comics form. Words and image don't share a path. They work on separate paths that can parallel, crisscross, and diverge.

You might instead delete the caption and let the image stand alone, maybe giving Philip a talk balloon of context-creating dialogue: "How was Paula's?" No redundancy, so a significant improvement. But while this one-panel image-text would be more interesting than the first, is it the best way to *develop* a comics story? Even though that originating sentence would not be included in the comic itself, the image is still an illustration of the deleted words. It began as an idea, one visually vague by virtue of being word-based. Cameron's sentence could produce literally thousands of necessarily specific variations, an infinite number of possible Philips drawn in varying angles and styles.

If Cameron were a comics writer, he might write a whole script this way, aware that each of his verbal descriptions would eventually be interpreted and made visually concrete by some future collaborating artist. His words would be akin to a song score to be later played by a musician whose performance would be the actual comic. But no one thinks of sheet music as music itself, and what composer writes music only through musical notation? Notes on a staff are only a method of representing sounds, ones tested, revised, and retested aloud on actual instruments during the composing process.

Though theoretically a composer could compose exclusively in her head—Mozart supposedly did—words are far less precise than notation. While comics writer Alan Moore is notorious for producing exceptionally detailed scripts for his collaborating artists, Nat Gertler's script for "Degeneration" nearly exceeds the a-picture-is-worth-a-thousand-words truism. Here is an excerpt describing a portion of the office setting to appear in the opening panel:

> There is a desk facing the entrance door. It has a heavy, polished black stone top, and space directly under that for about 4 inches of drawers. The desk is supported by black metal sides; instead they head from the edge of the top downward and inward, curving back at the bottom to provide feet. This has the effect of accentuating the information that the desk does not have file drawers on the side—this is not the desk of someone who is supposed to keep his own files, and heaven forbid that it looks as though he does.
>
> 2002: 163

Gertler seems to have a very specific desk in mind, and though artist Steve Lieber translates his descriptions dutifully, it's not possible for Lieber's drawn desk and Gertler's mentally imagined and then verbally described desk to be the same desk. For one, the desk is not described from one specific angle—a requirement of drawing. It is instead described in perspective-free details true from all possible angles. The desk isn't being looked at it—it simply *is*. Gertler later describes his preferred "angle" too: "we're looking toward the desk from the inside . . . we can be far enough back that we get a sense of the room" (2002: 164). But this isn't a single angle either, but a slightly reduced range of possible angles.

Not only are Gertler's words not a desk, they may not produce a specific image of desk in a reader's head either. Peter Mendelsund observes that "even the most . . . lushly described locales in naturalistic fiction, are, visually: flat" and "characters, in *all* types of fiction, [are] merely visual types, examplars of particular categories—sizes; body, shapes; hair colors"; and since we "don't have pictures in our minds when we read, then it is the interaction of ideas—the intermingling of abstract relationships—that catalyzes feeling in us readers" (2014: 371, 373, 245). That's why verbal descriptions can't achieve what drawings can. To visually represent something is to capture it from one specific perspective at one specific moment. Visual representations are inevitably spatiotemporal—which is why comics tend to be like storyboards or sequenced snapshots. Moving from image to image in a comic typically means also moving from moment to moment and perspective to perspective. That is a norm that can and should be overturned at times. No matter how detailed a visual description might be—Gertler could describe not only the desk but how it appears from one precise angle as though working from a photograph in his head—words are not images. The image in Gertler's head is not an image either. It's an idea. He then translates his mental ideas into words and Lieber translates those words into an image.

Image First

So why not just begin with the image?

Images are physical. They're ink on paper or pixels on screen or paint on canvas. Words can be physical too, but only to the degree that they are rendered lines and shapes. Their meanings are less grounded. Prose writers weigh not simply a word's overt definition, but its connotations too, including its sounds and associations. Cameron could have written that Philip was "reading a book." Instead he wrote "contemplating a book." Do the two verbs denote the same meaning? More or less, but the nuance of difference is the power of prose. Philip might instead be studying, flipping through, fingering, squinting at, clutching, or hunching over a book. Each has a slightly different connotation that subtlety shapes a reader's experience. And while some of these subtleties might be translatable to a drawn image, images acquire other qualities in the process, producing a range of additional connotations that couldn't be expressed in words. What is the attitude toward Philip implied by the angle of perspective? What is the expressive quality of the lines that compose his body? Do they convey the same low energy of his quiet activity or contradict it? Is he holding the book in one hand or two? Is his posture overall relaxed or stiff? And what do all those external details imply about Philip's internal state?

Images also are not simply information conduits. They contain ambiguities. A script writer can only state what she hopes the image will convey, not what the image will actually be. Even an artist can't control for every visual nuance and how those details—the unplanned slope of Philip's cartoonish shoulders, the slightly frenetic scribble of his hair shading—will shape the viewer's experience of the scene. A drawing is not simply an execution of an idea. Things happen in the drawing process itself, and so the composition of the comic doesn't fully begin until the artist commits pencil to paper (or paint to canvas or photograph to Photoshop, etc.). And yet a scripter first conceives and develops an imaginary comic through the medium of words—which is not the medium of the comic. Conceiving and developing a story in a different medium turns the actual comic into an adaptation, a secondary work that is dependent on the primary work. Script-based writing reduces comics art to illustrations. It also shapes the content in ways alien to image-making.

Consider the second sentence of Peter Cameron's short story:

> I know from experience that he is not reading.
>
> 2010: 266

How does an artist draw that? She doesn't. It's a visually unrepresentable fact. Like Gertler's desk, it simply *is*. To translate it, the adapter would have to invent a specific action—a single event in space and time—ideally one that implies a pattern of similar actions. The narrator could say, "I know you're not reading." Again, a good translation, but since comics are more than illustrated plays, it's better if an image does more than prop dialogue. Maybe Philips is holding his copy of *Pride and Prejudice* upside down. Not bad, but how does the humorous effect alter the intended tone? If the author were simply working with images as images and not as translations of text, there would be no intended tone. There would only be the drawn drafts of the comic itself.

If Peter Cameron were a comics artist-writer, his story's characters andsituations could have developed visually. The first time he sketched Philip he would have learned details about him, ones that are different from the kinds of details he created by working in the medium of words. The final draft of "The End of My Life in New York" doesn't reveal what book Philip was holding or what he was wearing as he sat up in bed. If, as described above, Philip is holding a mangled paperback of *Pride and Prejudice*, we can infer that, even though he is not currently reading it, he has read it at some point before, apparently many times before, suggesting a personal connection to the novel, the most famous and influential romance novel in English literature. That's a window into Philip's character. Cameron also doesn't describe his hair, build, or skin color. Does Philip work out in the gym to compensate for the hair loss? The life experiences of a dark-skinned man are going to be different from those of a light-skinned one. By shading Philip's face a degree darker, Cameron could trigger a range of social expectations in his viewer, ones he could then continue to explore and disrupt as his story develops image by image instead of word by word.

Even the most visually adept, artistically attentive scripter cannot describe in words what an artist discovers and achieves through the drawing process. A description of an image is an unexecuted idea, and visual art produced from the verbal descriptions of ideas is limited by its own creative process. Alan Moore and Dave Gibbons' *Watchmen*, the most acclaimed graphic novel of the twentieth century, is an illustrated script drawn in the semi-naturalistic style of the superhero art codified by Marvel and DC during the 1970s. The additional color art of John Higgins, while innovative for the mainstream genre and time period, is so limited by the production necessities of color separation boards that most viewers outside of comics would view it as unaesthetic. A black and white *Watchmen* might be a superior work of art. *Watchmen* drawn in a less derivative style would likely be superior too—unless you argue that Gibbons' largely standardized style produces visual commentary on the genre that parallels the story's deconstruction of superhero norms. Still, in literary terms—which is the way in which the novel has been read and appreciated—all rendered versions would be essentially equal. *Watchmen*, in other words, is a significant work of literature, but as a work of visual art, it is at best unremarkable.

Scripts Aren't Images

Comics writer Kurt Busiek rightfully considers his story "The Nearness of You" possibly "the best piece I've ever written," and while in literary terms it deserves praise as "the best to appear in [Busiek's series] *Astro City*" (Gertler 2002: 106), it is visually less effective in part because of penciller Brent Anderson's necessary adherence to Busiek's script. The comic's opening page captions are striking for their use of non-visual sensations and out-of-scene details:

> She has a low, throaty laugh, and a capped tooth from a bicycle accident when she was eight years old.
>
> Her shampoo makes her hair smell likes apples and wildflowers.
>
> GERTLER 2002: 108

But Busiek's visual description "THE BACKGROUND IS MISTY, INDISTINCT" is an idea not an image and it prompts Anderson toward the literal indistinctness of a white background and a visually generic swirl of mist. Busiek describes "MIKE" as only "A YOUNG MAN IN HIS LATE TWENTIES," a name and age range that Anderson adorns with short, non-descript hair and a generic tuxedo. When Busiek describes him later wearing "BOXERS AND A T-SHIRT," Anderson draws a white T-shirt and boxers with no pattern or other distinguishing characteristics. Busiek labels Mike's bedroom but offers no details, and so Anderson gives it rectangular furniture that suggests Platonic ideals more than physical objects with individual histories of manufacturing and use by specific people in specific circumstances. The scripted Mike is "GLUM," an idea translated into the same pose twice, his head slumped into his open palm as he stares down. Busiek's visual descriptions also produce redundant images, as when the captioned words "and then she's gone" accompany an image of Mike suddenly alone as his arms sweep the dissipating swirl of mist, an accurate rendering of the scripted instructions: "SUDDENLY, SHE'S GONE, AND HE'S PANICKY, GRASPING AT NOTHING" (Gertler 2002: 109). Anderson in short draws what he's told to draw, making additions to the extent required to form the impression of physical reality. That reality, however, reproduces the visual vagueness of written language. It is derived from ideas rather than things. This is why Ivan Brunetti warns that when "form and content diverge, only a specter remains, and nothing solid can be built," and so images must "organically evolve" rather than be "imposed by an external force" (2011: 6).

"The Nearness of You" includes a moment similar to a moment in David Mazzucchelli's *Asterios Polyp*. Like Mike, Mazzucchelli's main character, Asterios, sits in his underwear on the edge of a bed while staring off, haunted by the memory of a lost lover. Asterios is rendered more cartoonishly than Mike—no human skull could ever produce a head of that shape—yet the odd specificity of his pose, the way he's examining a blister on the sole of his upturned foot that he's holding in both hands, creates a more grounded reality. The furnishings—the pineapple-shaped bedposts, the zigzag-patterned comforter, the claw-footed dresser, the ornate base of the lamp set inexplicably on the floor, let alone all of the individual candles and decorations—these all create a sense of a specific reality, even though Mazzucchelli renders each in minimal detail.

A prose writer works in prose, literally thinks on paper, producing specific words in an order that she revises, subtracting old words, substituting in new ones, adding new sentences, repeatedly, until arriving at a finished product: the set of final words in the final order. Through that process, she discovers, tests, throws out, adds, and refines thousands of details about her characters and the world they inhabit and the events they experience. The story still may be conceptual—it happens in her and her readers' heads—but those concepts are shaped by and evolved through specific words. It all happens on paper.

Comics can happen on paper too. But the paper of comics is not the kind that rolls into a typewriter. A comics script is not a necessary stage in the process of writing a comic. It's often a creative detour, a side road that adds miles to the speedometer but through different terrain. Instead of a script, Ivan Brunetti recommends writing "a text summary" but only to "get them out of your system," since your "story will begin to change the second you put pencil to paper," a point Chris Ware further stresses:

> letting stories grow at their own momentum was a more natural and sympathetic way of working than carpentering them out of ideas and plans. And the images suggested the stories, not the other way around. I believe that allowing one's drawings to suggest the direction of a story is comics' single greatest formal advantage.
>
> qtd in BRUNETTI 2011: 66

The continuing development of the comics form requires further steps in such visual writing, allowing image to not only guide story but to determine it.

Busiek is the author of "The Nearness of You" and Anderson is, to quote Brian Michael Bendis, his "art monkey"—which does not describe Anderson's skill, only his industry's creative process. Its emphasis on visual storytelling over visual aesthetics also means that, as Pascal Lefèvre observes, "a lot of artists use stereotypical icons (like the Statue of Liberty for New York or the pyramids for Egypt) because such famous buildings or monuments can be easily recognized" (2009: 357). Could Busiek's script be rendered in a less expected, non-stereotypical way? Anderson would need to explore and articulate his own visual dialect, one that did not rely so fully on the customs of superhero comics art specifically and icons generally—something the commercial publishing needs of *Astro City* likely prohibited. He would also have to leave the role of assistant to become a co-writer by developing a visual universe rich with his own imaginings. Where did Mike buy that tux? Was it a rental? Was it his first choice? His fifth? Did he splurge? Did he go for a cheaper one and regret it later—or does he prefer off-brands? Are the shoulders a little too tight, the pant legs a little too long? How old are those boxers anyway? How did he rip the bottom seam of the T-shirt? Or is that crease from the package he pulled it out of yesterday? Was that dent in the bottom bookcase shelf there when he bought it second-hand at Goodwill or did he do that himself while following the Ikea assembly directions?

Those answers could come in part from real-world props—an actual bookcase and an actual tuxedo, ones the artist positions by hand. A composite of internet images might suffice if the Google search unearths more than catalogues and advertisements. Generic images produce generic worlds. While readers and scripters might visualize surprisingly little, a comics artist must visualize a universe as palpable and specific as her own world and then render it in her own expressive line. That richness will emerge not from ideas, but from physical marks on physical pages.

Media

But what kinds of marks on what kind of page? Mainstream comics are traditionally drawn in pencil on artboards and then separately inked, usually by two different artists at two distinct stages of production, which are then followed by lettering and coloring by additional artists. The assembly line approach suits the needs of mass-market publishers producing multiple monthly titles. It also allows a company's most valued artists, the pencillers, to work on the greatest number of issues—as Jack Kirby did at Marvel in the 1960s. But comics creators have a wide range of other approaches.

For *We Are On Our Own* (2006), Miriam Katin drew her World War II memoir in pencil but did not finish it in ink, creating a gray palette occasionally punctuated by pages in colored pencils that depict later events. Miriam Libicki also drew her comics essay "Towards a Hot Jew" (2016) in pencil but used watercolor paper for a textured effect. Alex Ross began *Kingdom Come* (1997) with pencil sketches, but instead of moving to ink, he painted his artboards with gouache, an opaque watercolor that eliminated the separate role of a colorist. For *Dracula: A Symphony in Moonlight and Nightmares* (1986), Jon J. Muth worked in pencils and watercolors, later placing dialogue in play format on facing pages to avoid inserting talk balloons over the art. For *Bindle* (2015), Elisabeth Frost and Dianne Kornberg inked and taped word collages onto damaged sheets of paper, which they then centered with physical bird nests and photographed. For *Iron Man: Crash* (1988), Mike Saenz used a Mac II to create what Marvel advertised as "the first computer generated graphic novel," composing low-resolution, black and white bitmaps that he uploaded into Lithographer to manipulate. Many of Saenz's pioneering processes are now standard practices. For *Book of No Ledge* (2016), Nance Van Winckel scanned pages of her childhood encyclopedia into Photoshop and then replaced the text with new words. Most contemporary artists scan and manipulate their artwork prior to publishing. For *Poetry Is Useless* (2015), Anders Nilsen photographed pages of a hard-bound sketchbook to create insets with additional scanned art added in the expansive margins. For his word- and image-combining book *Jazz* (1947), Henri Matisse used only sheets of colored paper and scissors.

Choices for page dimensions for drafting and publishing comics are equally eclectic. While a 3:4 ratio is standard for paintings, drawings tend to be smaller, with ratios between 3:4 and 2:3—though because there is no book spine, orientation is interchangeable. Begin with a sketchbook, hardbound, spiral-bound, any size. They're for drafting images, but even finished images can appear on various page sizes. Comics artists traditionally complete their work on 11" x 17" artboards, which are later reduced and trimmed, requiring an internal 10" x 15" safe area border and a bleed border that extends beyond the trim line used during the printing process. But, as Fantagraphics Books explain on their submission page: "We publish books of all dimensions and page counts (within reason) — there is no standard format."

Artboard sizes vary, but whatever its original dimensions, traditionally comics art is reduced when printed, usually by roughly a third, though there are plenty of exceptions. Bill Sienkiewicz drew 12" x 18" *Batman* covers that were reduced by half. Art Spiegelman drew *Maus* in the same roughly 6" x 9" dimensions as the pages it would be printed on. Tillie Walden draws all of her graphic novels in 1:1 proportions too. For *Truth: Red, White and Black* (2004), Kyle Baker enlarged his art, emphasizing rather than reducing attention to line qualities. Renée French also did to a more radical degree for *micrographica* (2007), drawing panels roughly half the size of postage stamps and then expanding them five times larger when printed.

In Illustration 1.1, Leigh Ann drew trees and fairies three times in different proportions, and then we scanned them (at 300 dpi, dots-per-inch, a standard resolution for book publishers) and resized them to fit into full-width panels. Notice how shrinking and enlarging alters the line and cross-hatch values. The top panel was originally drawn on a much larger sheet and then shrunk to 35 percent. Many artists like how shrinking transforms their artwork—though a too densely drawn image will collapse detail. The middle panel was drawn in roughly the size of the panel on the page, so reproduced here at 100 percent. The lines and values are the same as on the original. Notice that the lines that compose the identical fairy from the first panel are not as delicate the second time. The last image was drawn in a tiny panel and enlarged by 350 percent. The enlarging draws attention to the line width, making the lines of that same fairy even thicker. You should experiment, but know that whichever approach you choose for a given project, resizing will alter the finished product.

You can begin to make comics with very few art materials. Lots of equipment is made especially for the comics trade, such as photo blue pencils and premade comic boards, but all you really need to begin is paper, pencil and a few other common art supplies. Choose a soft but dark drawing pencil with a smooth glide. Black Micron pens, especially 05 and 08, work well for linear work, and black Micron brush tips are a great choice for filling in large areas of black. A white plastic Mars eraser and a good pencil sharpener are recommended. Strathmore drawing paper pads are useful for sketching

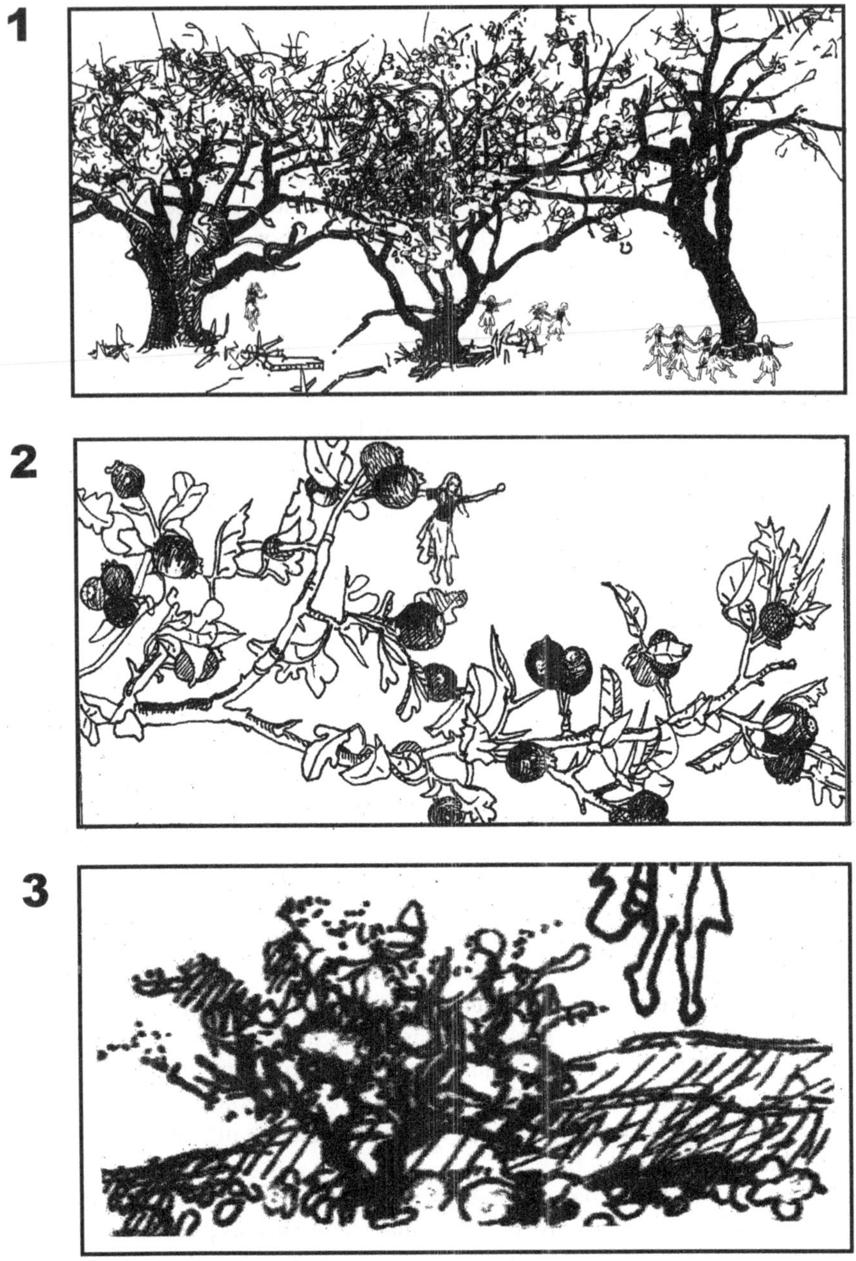

ILLUSTRATION 1.1 *Sizing options.*

out ideas, and Bristol board is perfect for finished copy. Panel templates with different-sized panels are handy as are handmade template shapes cut from mat board. T-squares, architectural templates (circles, squares, rectangles, common shapes), rulers, glue, good scissors and copious amounts of tape are all handy in a communal drawing situation. Finally, a light table is recommended for tracing over old drawings, photos, or combining drawings. A bright window is a perfectly good substitute. One piece of equipment that will make the whole process easier is a copier with scanning capabilities. The ability to shrink and enlarge drawings, cut and collage from copies, and recopy as a whole is a helpful addition to the drawing process. Shrinking and enlarging a drawing can instantly spotlight a drawing's potential and pinpoint weaknesses.

Reproductions

The fact that comics art can be resized when published distinguishes comics from most other visual art. Comics artists create art in order to create comics, but the object the artist creates—the physical paper and ink—is not the intended art. Traditionally, a comics artist draws on artboards, and then a printer uses those artboards to produce a comic. The comic is the work of art. The artboards can and should be called works of art too, but they are not the art that is the comic—which has no original. A comic is its multiple copies. This is similarly true for recording artists and film makers. An album (a term also used for European graphic novels) or a film released to multiple theaters and internet platforms is its multiple copies, as opposed to the master recording from which all other physical copies and digital downloads are made.

For a comics artist, the focus is on the artboard and its necessary reproducibility. That also affects how artists make their images—usually in a convenient way. The Society of Illustrators exhibited a Ralph Steadman retrospective in 2016. Steadman began his career as a freelance cartoonist in the 1960s for several British magazines (including *Punch*, where the term "cartoon" coincidentally originates). Cartoons don't usually hang in art galleries, which traditionally feature works such as Georges Seurat's *A Sunday Afternoon on the Island of La Grande Jatte*. Steadman's parody, *A Sunday Afternoon on the Serpentine*, appeared in *Town* magazine in 1967. Although the Society of Illustrators identified the piece hanging in its gallery by the same name, if "reproduced" is a defining quality of a comic, then the gallery piece was not that one-panel comic but its artboard. While other works of art are reproducible, Steadman's was created to be reproduced. It includes splotches of typewriter correction fluid and speech balloons cut from separate sheets of paper and affixed over the primary sheet, with faintly erased pencil marks visible under the inked lettering. The same techniques appeared in nearly all of the exhibited work, often to cover stray lines and reshape edges, though Steadman occasionally inked new figures onto dried correction fluid.

The art term for such corrections is "pentimento," Italian for "regrets" or "repentance," what artists presumably experience when painting over what they wish that had not painted in the first place. Except Steadman is not "painting" in these cases. According to the gallery plaques, his materials are only pen and ink—because the Society of Illustrators curators apparently did not consider typewriter correction fluid an "art" material.

One of Steadman's most famous images of Hunter S. Thompson appears on the retrospective's entrance poster, on postcards, and in framed prints in the gallery gift shop as *Vintage Dr. Gonzo*. Setting aside the considerable fact that these "reproductions" include color while the "original" in the exhibit does not (imagine if Seurat left coloring to his printers), the numerous whiteout blotches go from unsightly to unseen because the larger image was designed for reproduction. The *Vintage Dr. Gonzo* postcard is closer to the intended work of art than the work of art hanging on the gallery wall. So many of Steadman's framed pieces include correction fluid and scissored paper and faint pencil lines because those are the norms of artboards. Each is an artifact of the process of making the mass-produced image that in its multiple copies is the final art.

So a comics artist must decide early what kind of art to create: a) works designed to be exhibited and that might also be reproduced, or b) works designed to be reproduced that might also be exhibited. For practical reasons, we prefer the second. It allows for a lot more "regrets." Don't worry about making mistakes. Everything is correctable. So be fearless. In fact, some comics artists incorporate their process into their final work. Many of the drawings in Julie Delporte's *This Woman's Work* include lightly visible tape at their corners. Frank Santoro takes the aesthetic further in *Pittsburgh*, which features wrinkled yellow paper for backgrounds with panels and partial images affixed onto it with white tape.

Line Variation

As you begin to draw, your own style will begin to emerge. It's not what you draw but how you draw it. Photorealism is relatively rare in comics (Bill Sienkiewicz and Dave McKean are occasional exceptions), but even photos (check out *A Softer World* photo webcomics of Emily Horne and Joey Comeau) aren't simply "real." Still, photos often do feel more realistic than drawings. Transforming reality into a set of lines is itself a distortion, and those lines may be thick or thin, dark or light, short or long, angular or rounded, straight or squiggling, curved or jagged, continuous or broken, consistent or variable. Since everything in the world of a comic book is composed of lines and every line is an expressive line, every object has an expressive quality that an artist can manipulate. Illustration 1.2 provides a range of line examples, and our first exercise will guide you to create your own.

ILLUSTRATION 1.2 *Line variations.*

EXERCISE 1.1 *VARYING LINES*

Open to the first page of a new sketchbook (or any piece of paper will do). Make a grid of 24 panels using a black fine-tipped marker (we recommend a Micron 08 or Micron 05) and a ruler (or not). Fill the panels with the following lines: 1. Slow horizontal lines; 2. Slow vertical lines; 3. Slow crosshatch lines; 4. Slow closer together crosshatch lines; 5. Even closer together crosshatch lines; 6. Slow diagonal lines from top to bottom, left to right; 7. Slow diagonal lines from top to bottom, right to left; 8. Diagonal crosshatch using lines from 6 and 7; 9. Slow horizontal hesitating lines barely touching the surface; 10. Rapid diagonal right-to-left lines; 11. Rapid diagonal closer together right-to-left lines; 12. Rapid vertical/diagonal crosshatch lines; 13. Large quick horizontal left-to-right zigzags; 14. Rapid overlapping horizontal left-to-right zigzags; 15. Rapid overlapping close-together horizontal left-to-right zigzags; 16. Horizontal rows of dots close together; 17. Switching to Micron 05, light fast right-to-left diagonals close together; 18. Farther apart fast left-to-right diagonals; 19. Fast crosshatch vertical and diagonals left to right, top to bottom; 20. Fast horizontal squiggles close together; 21. Fast crosshatch verticals and diagonals right to left, top to bottom; 22. Loose free-form fast left-to-right, top-to-bottom diagonals; 23. Fast diagonal segments slotted into each other in three parts, left to right, top to bottom; and 24. Very close crosshatch diagonals.

The choice of lines controls the overall image which defines the overall story. Recall the opening sentence of Cameron's short story. A Philip composed of short, thick, jagged lines would be different from a Philip composed of long, thin, curving lines. Those details are another window into his character. They create impressions about his emotional state as he's sitting pretending to read. Is he calm or agitated? An artist might ask that question in advance and then choose a style to capture it. Or she might simply start sketching and, noticing the agitated feel of her short, thick, jagged lines, decide how upset Philip must be—and how much he is trying to repress it given the contrastingly calm shape of his posture. These choices may feel more like discoveries than inventions, but they can only happen if the story is developed visually.

Draw Reality

There are two general approaches to making images. Lynda Barry guides new comics artists to draw from their heads: a car, Batman, anything that fills your hand with the freeing energy of a child drawing for fun. That's a great approach, one we will explore soon, but first let's start with things outside of our heads. Practice drawing from reality. Whether or not your comic is realistic, having the ability to draw observationally will help you solidify even the most cartoonish reality.

Students in our class arrive with wildly different drawing skills. This has little to do with innate skill; it usually boils down to how much or how little experience they have had drawing. The only way to draw well is to draw and draw and draw. Every drawing you make is a learning experience, and all drawings have merit that can be capitalized on. Learning how to find shape, line, and value effectively takes time and sometimes a bit of instruction. Begin where you are now, practice, and, if you feel the need, get a few great drawing books or, better yet, take a drawing class, online or in person. Taking a class in traditional observational drawing isn't absolutely necessary, but it can make drawing comics easier and more satisfying. Any observational drawing book or beginning drawing technique class will give you information that you didn't already have and hopefully make your drawings more like *your* drawings. Online resources are rich and seemingly infinite. If you want to learn to draw an elephant, there is an online resource for it, either a step-by-step instruction or a YouTube video of an artist drawing. There are poster pages for drawing heads, feet, trees, bushes, cars, babies, swords, deer, etc. Don't hesitate to gather more information; it will always help your drawing. For a start point, look at Illustration 1.3 for some basic ideas about depth and contrast, and Illustration 1.4 for human anatomy.

Accepting what your drawings look like now is important. You cannot learn to make more effective drawings if you don't first draw. You have to have a drawing to react to, to change, to learn from. Sketchbooks are a splendid, time-honored way to practice drawing without the stress of an audience. Buy one. Fill it up. Buy another one. Keep filling them up. Draw all of the *Creating Comics* exercises in your sketchbook. Draw everywhere and anywhere, out of your head and from objects and scenes in front of you. Keep running lists of ideas and make fast sketches of your ideas at the same time. Trace other artists' comics to get a feeling for line, shape, and value potential. Make copies of favorite drawings and shrink them to go in your sketchbook for inspiration. Think of something that you have always wanted to draw, like a horse or a dragon or just a believable box, find an online source that will teach you how, and do it in your sketchbook.

The point isn't to make "good" drawings. The point is to draw. Learn the feel of the pencil against the paper, the different angles you hold your wrist, the motion of your whole arm when you draw from your shoulder. The more you draw, the more confident you will feel drawing. Arrange a still life on a table and draw. Find an interesting place inside and draw. Find an interesting place outside and draw. Ask a friend to pose and draw. When you flip back through your pages and find something you like, great—that image may end up in one of your comics. You'll also see that you have your own

ILLUSTRATION 1.3 *Depth and contrast.*

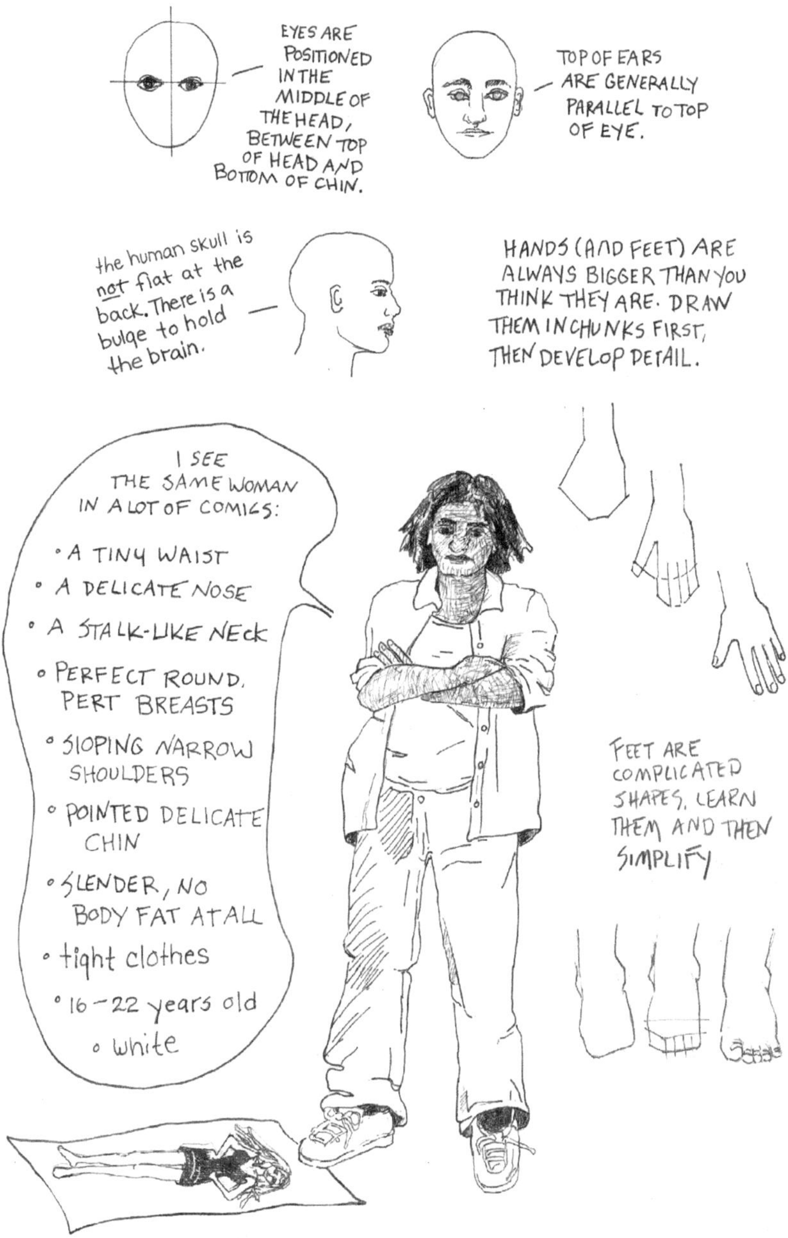

ILLUSTRATION 1.4 *Anatomy basics.*

way of making lines and shapes and values, of interpreting visual information and translating it into your own kind of mark. You have your own style.

Manipulate Reality

Your comic doesn't need to have a drawn-from-reality feel, but your drawings will create their own reality. The lines that compose Philip would have overall shapes that are understood to be the actual shapes of Philip's body. If the drawings are veering toward realism, those shapes will fall within the range of human beings. Many comic images are well outside that range. If, for instance, Philip's head is more than a seventh or eighth of his height or is more rounded than a human skull, then he will appear cartoonish. If his head is a third or more of his height and perfectly round, he will be extremely cartoonish, probably resembling Charlie Brown or a character from *South Park* more than an actual person. A realistic Philip would have more descriptive line and value. In *99 Ways to Tell a Story*, Matt Madden illustrates differences in line quantity by drawing the same one-page scene in "Silhouette," "Minimalist," "Maximalist" and even "No Line" styles, all with the same objects using the same contours but varying the number of internal lines (2005: 176–83).

Cartoons tend to be composed of fewer lines, with less internal shading to indicate musculature or the complexities of fabric folds in clothing. They're "flat." This would also affect a viewer's understanding of Philip and his situation. A realistically drawn Philip might produce an expectation that his internal world is similarly complex, that he has the same psychological depth as a three-dimensional person. A cartoon Philip is more ambiguous. His emotions may seem simpler. Upset over his spouse going to a dinner party without him requires a fair amount of psychological shading. So subject and style are not always separable. When creating stories through images, external appearance can be the same as internal characterization.

Analyze other artists' styles. The best way for artists to analyze is with their hands. In Illustration 1.5, students in our class browsed our library of comics, selected panels they liked, and copied them. This is one of the very best drawing exercises. Not only does a student get a feel for another artist's lines but they also learn to measure and keep proportion in their head, a necessary skill that only comes with practice. If you flip forward to the Anthology, you'll see that Marguerite Dabaie recreates cartoons by Naji al-Ali, and Gina Siciliano recreates paintings by Renaissance painter Artemisia Gentileschi. Reproducing another artist's lines gives you a feeling for what is possible. While tracing, be conscious of the way the line is used, how fast or slow you have to draw, how detailed, what detail, what sort of value is used, etc. Be present to the process, and your hand and eye will learn something every time you copy.

ILLUSTRATION 1.5 *Student copies of Seiichi Hayashi, Sophia Dimino-Foster, Julie Doucet, Alison Bechdel, Craig Thompson, Tillie Walden, Adrian Tomine, Richard McGuire, and David Small.*

EXERCISE 1.2 *COPYING OTHERS*

Browse a large selection of comics (starting with this book's anthology) and choose one panel from six artists with very different styles. Write down what you see in the panel. Describe the setting. List each object. Describe the types of line used. Describe the demeanor of the drawing—quick or slow, detailed or spare, etc. Trace the six panels, using a medium soft drawing pencil or a black felt-tipped marker and a light table (you can also improvise one with a large Tupperware container and the flashlight app on a phone). Be aware of the lines you are tracing. What do they describe? How were they made? *Think* as you trace. Tape your traces into your sketchbook later, but first place your sketchbook and the panel copies side by side. Draw the panels in your sketchbook free hand. Keep the drawings the same size as the originals. Remember what you learned from tracing the panels. And again, *think* as you draw.

Though there is an enormous range of styles among comics artists, sometimes all comics art is called "cartoon." The term originally referred to a cardboard-like paper used for preliminary sketches. When England's *Punch* magazine published a series of "cartoons" lampooning Parliament's planned murals in 1843, the word became associated with both satire and a specific drawing style: simplified and exaggerated. A cartoon has fewer details than a naturalistic drawing, and those details—the contours of the lines—are distorted. Realism requires more lines, and those lines are derived directly from their subject matter. Images that combine those two categories are harder to classify. An exaggerated but detailed image isn't realistic, but it might not connote "cartoon" to a viewer either, and images made of very few but observationally accurate lines might strike some viewers as a cartoon and others as realistic.

In Illustration 1.6, Leigh Ann has drawn our student Henry six times. The top row is realistic in the sense that the line shapes of the image match the photograph they're based on. But as you move left to right, each image changes in terms of detail. The first is heavily crosshatched; the second uses value blocks of uniformly rendered black; and the third includes only contour line. The second row follows the same progression, but the figure is distorted. Leigh Ann exaggerated Henry's feet, hands, and head. She could exaggerate different features instead and to any of a range of possible levels. She could also alter the shapes, making the head rounder, the feet squarer, the hands longer, etc. Simplification (the reduction) of details can vary more too, with different areas contrasting. As far as style, Henry 1. is the most realistic, and Henry 2. is the most cartoonish. All nine images began as a photo taken on a phone, emailed to Leigh Ann's Mac, printed on her laser printer, traced on a lightboard, and photocopied and resized multiple times, with body parts

ILLUSTRATION 1.6 *Simplifying and exaggerating Henry.*

cut out and glued on by hand, before being rescanned and digitally cleaned up to eliminate traces of white-out and internal paper edges.

EXERCISE 1.3 *SIMPLIFYING AND EXAGGERATING FIGURES*

In addition to previous materials, you'll need access to a photocopier, plus scissors and glue.

1 Start by taking a photo of a friend with your cellphone, preferably a head-to-toe shot. Heighten the contrast without losing too much detail. Print this off and shrink the image on a copier to around six inches.

2 Trace this image on a light table with a black Micron pen. Simplify any patterns. Use black, white and gray (hatching or dotting). Simplify shapes to your liking. For instance, make the hair one large specific shape. Take care with the face, simplifying the eyes and nose. If your copy is hard to make out on the lightboard, deepen the contrast, print off a new copy, shrink and start again. Take your time.

3 Photocopy the above image, put it on the light table and trace it again, but this time simplify the contrast to only black and white. In other words, lump all the darker halftones with black and the lighter halftones with white. If you have trouble visualizing this, go back to Illustration 1.6 and compare 1. and 2.

4 Photocopy the above finished image and make a contour drawing that uses only lines. Outline the major shapes and *some* of the details. Losing the value will simplify your figure considerably. Make several of these and see which has the most essential linear information and keep that one. Let the line disappear in places that just feel right. It shouldn't be one unbroken line. Go back and look at 3. in Illustration 1.6 again.

5 Photocopy the first image you made but 50 percent larger. Cut off the head, hands, and feet and attach them to the normal-size figure. Now copy this again, put it on a light table, and trace with only black and white value shapes.

6 Photocopy this last image and trace again using only lines, simplifying but still retaining interesting, specific information.

You should have six finished drawings on separate pieces of paper. Shrink each of the drawings on the copier by 50 percent. Paste all of these drawings on one piece of paper, three on top row, three on bottom, and paste this sheet in your sketchbook. If you have to shrink them more than 50 percent to fit them on the page, then do it.

Few people outside of comics would call reduction and alteration of details "cartooning," but Picasso's eleven-lithograph *Bull* series demonstrates the same two qualities. Though his final minimally detailed and maximally distorted image is not a cartoon in the sense of a shared set of drawing norms, it is expressed in a set of instantly recognizable visual norms. It is a Picasso bull. It is drawn in a Picasso style. A face drawn in a manga style resembles other drawings of manga-style faces more than it resembles any actual face. This affects a viewer's understanding of the character and situation at yet another level. A manga Philip would create a different impression and set of expectations than a Philip drawn in the style of Robert Crumb or Jack Kirby. Both styles tell viewers what kind of world they're entering, and so what norms are in play. Suddenly Philip is not just a character, but a character in a *kind* of story with an entire genre history behind it.

Group style norms also further explain the "non-art" prejudice against comics from Art departments, since an artist who only imitates another artist may be considered no artist at all. A manga face or Kirbyan foot are generic in the literal and pejorative senses. They place a story's genre before the story itself, and they use what Lefèvre called "stereotypical icons," only now the icons aren't from the real world but from other images. The new artist renders her lines to resemble the qualities of other artists' lines, making the subject matter twice removed. This is especially true of invented images, ones drawn from mental impressions, because all artists are influenced by other art, consciously and unconsciously. Better to begin with reality and then discover the style of your story—which may vary with each story you draw—as you develop it, allowing subject matter to influence rendering and rendering to influence subject matter in a virtuous circle.

Use References

Don't rely on your memory or your imagination. Look for examples to draw tigers, corvettes, bras, eyeglasses, oak trees, babies, etc. Be specific. Details are crucial. Windowsills on windows, buttons on shirts, lines in sidewalks, stretch marks on stomachs, condensation on iced-tea glasses. Overly familiar forms are boring. Working from photographs (preferably your own) gives a comic real-world specificity. Comics creators from a full range of genres and styles begin by staging a photo shoot. Robyn Warhol describes Alison Bechdel's "practice of taking snapshots of herself posing for each of the characters in every frame, then draw from the snapshots . . . to get every bodily gesture, every wrinkle in the clothing, every angle just right" (2011: 7). Bechdel does not actually reproduce every wrinkle in her actual drawings (her style in *Fun Home* is relatively sparse), but the poses add realism to what might otherwise appear cartoonish in its simplicity. Bernie Wrightson created the premiere Swamp Thing episode in *House of Secrets* #92 (July 1971) by posing friends in the roles of villain, damsel, and hero-monster (Cooke and Khoury 2014:

96–7). Bechdel dressed in a man's suit and tie looks a lot more like her father than Wrightson's friend looks like a mud-encrusted swamp creature, but the photographs still provided the necessary gestures and angles to give the comic a naturalistic edge. For his comics adaption of the silent film classic *M*, Jon J. Muth takes the photographic approach to its extreme:

> All of the scenes in *M* were enacted by people in character. I cast friends, family, and strangers, gathered clothes and props, and decided where each scene would be shot. . . After directing and photographing a scene, I would make my drawings from the photographs. . . If I took a poor photograph—one that was over- or underexposed or blurry—then I did a drawing of a poor photo. I didn't correct anything. . . . When I duplicated a photograph by drawing it, the drawing extracted a different range of emotions than the photo. This happened though I tried to be as faithful to the photograph as possible . . . This was a discovery, and not by design.
>
> 2008: 192

Again, this is the kind of discovery possible only through image making. No script can produce it.

Illustration 1.7 demonstrates a range of photo research examples. Each includes an original photograph and a drawing made from it. The goal isn't fidelity—unless that's your particular goal. Sometimes the drawn image varies significantly, referencing the photo for general ideas. Other times the references are exact but edited, like Leigh Ann's sparsely arranged bricks. Some of the images are traced on a lightboard; others are freehand. Chris made the tree and fence in Microsoft Paint. Some of the images add details—Leigh Ann invented those beach balls but copied Godzilla from a website. She also photographed a colleague to paint in watercolor, showing the differences of media too. Our student Anna pulled a photo from her phone to use in her memoir about running, and Mims snapped pictures of her own legs while in class to use for a character stepping into water. Emily's four-panel strip at the bottom was taken from a class photoshoot with students posed with instruments and in animal masks.

If Peter Cameron were a comics creator, he could find a friend to pose with a book in bed. Philip might end up looking a lot like the friend, though not necessarily more than Bechdel looks like her father or any human being like Swamp Thing. Cameron's actual bed and covers will become Philip's too, as well as other contents and architecture of the bedroom. Holding a camera also forces other creative decisions. Do we look down at Philip? If so, that might imply an attitude, meaning we are figuratively looking down at him, judging him negatively. Or do we snap the picture from below and so look up at Philip, possibly implying a positive and even admiring attitude. If the camera and Philip are on the same level, they are equals, which could imply that Philip and the narrator are equals in terms of the power dynamics of their relationship, especially if the point-of-view is understood to be the

ILLUSTRATION 1.7 *Photo research.*

narrator's. Or is the narrator in the image too? Are we looking over the narrator's shoulder from the doorway? We might instead view Philip from the opposite side of the bed, with the doorway and narrator in the background. Maybe Philip's comforter-covered foot is in the foreground. Or maybe we move the camera closer so only Philip's head and the book are visible in the foreground, and the narrator is framed between them. The more you experiment the more nearly infinite the possibilities are.

If you were an artist adapting Peter Cameron's short story, you'd take a dozen variations, study them and chose one shot or a combination of shots that most appealed to you. That's the basis of your first image. Because the photograph has already flattened reality into shapes and shades, it's easier to draw than from a live model or even a still life. Now is your chance to experiment with style. How true-to-life should your shapes be? Your drawn Philip might be cartoonishly thinner or thicker than the human model or otherwise disproportionate. How detailed is he? Does he have just enough lines to define his basic anatomy or does he possess three-dimensional crosshatched depth? And those crosshatches and outlines, what are the qualities of those lines and how do they create a sense of Philip? Also think about his relationship to his drawn environment. Are the lines of his body and the lines of the bedroom roughly the same in terms of style or do they contrast? Though degree of detail can suggest significance—the more detailed a character or object is the more important they seem by comparison—some comics place minimally detailed characters in highly detailed surroundings. Try both approaches. Draw Philip several times, until he begins to accrue a sense of permanence in your own mind. Eventually those drawn qualities will become part of your mental understanding of his character, and then when you draw him in different moments and actions, he will still look like and so be "Philip."

Whatever the framing effect of the photo, when you draw from it you also control the positioning of elements within the new frame. First consider centering. Do you want Philip in the middle of the frame? If so, he's likely to seem more significant than if he's closer to an edge, making him literally but also figuratively "marginal." You can even crop Philip partially or entirely out of frame, reducing his presence in the image and suggesting his reduced role in the story's power dynamic. Or, introducing a technique not available to photographers, Philip's body could break the frame and extend either into the margin of the gutter between images or into the drawn content of an adjacent image. If so, Philip will likely seem more powerful, able to break through the boundaries of his visual container even though within the storyworld he is stationary.

Also consider how fully Philip fills the image. Does he take up the most two-dimensional space and so figuratively dominate too? Or does the positioning and angling of the bed make it more powerful, turning Philip into its tiny occupant? If so, the bed may take on metaphorical meaning, suggesting perhaps the couple's relationship overall. Or both Philip and the bed may just be elements in an expansively framed bedroom. The more expansive the framing, the less space Philip occupies and the less powerful his character will seem.

EXERCISE 1.4 *USING PHOTOSHOOTS*

Make a three-panel comic, using a phone camera as a drawing tool. Refine images as well as create original content through your own photoshoots. Ask friends to dress up and perform or document some actual event: a sports game, a poetry reading, a birthday party. Be sure to include at least one individual. Take lots of photos. Experiment with framing. Try cropping and centering the same figure. Vary distance to make the figure seem larger and smaller. Afterwards flip through them and find three that appeal to you. They might be three that together create a sense of a single action, or they might be three isolated moments. Use them as your source material and draw a three-panel comic in any style, simplifying and distorting as much or as little as you like.

Frames

Unlike photography, the frame of a comic panel can be any shape. There's no default form. You have to decide the shape relationship of the frame to the content it encloses. To emphasize Philip, draw the frame to match his body. Sitting up in bed probably gives him a roughly upright rectangular shape, which the frame can duplicate and so produce a panel shape that reflects its content. To emphasize the bed instead, draw a frame that matches it, probably a longer, vertical rectangle, one not dominated by Philip. You can also extend panel dimensions to contrast content. If that first frame is a thinner, taller rectangle, it will either end up cropping Philip or include more content above or below him, making him seem less important even if he's still centered. And panels needn't be rectangles at all. Design a shape that suits the needs of the image.

Illustration 1.8 includes a range of framing examples by our students. There are two major approaches. The top section features images (by Anna, Katie, Mims, and Emily) with frames that match the subject's proportions. That tends to be the default setting. We tend to draw tall figures in tall frames and wide figures in wide frames. That's fine, but the uniformity can get boring. Find interesting contradictions, ways that the frame and the subject can be mismatched instead. If the figure is wide, what happens when you use a tall frame? Either you have to crop the subject or you have to shrink it, creating additional space within the frame to fill with additional subject matter, expanding the surrounding or background content. You can

ILLUSTRATION 1.8 *Frame and subject relationships.*

misalign too, using the frame to crop content that could be centered but isn't. The bottom images (by Coleman, Maddie, Anna, and Grace) include a range of intentionally mismatched framing choices. They all appeared in our students' comics, so they are mismatched for specific reasons—often to convey a negative connotation in the story situation. A centered, proportionately framed subject creates an impression of balance and control. De-centered, cropped, and disproportionately framed subjects seem less balanced and less in control. Choose accordingly.

Finally, there's the frame itself—which isn't a frame but a drawing of one. Illustration 1.9 includes a range of frames suggested by the image content: Leigh Ann's tree branches, Chris's beakers, coffee mugs, and legs, and Daisy's dominoes. Like the rest of the image, you control all of a frame's qualities. A thick, ruler-sharp line carries a different connotation than a barely discernable, free-form line. In *I'm Not Here* (2017), GG includes no frame lines at all, allowing white areas within her images to merge with the white of the gutters. In *Red Winter* (2018), Anneli Furmark demonstrates the opposite extremes with wide frame lines that are thicker and blacker than any of the image elements they contain. As a result, Furmark's characters seem trapped while GG's seem to float in a ghostly world. Instead of drawing panel frames, Kate Evans scans and digitally inserts strips of fabric to define the gutters for her graphic nonfiction *Threads* (2017).

Though not part of the story-world, the frame can still reflect and reinforce story elements by duplicating style or visual motifs. What if Philip's frame repeats the pattern in his comforter? Or the design of the book cover he's holding in his hands? Is he metaphorically in control of the scene as if able to hold it all too? What if there's no frame, just the lines of the image petering into the undrawn white of the page? That carries connotations too, ones that, like all the other connotations of image, you can only discover through the drawing process.

EXERCISE 1.5 *FRAMING*

Pick a subject. It can be anything, a bicycle, a palm tree, the Empire State Building. Look it up online for a visual reference. You're going to draw it four times. First, frame it inside a panel that matches its proportions, leaving some space but not too much between it and the frame. Second, draw it again, beginning with a frame that's either too tall or too wide and so requires including more than just the immediate subject in the drawing. Third, use that frame again, but this time crop the subject so that it doesn't all fit. Look over your three drawings. Pick your favorite and redraw it, this time developing the frame, too. If the frame were real, what would it be made of? Make it relate in some way to the subject.

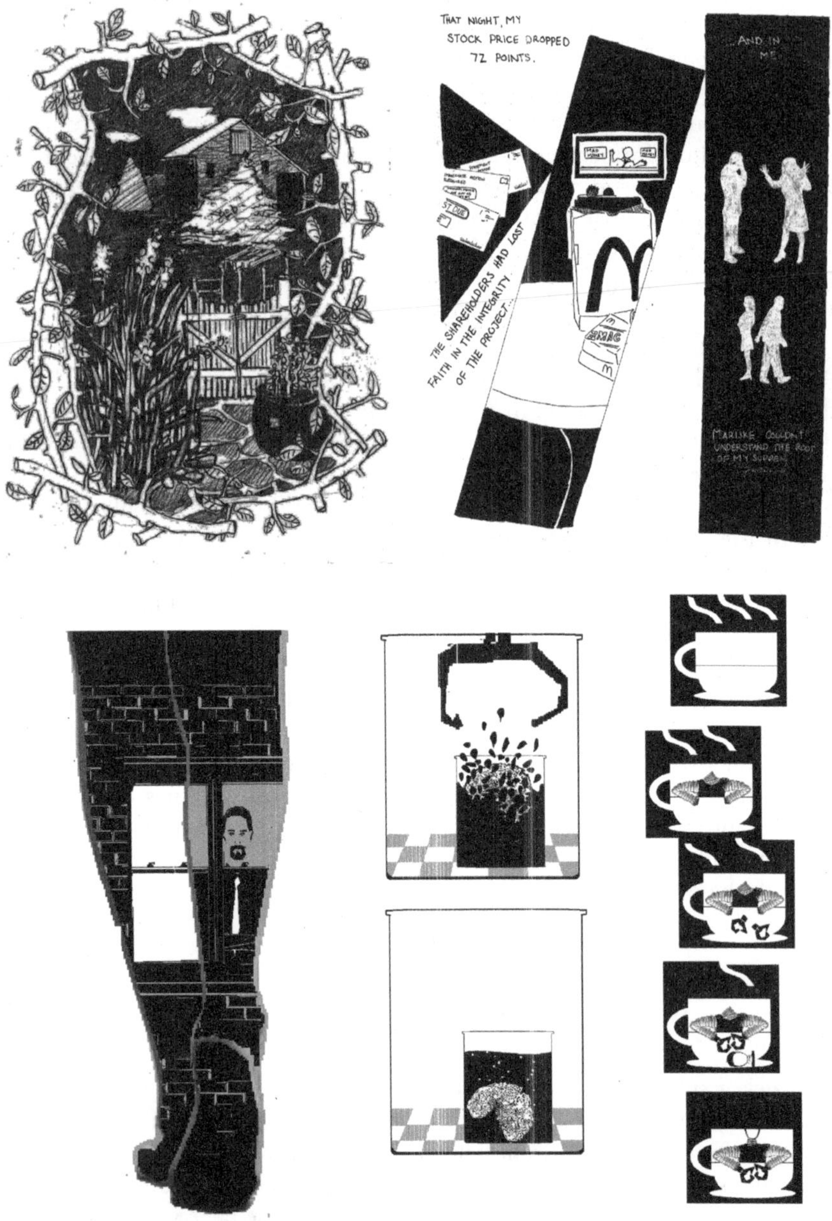

ILLUSTRATION 1.9 *Frame styles.*

Revision

On the first day of class, we told students to draw a kangaroo in a rocking chair in front of a window. The top half of Illustration 1.10 includes six rough drafts by Coleman, Anna, Henry, Mims, Grace, and Katie, students ranging from those with plenty of art studio experience to those who had never picked up a drawing pencil before. It doesn't matter what experience you've had. Everyone can produce interesting art through revision. We said a kangaroo because people tend not to have a clear picture of one already in their heads, so they can't draw a generic "idea." Their rocking chairs tend to be fairly generic too. And the idea of a window tends to be a 2 x 2 frame—which is oddly rare for actual windows.

Revising the first draft requires image research. Since we have no rocking chairs and kangaroos in our art studio, students Googled "kangaroo" and "rocking chair" on their phones and found images that appealed to them, studied them, sketched variations, redrew their first drafts, and inked them. The bottom six images are those revisions. Further revision is always possible (some of those lamps are still pretty generic), but they all became much more specific and so more interesting. You will follow this process with all of your panels, identifying objects, researching images, and revising for specificity. That doesn't mean realism. It doesn't even mean adding more lines. Your final images may be cartoonishly sparse, but their lines will create objects with individual character.

Unless you intend to create a comic about a kangaroo with a rocking chair, this assignment won't be of any immediate use to you. But the process will be. Illustration 1.11 breaks Henry's process into five steps. Even if you already have a specific character and story in mind, begin by "doodling." Draw anything in any style anywhere on the page with no plan. Let your hand do what it wants. This can teach you some of your own preferences for both style and subject matter. What do you like to draw? If the shapes of fish or robots come easily off your pencil tip, fish or robots probably belong in your comic. If you doodle flowers or geometric shapes, that might tell you something about your settings.

Our students doodled for fifteen minutes before stopping and looking over their pages. They all included rough drafts of their first characters. Some included many characters, but everyone chose one to develop first. Developing an image means making it more specific. Henry began by drawing a fantastical semi-human creature with wings and bird feet. He added more reality to that fantasy by going online and selecting related images: bird talons, bat wings, a male torso. If you drew a fish, search for specific fish and study their tails and gills and fins and mouths. If you drew a robot, search for machines and study their hinges and wheels and bolts and wires. You may want to copy and paste your researched images into a document and print it out for easy access.

1

2

ILLUSTRATION 1.10 *Revision.*

ILLUSTRATION 1.11 *Five-step character creation.*

EXERCISE 1.6 *CREATING A CHARACTER*

1 Begin by drawing with no plan in mind. Draw anything. Doodle for fifteen minutes before stopping to look over the page.

2 Select a particularly successful or interesting or personal section from the page to be your character. If this is difficult, have a friend pick. Draw it larger on a separate piece of paper. Feel free to change it as you draw it a second time.

3 Take inventory of your character's specific characteristics. Hands? Body? Clothes? Wings? Feet? Accessory objects? Research them all by finding visual references. Make a page of drawings that reflect your research. Feel free to trace anything from copies until you know how to draw them.

4 Now draw your character again, using your research to make it as specific as possible. Experiment with distortion and detail – how little, how much, where and where not to change the original drawing. Once you are satisfied with the general appearance of your character, revise it again, making the specific details more concrete, more confident. For example, if you've used a hesitant line, make it solid. If at this time you want to simplify the character, then take out extra detail and reassess. Be flexible. You may have to put some detail back in. Remember that revision can happen at any time during your drawing process. When you are happy with your revised drawing, go over the pencil lines with black marker.

5 You have a character. Now you need to know what it looks like from any point of view. Draw it fifty times (yes, fifty!). You'll be the world's expert by the end of this exercise. Use three or more sheets of paper. Draw in pencil. Here is a starter list of prompts. Some may not be practical or possible, so add more that are. Draw your character from behind, from the side, from above, from below, sitting, jumping, walking, kneeling, kicking, slouching, stretching, laughing, eating, sneezing, crying, crawling. Researching any necessary objects, draw your character playing tennis, playing trumpet, weightlifting, making bread, changing a diaper, drawing themselves, making coffee, tying hiking boots Add partial environments: teetering on a cliff, behind jail bars, at a protest, getting a facial. Zoom in for close-ups. Remember to fill in new details when zooming into eyes, hands, torso, lap, shoes or feet from the character's perspective. Zoom out: from above, from very far away, from inside a tunnel, from above with the character underwater, from afar skiing downhill, from outside a window with the character inside reading, from outside of a car with the character driving, from outside an airplane with the character as a passenger.

6 Look over your drawings. What do the images say about your character? What information do they convey? What possibilities about their lives and pasts and preferences and goals might they suggest? Write a list of possible facts about them. If you were working from a script, this list might have been your starting point, but now characters, stories, and whole worlds can originate from the images themselves. Begin with these prompts, responding in bullet points or in a steam-of-consciousness paragraph, expanding and moving between questions however you like. But be specific:

Describe your character's appearance.
What are their most striking physical characteristics?
How does it feel to be in their body?
How old are they?
What physical activity do they most enjoy?
What activity do they avoid?
What is their full name?
What does their signature look like? Sign their name as they would.
Do they have parents and siblings?
Name a fact about a grandparent.
Describe their worst fight with a family member.
Describe an odd childhood memory, one they're not even sure why it stays with them.
Do they have any birthmarks, scars, tattoos, injuries, or recent wounds?
Where do they live now? What sort of dwelling? Do they own or rent it?
What do you smell when you walk in?
Do they live alone or with others?
Do they have a pet?
What sort of animals do they come in contact with?
What sort of bed do they sleep in? What is their sleeping position?
What is on the bedside table or near them when they sleep?
Describe a fragment from a dream they had last night.
Name items in their medicine cabinet.
What clothing do they own other than what they're currently wearing?
What is their clothing made of?
Describe their shoes.
Do they wear underwear?
Where do they get their clothes?
Do they wear a ring or other specific piece of jewelry? Where did they get it?

What do they eat? Do they cook? What is their favorite food? Where do they get it?
What is the best meal they ever had?
Do they have neighbors? How would neighbors describe their personality? Would all the neighbors agree?
Are there any people or places they avoid?
When they want to be alone, where do they go?
When they want to be with others, where do they go?
List five actions they perform daily.
What happened yesterday at work?
Describe their workplace—the physical structure, the quality of light, the noise level. How do they feel when they're there?
What is the last lie they told?
Name something they lost and how they lost it.
Describe a secret they've told only once.
Name two of their regrets, one big, one small.
What is the most violent event they ever witnessed or experienced?
What was the highpoint of their week?
Describe an odd way they have of killing time and the first and most recent times they did it.
Describe a smell, taste, or texture they hate and why.
Describe the last time they laughed.
Describe something contradictory about them.
Describe an ambition they no longer have.
When they close their eyes, what do they picture?
Name two things they worry about, one small, one big.
What is one of their biggest goals? Name something specific they would sacrifice to achieve it. Name something they would not sacrifice. Name something they're not sure they could sacrifice or not.
What do they think will happen to them when they grow older?
They have a nagging feeling that they forgot something. What was it?
Reach into one their pockets and pull something out. What is it?
What are they doing right now? Describe the location.
Are they having a good time?
What do they most want at this moment?
Describe your character in one sentence.

You now should have a pretty interesting character. By developing it visually, you likely spurred yourself to invent details, both visual and non-visual, that you wouldn't have if you'd approached character development only through words. You also probably have a range of situations, plots, and other story material to build on for the next chapters. Add anything you want at any time.

Anthology

Turn to the anthology section now, and as you look through the excerpts, consider the following questions: How would you describe each artist's style? How do the images appear to have been made—with what media? What hint of drawing process remains in the final products? Describe the line qualities and what they connote. Where in the range of realism and cartoon do the images fall? How exaggerated are the details? How simplified are they overall? Is the style consistent? If it varies, where and to what effect?

Beginning with line quality, note the difference between Tsai's thin sharp continuous contour lines and Alagbé's more varied expressive lines. French's even thicker lines were originally drawn in square centimeters and then enlarged, resulting in little detail. Ma's art was instead significantly shrunk when printed, producing dense detailing. Katin's soft gestural lines produce porous forms and an illusion of movement. Libicki's forms are planar with hard linear edges and higher contrast.

Even "black" varies between artists. Finck's darkest panels preserve a record of her filling them with random sets of angled pen strokes that leave some portion of the page untouched and so create a textured and tactile black. Johnson and Hernandez instead fill areas with opaque black that creates unified shapes without texture or gradation. D'Salate combines approaches, sometimes roughly crosshatching and sometimes filling in area with opaque black. GG uses almost no lines, instead creating sharp-edged shapes that vary by digital value gradations. Nickerson uses black contour lines to define shapes in the foreground of a varied gray background. Bechdel and Corman use four values (black, white, and two shades of neutral gray) but Bechdel's grays are transparent and often wash over or do not quite reach the edge of the shape, while Corman's uniform grays fill the shapes precisely.

Whatever the qualities of line, shape, and value gradation, artists can combine them in a spectrum of styles ranging from realistic to the most exaggerated and simplified of cartoons. As a photographer, Bick's images are by far the most realistic in the anthology, but Comeau also incorporates photography for radically different and non-realistic effects. Combining density of detail and realistic proportion, Ma's art is probably the most realistic, followed perhaps by Hogarth and Estrada. Ott and Siciliano aren't far behind. Hankiewicz's style is meticulously textured to create value, but the simplified shapes flatten the depth of field for an overall surreal effect. Ernst extracts illustrations by uncredited artists from Victorian novels and encyclopedias and arranges them in surreal collages. Lightman's intentionally incomplete images undercut their realistic accuracy. Katin and D'Salate, though stylistically distinct, employ similarly mid-range levels of distortion and detail. Abel, Alagbé, GG, Hernandez, Johnson, Powell, Radtke, Roberts, Thompson, Tomine, and Vallotton simplify but mostly avoid exaggeration for overall naturalistic effects.

The cartoon end of the style spectrum is equally diverse. Tsai's figures are perhaps the most exaggerated, and Nickerson's the most simplified, eliminating most details including even facial features. Finck's cartooning involves a looser line quality for intentionally imprecise shapes, while Dhaliwal's more precise lines create consistently specific shapes and so characters. Tobocman's figures are simplified and exaggerated too, but in a style that evokes expressionistic woodcuts because the shapes are blocky and limited to two values. Barry, Davis, Muñoz, Smyth, and Satrapi each create their own style within the larger category of cartooning.

Other artists vary their style. While Tamaki's *Everlasting Boy* strip is cartoony, Tamaki's full-page image is more precise in its line quality and details, producing a comparatively realistic effect despite the cartoon qualities of the character's faces. Dabaie varies style by redrawing another artist's cartoons, which are distinguishable from her own self-portrait. Libicki cartoons herself and the people she interacts with privately, but images that portray national events are more realistic. Bechdel includes images from earlier in her career that contrast with her current style. Corman's style varies within images, with naturalistic settings but cartoon faces. Interestingly, Siciliano does not vary her style, even though the content of her images vacillates between an artist and the canvas the artist is painting. Hopkins, as the only artist drawing non-representationally, is not on the naturalistic-cartoon spectrum.

What other stylistic qualities strike your attention? Keep looking through the anthology, pausing over favorite images. They could serve as inspiration as you continue to experiment and develop your own visual style.

2

Hinges

CHAPTER OUTLINE

"If you're a literary writer trying to write your first comic," explains literary and comics writer Benjamin Percy, "it might go something like this:

> Here is a panel of a man talking to his wife. He pulls some milk out of the fridge as she sits at the kitchen table, ashing a cigarette onto a plate.
>
> In the next panel, they're both sitting down, and now he's got his head in his hands and a full glass of milk in front of him.
>
> The next panel? They're sitting there, still talking, the cigarette burned down to the filter and glass now empty except for the white suds at its bottom.
>
> The next panel: Still sitting there.
>
> The next panel and the next panel and the next: Maybe by this point, someone has pushed away from the table, but the couple remain in the kitchen.

> The next panel, they're putting on their coats.
> The next panel, they're on the stoop, locking the door.
> The next panel, they're walking to the bus stop.
> The next panel, they're waiting for the bus.
> The next panel, they're still waiting for the bus.
> The next panel, they're on the bus.
>
> 2016: 28

This, according to Percy, is a bad script—or really the skeleton of a draft of a bad script since the actual dialogue doesn't exist yet. But that's his point: dialogue doesn't matter. Comics are about action, and this comic will have none. In addition to publishing prose novels, Percy writes for DC's *Green Lantern* and *Teen Titans* series. DC revolutionized the industry with the publication of *Action Comics* #1 in 1938, so it's no wonder that "action" still defines the company.

But Percy is only partially right about his sample script. If drawn, it might well result in a dull couple of comics pages. Or an inspired artist might take this skeleton and achieve a visually compelling two-page spread that seizes a viewer's attention with the power of its rendering by depicting complex character conflict in the nuanced connotations of its details. We can't know, since the actual images don't exist. And that's our point: scripts aren't comics. Since Percy isn't the artist and so can't determine any of the qualities of the eventual comic he's "writing," he controls what he can: drawing instructions. Since drawing instructions are not drawings, a script's word-based visual concepts limit both the process and the product.

Still, Percy has a point. Comics—even non-superhero comics—do emphasize action, though not necessarily in the sense Percy means. He says to "Open big" and provides examples of a zombie hand shoving out of a grave and a jet crashing into an airport terminal. But his script skeleton includes action too. He discounts speech and the image of the wife removing ash from her cigarette, and for the most part we agree. The real action would take place *between* these described images.

In the first panel, the husband would be standing in front of an open refrigerator with a container of milk in his hand. Percy says he "pulls" the milk from the fridge. Perhaps his arm and the angle of the container are drawn to suggest movement, but movement in which direction? Taken alone, the image might be ambiguous. Maybe he is angling the container back onto a shelf? A viewer can't determine that until the second image. The husband would now be seated with a glass of milk in front of him. What actions happened between these two snapshot-like instances of frozen time? Well, a lot, and though they are all undrawn, the juxtaposition of the two images does the work of implying them—though ultimately all "actions" are the inferences of the viewer. They happen not on the page but in the story-world inside the viewer's mind.

In Percy's third panel description, there are only white suds in the glass and the cigarette is burnt down to its filter. What happened between those two images? Presumably the husband drank the milk and the wife smoked the cigarette. We assume this even though no artist draws the cigarette touching the wife's lips or the glass touching the husband's. We also assume these specific actions despite a range of other possible actions. Maybe the husband spilled the milk on the floor and the puddle is out of frame? Maybe the wife handed the cigarette to the husband who smoked it and then handed the butt back to her? While neither of these possibilities are precluded by the juxtaposition of the two images, neither seems likely. Viewers tend to imagine the simplest solution to the puzzles created by placing two images next to each other.

Since Scott McCloud published *Understanding Comics* in 1993, those puzzle-solving inferences have been called "closure." McCloud borrowed the term from Gestalt psychology, which describes how, for example, a viewer mentally fills in the gaps between dots to perceive a dotted line as a "line" and not simply disconnected dots. In comics, viewers fill in gaps in a metaphorical sense—even if there's a literal gap, or gutter, between the images too. Filling that conceptual space doesn't involve imagining more images though. We don't mentally draw new panels of the husband and wife drinking and smoking. We just understand that they did. The information is image-less.

McCloud insists that "comics is closure!" (67), meaning that the inferences that juxtaposed images create are the form's most defining qualities. Though definitions of comics vary, almost all definers agree that a comic isn't a comic unless it combines at least two images. This is why a comics creator needs to understand the full range of inferences that two juxtaposed images can trigger.

Medieval diptychs include literal panels joined by literal hinges—which is another metaphor for the gutter (which is itself a metaphor). Since the term "closure" is confusing (because comics closure isn't the same as the Gestalt effect it's named after, plus "closure" is also a term for how a story achieves its ending), we're going to talk about "hinged" images instead. What holds two images together? We identify ten kinds of inferences, or hinges, all of which can occur in combination.

Recurrence

This is probably the most basic building block of comics. Since the majority of visual art consists of single images, the majority of visual art also consists of single representations of subjects. Comics almost inevitably include multiple depictions of the same things—people, objects, environments, you name it. Though an artist might reuse an exact image, usually each representation is a new image consisting entirely of new lines. And yet a viewer understands each set of lines to "be" the same thing.

Consider Percy's script. In the first image, the husband would be standing at a refrigerator, but in the second, he would be seated at a table. In the first image, his entire body might be visible, but in the second perhaps only his upper torso. In the first he might be viewed in profile, but in the second head-on. Despite these and other differences in the actual drawings, the two representations would need to be similar enough that a viewer understands them to be a recurring character.

Sometimes the differences are extreme and may also indicate a change in the character within the story-world. The husband in Percy's later panels might be wearing a long winter coat with the collar up; add a hat, gloves, and a hunching posture as he braces against wind, and the figure may bear only the most rudimentary resemblance to the figure in the first panel. When Joe Shuster drew Clark Kent cowering in one panel and then Superman leaping powerfully in the next, he needed viewers to understand that the two images were of the same person playing different roles in different clothes. When Robert McKimson draws the Tasmanian Devil first in cartoonishly anthropomorphic proportions and then as tornado-shaped scribbles, we still need to know it's the same character—even though there is zero visual resemblance.

Fortunately, viewers are capable of ignoring a surprising amount of visual information in order to maintain a sense of object permanence. Recurrence means we have a stored mental schema of characters and objects, and as long as some visual detail triggers the schema, we superimpose it over the actual drawing, ignoring anything that doesn't match. Once an artist has settled on and communicated the defining visual elements, viewers' desire to infer recurrence creates a margin of error safety net. This is also why cartoonist Mort Walker advises: "A good comic character should have such a definite morf that it is recognizable even in silhouette" (2000: 19). By "morf," Walker means a reproducible body shape, and for examples he gives Dagwood, Popeye, Li'l Abner, Charlie Brown, Dick Tracy, and Mickey Mouse. Such iconic silhouettes are less possible in more realistic styles, but the principle is the same: draw your characters from multiple angles, positions, and conditions, until they accrue a recognizable permanence in your own drawing repertoire.

Recurrence can also be thematic or non-representational. If the first image features a door—say, the double arching doors of a church—and the second image features a screen door to a suburban porch, a viewer will presumably recognize both as examples of the category "doors." Connections might be more abstract— "love," "isolation," "things that form triangular shapes"—and the images don't even have to represent real-world subjects. Two completely abstract images can produce a sense of recurrence through repeated shapes, colors, line qualities and any other non-representational elements that a viewer experiences as visual echoes. An artist can even relate two otherwise unrelated representational images by repeating line and shape qualities. In fact, place *any* two images side-by-side and viewers will search for—and probably find—connections. But if a viewer doesn't experience any sense of recurrence, then she sees no relationship between the two images. They're non-sequiturs and so "unhinged."

Spatial

Recurrence applies to settings too. The first two images of Percy's script might show the kitchen from opposite perspectives, repeating no content, but we would still understand both to be drawings of *the* kitchen. This, coincidentally, matches McCloud's example of "a four-panel establishing shot of an old-fashioned kitchen scene . . . With a high degree of closure, your mind is taking four picture fragments and constructing an entire scene out of those fragments" (1993: 88–9). When a viewer infers that two images represent different areas or angles of a shared story space, the hinge is spatial. This occurs whether the setting is meticulously detailed or entirely undrawn but implied by characters having to occupy some location. It also occurs when two images reproduce the same angle of the same setting, creating the impression of a continuing line of vision—even though the viewer's actual line of vision is interrupted by the physical act of her eyes moving from the first area of the page to the second.

Some image pairings require greater spatial inferences. Imagine if the first image of Percy's script featured only the man in the kitchen and the second described the woman smoking in a bedroom. When paired a viewer might conclude—or at least hypothesize until able to confirm later—that the two rooms are located in the same house. If the story is futuristic, the two locations might be on different planets, and yet we can still understand them to have some sort of known physical relationship. But if a second image features an unfamiliar or ambiguous setting, a viewer experiences no spatial hinge. We either don't know where we are—or setting just isn't important for understanding how the two images relate.

Temporal

The two images take place at moments along a shared timeline. Typically a temporal hinge is forward-moving: we infer that the second image occurs after the first. The husband was *first* standing at the fridge, and *then* he was sitting at the table. That default assumption may be related to the viewer experiencing the passage of actual time as she moves from one image to the next. But a second image could instead indicate somehow that it takes place earlier or even simultaneously, either of which involves a kind of temporal hinge.

Even if two images are identical—when, for instance, Percy says the couple continues to sit at the table, the artist might duplicate the same drawing—we assume some amount of time has passed within the storyworld: they are *still* sitting. Inferring how much time is another puzzle. Even without the minutes-indicating clue of the cigarette, viewers tend toward shorter leaps. An hour or even a day *could* have passed, but we probably think only minutes have. Other passages could be weeks or centuries, depending on the visual clues. Viewers might also infer a temporal hinge even without any character or setting recurrence. Two images representing two otherwise unrelated locations may be understood as taking place one after the other, and so then they are related temporally and so not entirely unhinged.

Causal

Some visual clues that trigger a temporal hinge are changes in subjects that require a passage of time to have happened. Percy first describes a glass that is full of milk, and then he describes the glass as filled with only white suds. That change must have a cause, and so a viewer assumes that the husband drank the milk. Much of what we call "action" in comics is a product of causal hinges since still images can only indirectly evoke movement-requiring actions. Similarly, the shortened cigarette was presumably caused by the wife smoking it. There are probably other possible causes, but a causal hinge usually produces the simplest answer to the question "What happened?" In his final descriptions, Percy says the couple is sitting at a bus stop and then sitting on a bus. There's no image of their getting on the bus, but we would conclude that they did. We also conclude that they did nothing else of significance between the two drawn moments. They did not, for instance, have dinner at a nearby restaurant. They didn't even catch a different bus and then transfer to the drawn bus. They got on this bus and only this bus.

Sometimes implied causality is the main point of the juxtaposition. Imagine if the first image is of the couple seated with their glass of milk and ash-flicked plate, and in the second image the couple is absent and the cup and plate are upside down in a dish rack beside the sink. By inferring the cause—one or both of them cleaned the items—we also know the minimum amount of time that has passed during the temporal hinge.

Embedded

We usually think of an image as a set of lines drawn together. But it's possible, and relatively common, for a set of lines to consist of two images instead. This is also where we get to toss out panels and gutters. They're not necessary. Since frames aren't frames—they're drawings of frames—the spaces between frames are a kind of drawing too. They're drawings of literally nothing, a make-believe emptiness beyond the reality of the other drawings. That's a convenient method for separating images, but it's only a convenience. There's no reason why images can't overlap—as they do when an element of one image is drawn as though breaking or extending beyond its drawn frame. Or when panels are drawn as though each were a card-like object that can be layered and arranged as if the "top" image were blocking the content of another image "underneath" it. In that case, the lines of the frame edges define the image boundaries, but if you don't draw frames, the content can mingle. Technically there would only be one image—but that's always true. A comics page is a *single* drawing. The experience of separate units happens in the viewer's head. We experience an embedded hinge by seeing "separate" images. The convention of panels and gutters obscures that fact by making the effect so instantaneous we don't register any other possibility.

An artist could apply a similar technique to Percy's script. Instead of a row of three panels, imagine a full-width panel that includes an image of the husband at the refrigerator and a second image of him seated at the table. Or the wife seated as she inhales from her cigarette and also her standing at the sink behind herself cleaning the ash off of her plate. Without an embedded hinge, we would have to understand the single image as a single moment and so a representation of four people, two sets of identical twins apparently. Instead, we'd understand that there are two moments of time superimposed on one space viewed from one angle. An embedded hinge then often includes a temporal hinge, since it's the division of time that allows the division of the images.

Associative

Even though two images are different, they're understood as representing the same thing. This is a form of thematic recurrence, and it includes visual metaphors. Instead of drawing a murder victim's head being struck in *Watchmen*, Dave Gibbons draws a falling Jack-o-Lantern smashing open on the ground. Instead of drawing lovers having intercourse in *Nick Fury, Agent of S.H.I.E.L.D.*, Jim Steranko draws a close-up of a gun inside its holster. Because the pumpkin and holstered gun were previously drawn as part of the settings, the associative hinge involves a spatial hinge too. And because we understand the second images to take place simultaneously, serving as a kind of curtain placed in front of the evoked but undrawn actions (sex and violence), it also involves a temporal hinge.

Percy doesn't tell us much about his married couple, but imagine if an artist drew them seated at the bus stop in exactly the same positions and postures as they were when seated in their kitchen. And if the artist developed other visual parallels—the shapes of the bus stop enclosure and the shapes of the kitchen counters and window—viewers would associate not only the two locations but the two moments and behaviors, perhaps concluding that this couple, even when together in their home doing nothing, are always psychologically "waiting." Their marriage is a metaphorical bus stop. That possibility doesn't find its way into Percy's or anyone else's script because it needs to develop on the page at the level of the drawn image. Which is to say: it's a perfectly good idea, but let's see what actually happens when you start drawing.

An associative hinge can include images not in the story-world too. These metaphors are harder to miss since they eliminate spatial and temporal hinges, leaving no other way to understand them. If a realistic image of the wife exhaling cigarette smoke is followed by an image of smoke billowing from a cartoon chimney, it's not hard to get the implied connection. Add an image of the husband frowning as he looks at her, and we'll probably infer that he's thinking: "She smokes like a chimney."

Non-sensory

If a character can sense something—the glint on the glass of milk, the smell of the cigarette, the cold winter air—then it's real. But if the cigarette-like chimney exists only in the husband's thoughts, then it's non-sensory. It's not part of the physical world of the story. Dreams and memories can use non-sensory hinges, allowing viewers to make sense of images that would otherwise violate basic principles of a stable reality.

In *The Oven* (2015), Sophie Goldstein uses this kind of visual metaphor not to obscure violent or sexual content, but to evoke emotional and psychological meanings. When a husband leaves his wife for the last time, Goldstein draws his figure dissolving into a stream of flying insects. Although such insects were previously established as existing in the story-world, this particular image does not represent a moment in time in which they are in flight. The image only represents the abstract idea of a dissolving marriage. Visual poetry, especially when it avoids temporal and spatial hinges, employs a lot of non-sensory hinges. Bianca Stone begins "Because You Love You Come Apart" with an image of the speaker in a mask breaking the back of another identically dressed version of herself (2016: 3–4). When in the next image the figure is singular, unharmed, and unmasked and in an apparently different location, a viewer understands those changes as non-sensory; Stone is representing things other than the physical world.

Returning to Percy's script, imagine after an image of the couple sitting at the bus stop, an artist draws a closely cropped cigarette being crushed out. Because no one in the first image is smoking, the transition to the crushed cigarette might be non-sensory. It might instead be a memory from earlier in the kitchen. Either character might be experiencing it. The connotations of the image—the remnants of something being forcefully ended—might be one of the character's unspoken impressions, or it might seem unconnected to either's thoughts and so the equivalent of a third-person narrator expressing an opinion about the couple.

Gestalt

This is the only kind of hinge that matches the meaning of "closure" that McCloud borrowed from Gestalt psychology. By turning closure into a metaphor, McCloud overlooked the one case when an inference does bridge a literal gap.

Imagine Percy's kitchen divided into two panels. In the first image the husband is standing at the fridge; in the second the wife is sitting at the table. Though there may be a traditional gutter dividing the panels, a viewer understands the space represented in each to be continuous, usually because objects—perhaps the lines of the table in the foreground and the lines of the counter and cabinets in the background—appear to connect, or they would if not interrupted by the frames and the blank area between them. It's as if the two panels were originally one panel that was cut apart by a pair of scissors the size of the gutter. In one sense, a gestalt hinge isn't a kind of hinge because the viewer doesn't experience two images but only one. In another sense, it's the most extreme kind of hinge because the two images are so connected they cease to be understood as separate at all. Gestalt hinges may also be partial. Some, but not all, objects might line up, usually indicating some kind of change within the story-world due to the objects moving or transforming. Take that two-panel view of Percy's kitchen again. What if the husband is standing at the fridge in the first panel and sitting at the table in the second? Or, better, what if only half of his seated body appears in the second, while the chair—which we're picturing divided in half by the vertical gutter—is empty in the first? Alternatively, picture the gutter dividing his face in half, but the backgrounds behind him differ. There's the kitchen in the left panel, but maybe it's the bus stop on the right, indicating a change in location, but, because the angle of perspective relative to his face is the same, we experience the two halves as a single face.

Pseudo-gestalt

These hinges connect otherwise unconnected things by drawing them not only side by side but with lines and shapes that appear to be interrupted by the gutter—even though in the story-world they're nowhere near each other. This is a kind of spatial hinge, since it forces us to understand two images as not spatially connected even though they are drawn as if they were. The first panel could show the couple stepping through the left side of their front door, and the second could show them stepping through the right side of the bus door, making the two doors look like one door.

Or, stranger still, why not make the left panel the husband's face, and the right panel the wife's? The gestalt hinge would produce the experience of a unified face, though it would not be an actual face in the story-world. This is a relatively common effect used, for example, by David Small in *Stitches*, J. H. Williams III in *Batwoman*, Kevin Pyle in *Take What You Can Carry*, and Charles Burns in *Black Hole*. What would the combination suggest about the couple's marriage? It depends on how you draw it, but the effect would likely suggest *something*.

Linguistic

Sometimes two images will produce few or no inferences because, despite being side by side, they are not primarily related to each other visually. Instead, each is linked to its own set of words, and the juxtaposition of those words bridges the visual leap. Imagine just the first and final images of Percy's script next to each other: a couple is in a kitchen, then a bus is driving away. There are too many causal leaps to bridge, or, if the artist draws the bus at a greater distance so the couple's faces aren't recognizable in the window, the juxtaposition is a non-sequitur. But if the first image includes the caption, "We killed a few minutes . . .," and the second, ". . . before catching the 5:15," there's no confusion.

The problem with linguistic hinges is their emphasis on words over image. Both images become an illustration of the narration. We're told they're killing time and we see them killing time; we're told they catch a bus and we see the bus they've caught. But linguistic hinges are more effective when paired with images that do not reproduce the same information as their paired words—a topic we will discuss more in a later chapter.

First, we need to explore drawn examples of the kinds of hinges we just described. The following six pages are divided into eighteen pairs of images. For each pair, list every kind of hinge you experience. When you're done listing, read our descriptions and compare.

Hinge Examples

Example 1 illustrates complete recurrence. The full image repeats and so produces no change in perspective—which is a kind of inference and so a spatial hinge. The temporal hinge might be ambiguous, but the second caption indicates that despite the two images being identical, time in the story-world has moved forward between Noa not hearing her name called and then not hearing the class leave.

Because viewers may experience a forward movement in time due only to panel progression even when image content is temporally ambiguous, **example 2** illustrates a temporal hinge that prevents that assumption by

1

2

3

ILLUSTRATIONS 2.1–6 *Hinge examples 1–18.*

4

5

6

ILLUSTRATIONS 2.1–6 *Hinge examples 1–18.*

7

8

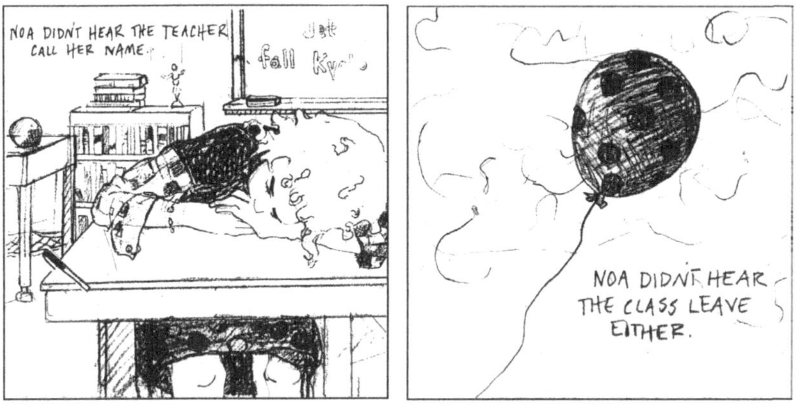

9

ILLUSTRATIONS 2.1–6 *Hinge examples 1–18.*

ILLUSTRATIONS 2.1–6 *Hinge examples 1–18.*

13

14

15

ILLUSTRATIONS 2.1–6 *Hinge examples 1–18.*

16

17

18

ILLUSTRATIONS 2.1–6 *Hinge examples 1–18.*

representing the same moment (or nearly the same moment) from different angles, producing a spatial hinge instead.

Example 3 produces recurrent, spatial, temporal, and causal hinges. The image repeats except for one element: the pen appears on the desktop in the first panel and on the ground in the second, triggering the causal inference that the pen rolled off the desktop and fell to the floor in the time gap between the drawn moments. Since movements in time are often represented by visual changes, the causal hinge also produces a temporal hinge, eliminating the need for the captioned text used in the first example.

In **example 4** the identical figure repeats in both panels, but the setting does not. The partial recurrence is understood through temporal, spatial, and causal hinges: the character, though reproduced identically, is understood not to be identical within the story-world because she has moved herself forward in time. It's as if the second image just happens to catch her arms and legs in the same positions.

Example 5 creates recurrent, temporal, and embedded hinges. The single, full-width panel requires an embedded hinge to be understood as two moments in time, an effect triggered by the recurrent figure. If the story provided a different explanation (a pair of identically dressed twins are walking home from school), the single panel would be understood as a single moment in time and so produce no embedded hinge and so no other kind of hinge either.

Example 6 creates an embedded hinge within each of the two panels. Most temporal and spatial hinges align with left-to-right reading. This pairing instead depicts the right-to-left movement of the softball, and the embedded hinges allow for both forward and backward temporal shifts. In the left panel, the recurrent and overlapping figures of the batter moves from a batting stance to a swing, while in the right panel, the recurrent and overlapping figures of the pitcher move from a wind-up to a completed pitch. The batting stance could depict a moment just before the wind-up, a simultaneous moment, or a moment just after, as well as just after the pitch. The swing, however, must occur fourth, even though the image is placed before both images of the pitcher.

If two images produce no closure, then the juxtaposition is a non-sequitur. This is uncommon because juxtapositions draw attention to similarities. **Example 7** could produce an associative hinge and so thematic recurrence. While the image of Noa cleaning a table has no overt relationship to the image of a softball pitcher on a pitcher's mound beside it, a reader might still feel an associative hinge by inferring that Noa is in some way *like* a softball pitcher preparing to throw a pitch.

Example 8 creates recurrent, temporal, non-sensory, and associative hinges. The balloon floating in the clouds represents the figure in the first panel, creating recurrence through an associative hinge with no drawn similarities but the dotted pattern on the clothes and balloon. While these elements change, none of those changes produce a causal hinge if a non-sensory hinge blocks it. The captions also help to bridge the visual ambiguity to produce a temporal hinge.

Though drawn very differently, both panels in **example 9** are understood to represent the same individual through partial recurrence. In addition to the temporal, spatial, and causal hinges, this juxtaposition also produces a non-sensory hinge by implying that the figure—even though she is drawn with wavy lines and depicted as defying gravity by floating out of her seat—is not literally wavy nor literally floating, qualities that instead suggest her internal experience of sleep.

Example 10 produces recurrent, non-sensory, and associative hinges. Although another interpretation is possible (perhaps the character walked for so long she entered a radically different landscape), naturalistic norms might produce a non-sensory hinge where the altered landscape represents the character's internal experience: it's *like* she's walking through a desert. Since the second landscape represents the first, the hinge is also associative. But because the identical figure may produce no causal hinge, the temporal hinge between the two images might be ambiguous, suggesting either a forward movement or a simultaneous moment.

Example 11 has seven kinds of hinges: recurrent, non-sensory, embedded, associative, spatial, causal, and temporal. Both panels produce embedded hinges, dividing the figures from the maps. Though the figure and the maps are both representational, the combinations are non-sensory because they don't show external reality. The map instead represents the undrawn but implied landscape that the figure is crossing, producing an associative hinge. Though expanded and cropped, the second figure is recurrent with the first. The second figure also occupies a different area of the map, implying a corresponding spatial relationship to the undrawn setting and so also a temporal hinge in order to have traveled it. Finally, the recurrent figure features one change that produces a causal hinge: a strand of hair fell loose as she was walking.

Example 12 produces recurrent, temporal, causal, gestalt, and embedded hinges. The three figures are understood to be the same character walking forward at three different moments in time. Although the middle figure is divided by the gutter, it is understood to be a single figure at a single moment. Each half figure also shares a panel with another figure, producing embedded hinges to divide them into separate moments. The background is also continuous across the gutter, producing a gestalt hinge.

In **example 13** gestalt and spatial hinges produce a paradoxical effect. The front half of the car in the first panel is stationary, while the back half of the same car in the second panel is moving. The movement of the car is also from right to left, the reverse of both reading and temporal order. The recurrence of the character in the backseat also produces the causal inferences of her having climbed into the cab and told the driver where to go.

Example 14 uses recurrent, temporal, spatial, and pseudo-gestalt hinges. As the identical figure moves herself forward, the change in setting implies that the second location is a later point in her walk. The pseudo-gestalt arrangement of the lines that form the streetlamp and the lines that form the tree branch seem continuous, suggesting that the tree and streetlight are more alike than they would otherwise seem.

Example 15 features a gestalt hinge for setting and a pseudo-gestalt hinge for the two figures. While the counter is continuous across the gutter, the two arms line up to create a double-handed pseudo-gestalt arm at the center of the combined panels. The individual hands are sufficient to create recurrence for each character, and the temporal hinge is aided by the dialogue.

While previous examples use some visual recurrence, **example 16** uses none, relying only on captions to establish the undrawn character of Noa. The captions also produce the spatiotemporal hinges needed to understand that Noa moved from the location of the first panel to the location of the second panel. Since the effect is achieved through words, and since the images alone would likely produce no clear inference, this juxtaposition needs a linguistic hinge to make sense.

While again illustrating a simultaneous temporal hinge through the complete recurrence of the pitcher, **example 17** also triggers retroactive hinges with a previous image. The first panel reveals that the softball pitcher appears on a TV screen and the second panel reveals the TV is in the coffee shop. The combined spatial hinges retroactively alter the initial associative hinge or non-sequitur effect in example 7.

Some juxtapositions produce no clear inferences and so are unhinged. In **example 18**, Noa's empty school chair could signify a range of possibilities. The second panel could occur at the next moment, simultaneously, or, if it is understood as a flashback, at an earlier moment than the first panel. Since Noa previously slept in the school chair, the empty chair could be from a moment after Noa left school. Or maybe through thematic recurrence it suggests the similar event of Noa having woken up at work and left there too. If so, it could associatively suggest that she is walking again, so both spatial and causal inferences. The image could also defy spatiotemporal logic and instead suggest Noa's non-sensory dreaming while still in the café. Even if a reader doesn't determine a precise relationship between the images, the juxtaposition is evocative because it triggers a search for hinges. At minimum this one creates the thematic recurrence of two tables and chairs.

Student Examples

Now before drawing your own hinged panels, look at the examples from comics pages drawn by our students in Illustration 2.7.

1. Emily juxtaposes two identical images. The spatial hinge is obvious: we're looking at the same cube on the same shelf from the same angle. The temporal hinge is harder. How much time passed between the images: an

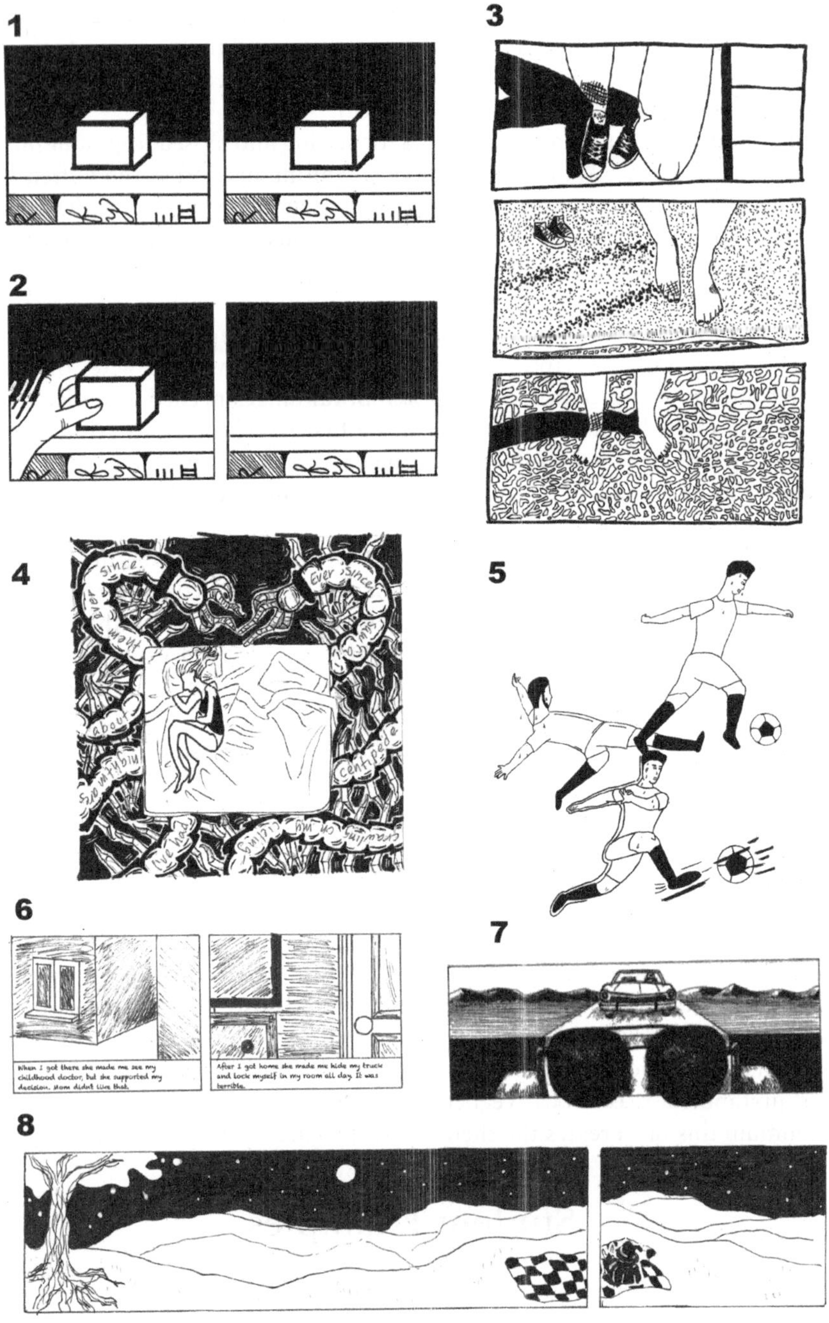

ILLUSTRATION 2.7 *Hinged panels.*

hour, day, minute, week, second, month? Or did no time pass, and the images are the same because they show the same moment? Or how do we know the second image doesn't happen first in the story-world and the images are arranged to reverse chronology? Technically we don't, but comics norms imply a forward movement in time—unless something drawn prevents that assumption.

2. Emily's second pairing repeats the same spatial hinge, and though it's still ambiguous how much time passes between them, the appearance of a hand means that the two images are not showing the same moment. A causal hinge also explains why the block is gone in the second image: after grabbing it (as drawn in the first image), the hand then removed it (not drawn), leaving the shelf empty (drawn in the second).

3. Mims' first two panels use spatial, temporal, and causal hinges. We don't know how far apart the sidewalk in the first panel and the sand in the second are, but we infer they're in walking distance and that minutes pass between them. We also assume that the person wearing the shoes in the first panel removed and discarded them during that same period of time. We make similar inferences between the second and third panels—though note the addition of a gestalt hinge: the water line appears at the bottom of the second panel. So spatially the second and third panels are continuous—though time passes between them to allow the figure to have stepped into the water. An astute viewer might also notice that the figure's shadow changes—in ways that could confuse things (since the sun seems to have moved backwards to its former position) and so might then be ignored, consciously or unconsciously.

4. Anna draws a figure on a bed surrounded by giant, writhing centipedes. Though it's possible to see this as a single image, the bed is more likely a panel inset placed "over" the image of the centipedes—which, if understood as a close-up, means the centipedes aren't giant. Though if the story is fantastical, giant centipedes could exist in the same room as the bed, the spatial hinge is ambiguous. That's because the centipedes are most likely not real. This is the dreamed or otherwise imagined fear of the figure in the bed—and so an example of a non-sensory hinge.

5. Hung draws no panel frames, and so his image has no gutters either. Is this an image of three players practicing soccer? Probably not. First, all three are drawn so similarly, they create a recurrent hinge. Plus each figure implies a different angle of perspective on the undrawn field or fields, and so three different moments in time. Though the figures overlap and are in a sense one image, they create the impression of three images through embedded hinges. Notice that the third figure includes a half-outline, a kind of partially embedded image that suggests movement. But if it's understood as a blur—like the movement lines of the ball—then it's experienced as one moment in time and so is not embedded.

6. The corner of a house viewed from outside and an off-centered close-up on an interior doorknob—how do these relate? Presumably they're parts

of the same house, but why are they side-by-side? Any spatial hinge doesn't tell us much. But if you read Coleman's two captions, the images take on a clearer relationship, including the presence of multiple undrawn characters at the center of the story. But without the words there is no story. The images relate primarily through linguistic hinges.

7. Lindsay's two images require a spatial hinge to understand that the second is a close-up of the driver operating the car in the first. Though a temporal hinge might suggest either two consecutive moments or a single moment, the effect is roughly the same. More interestingly, she lines up the edges of the road to the edges of the driver's head, creating a pseudo-gestalt effect. The road and head have no close spatial relation within the story, but they're drawn as though they're connected—perhaps suggesting something about the driver's character too. Since Lindsay uses no gutter, just a single line framing and dividing the images, the pseudo-gestalt hinge is even stronger. She also draws the driver's sunglasses breaking the second frame, further connecting the two images.

8. Finally, Grace connects her two panels with a gestalt hinge. It's as if the gutter interrupts a single image, imposing a break where we understand there is none in the story-world. Though the story context would tell us more, the half-empty picnic blanket in the left panel and the lone figure on the right are suggestive—more so than if the gutter didn't highlight her isolation and imply the absence of someone beside her.

EXERCISE 2.1 *HINGING PANELS*

Look back at the character you created at the end of Chapter 1, including all of your drawings and all of your answers to the character development questions. Use these to select and create content for these next exercises. For each, draw two images side by side in pencil. If you like panels and gutters, then draw frames for your images, but unframed images will work as well.

1 **Complete recurrence:** Draw the same image twice. Have the objects in the repeated image not moved or is time frozen? If time is moving forward, how much time has passed—a second, a day, a century? What elements in the images can guide us? Unless you repeated the first image by photocopying it, the two will not be perfectly identical. What differences are viewers likely to ignore as not indicating an actual change in the story-world?

2 **Partial recurrence:** Change something about your character in the second image, while making sure we still recognize it as a drawing of the same character. Maybe they've changed clothes or hair style, but

their face or body shape are still distinct? This might also trigger a causal hinge in order to explain the changes.

3 **Thematic recurrence:** Juxtapose your character in the first image with someone or something else in the second to suggest that the two share some important characteristic. This might turn into a visual metaphor, so an associative hinge too.

4 **Temporal hinge:** Draw your character at the same angle in both images but at different moments. How far apart in time are the two moments? If the character is in diapers in the first, and using a cane in the second, that would be a clue. So would a change of settings that doesn't alter the drawing of the character at all.

5 **Spatial hinge:** How little of a setting can you repeat and still imply that it's the same in both images? Change angles, zoom in or zoom out, focus on two different isolated corners, or two different rooms or areas of a shared building or larger space.

6 **Causal hinge:** Instead of drawing your character in mid-action, draw before and after images, implying the action between them. Or select some smaller detail and change it in a way that suggests a missing action.

7 **Non-sensory hinge:** Is your character dreaming or recalling a past event or imagining a future event? Or is the second image not filtered through the character but a kind of omniscient opinion about the character through an image that isn't supposed to be literal?

8 **Associative hinge:** Draw something that suggests your character's emotional state. It can use things from the story-world to make a comparison or the comparison can be non-sensory again.

9 **Embedded hinge:** If you've been using frames and a gutter, this time draw only one frame, but communicate that the single panel actually includes two different images. That might require partial recurrence of one or more characters, and probably spatial and temporal hinges too.

10 **Gestalt hinge:** If you've not been using frames and a gutter, this time you need to. Make all or some of the first panel continue into the second panel. If the background is continuous but something in the foreground changes, then you'll trigger a temporal and maybe a causal hinge too.

11 **Pseudo-gestalt hinge:** Again, you need frames and a gutter for this one. Select two locations, objects, or figures that are not connected and draw them as if they are connected—or would be if the gutter didn't interrupt them.

EXERCISE 2.2 *TAKE TWO*

When you're done with the above, you'll have eleven hinged panels. Now go back through the list and come up with another hinged panel for each prompt, something as different as possible from your first one. Interpret the prompt in a new way. Please bend the instructions if they are in your way. All that matters is that you explore juxtapositions and discover and invent your own approaches for combining images. Try getting rid of panel frames if you are using them, or using frames if you haven't.

When you are done, you'll have twenty-four hinged panels. Like the fifty character variations that you drew in Chapter 1, these images should be a gold mine of possibilities to develop further in later chapters. Some probably already go together, while others diverge down different paths.

EXERCISE 2.3 *REVISING HINGES*

Select one of your hinged panels to revise. It doesn't have to be your very favorite, just one that for whatever reason appeals to you right now. Maybe the hinge effect is particularly striking, or maybe the story content jumps out at you, or maybe it's something about the drawn qualities that make the images so interesting. Think about ways to redraw it to make it even stronger. Do the images have clear locations? What would make them more specific? List the objects currently in the images. Are some of them generic? Could they be replaced with more specific ones? Describe the clothing worn by any characters. Does it help define them? A visual character is its external appearance, so make every detail count—especially when a character is simplified. How are the characters posed? Even if the character isn't based on realistic anatomy, are its shape and posture interesting to look at? How could they be altered or refined to create more dynamic visual effects?

Gather research to revise. Go online. Find examples of each location, object, clothing, pose, anything that could make your imagery more specific. Place them into a file on your computer or print them off and keep them in a paper file. If you are revising a lamp, find a dozen lamps that interest you and then combine details to create your own lamp, one that is unlike anything in the real world but yet still feels real. Another option is to get out your camera, snap photos of objects or people or poses.

Once you have your research assembled, start drawing again. When you have revised your hinged panels to your satisfaction, go over the pencil lines with ink.

Leigh Ann wasn't happy with her original illustration for **example 15**, so she researched and redrew it:

The original focus wasn't on the exchange of money and coffee, and the characters were static and unessential. She decided to zoom in and focus on the essential information for that panel—the hands, the cup and saucer, and the money. Because those details would now be larger and so require more detail, she decided to get a model. A friend posed against a white wall, first with a white cup and saucer coming from the left and then a hand with a $5 bill coming from the right. Leigh Ann traced the black and white photographic images, editing out excess detail and heightening the contrast so that the cup and saucer and money stand out.

You can revise your work just as much.

Anthology

Flip to the anthology section again and you'll find a full range of hinges. Even Ernst's surreal collages, which repeat visual elements, create thematic recurrence. Since forward-moving spatiotemporal relationships are by far the most common hinges (Bick's "Street Ballet IV, New York, NY" and "Street Ballet XIII, Houston, TX" are rare photographic examples), we will highlight less common ones.

Tamaki's six-panel comic strip of *Everlasting Boy* creates unusual temporal hinges by inserting a fifth image that breaks chronological order and leaps backwards in time to what would appear to be the third moment in the sequence before leaping forward again. Tomine and Abel create extended flashbacks triggered by similar backward-moving hinges. Thompson's second page includes five images that use temporally simultaneous hinges with complex spatial hinges: the two insets depict areas near the images surrounding them, while the center panel is a word container framing a sound effect heard in both inset locations but not the wider ones. The wide middle gutter suggests the vast physical (and perhaps emotional) distance between the characters. The hinge between Hogarth's *Gin Alley* and *Beer Street* is temporally ambiguous since the two images could occur simultaneously or sequentially in either order and reading direction.

Johnson draws an essentially identical panel four times in his excerpt. The complete recurrence produces a partially ambiguous temporal hinge, especially between the final two directly juxtaposed repetitions since the father could remain in that posture for seconds, minutes, or even longer, adding to the emotional impact. Radtke creates recurrence by drawing the same angle of the same bedroom (spatial hinges) that changes over what appears to be months (temporal hinges). If the black marks growing mold-like up the walls are non-literal but a metaphor for the couple's growing tension, the panels may also be linked by non-sensory, associative hinges. Ma uses similar recurrent and spatial hinges, but the temporal hinges between his evolving neighborhood link moments separated by years if not decades. Siciliano creates an especially challenging spatial hinge between the second and third panels of her first page by framing an interior portion of the canvas so that the two images have no immediate connection; she then resolves that tension by including both the artist and the canvas in the next panel, revealing their spatial relationship.

The final panel of the first page of Hernandez's comic shows a balled-up piece of paper above a garbage can. Because of the causal hinge, we understand that this is the same piece of paper (recurrence) that appears in the typewriter at the start of the same row and that the woman in that same frame pulled it out, crumpled it, and threw it, even though none of those actions are drawn. Libicki creates an extended causal hinge between the middle two panels of her first page, first showing herself on a bus and next entering a kitchen door—implying a range of undrawn events that must have occurred between the two drawn ones.

Smyth's second two-page comic produces no clear spatiotemporal hinges or even reading order because the images are all ambiguously related. Though most readers will likely read Barry's 2 x 2 grids as rows, the themed but unhinged images allow column reading too. Though they have no spatiotemporal hinges, Vallotton depicts thematically related scenes of intimate couples (which we have placed in grid layouts), while also creating recurrent qualities in the woodcut shapes. Though his images do create spatiotemporal hinges, D'Salete also explores partial recurrence with repeated shapes: the circular plate, hut, and eye; the triangular doorway and roof.

Corman's fourth page changes framing style to trigger non-sensory hinges as the main character dreams. Though the final image is similarly unframed, the return to her waking state produces little confusion since we understand the previous images to be dreams. Muñoz's non-sensory hinges communicate that the protagonist is only imagining that he is being threatened and attacked as he walks by a group of men. The slight changes in their appearances in panels three and five indicate no actual change within the story-world.

In the excerpt from Lewis' memoir, Powell uses a gestalt hinge to connect the top two panels of the second page. Though *Found Forest Floor* is both visually and linguistically abstract, some image content repeats across the four pages, producing recurrence. The six panels of the first page are unhinged, but when they appear on later pages with additional panels, they develop gestalt hinges. GG draws an unusual gestalt hinge on the sixth page of her excerpt. The figure in the second panel continues in the fourth as though not only the gutters but the third panel were laid across a larger image. Each of Hankiewicz's four two-panel pages produces gestalt hinges, leaving the relationships of the images to each other and to the text ambiguous and possibly unhinged.

The final panel in Satrapi's excerpt produces an embedded hinge since viewers understand that the narrator is a single individual despite being drawn three times. Doucet's "I Was Dancing My Way to the Mall" uses both gestalt and embedded hinges on the first and second rows of the second page. While the environment is continuous across the three-panel rows, the figure's leg and the dog's tail appear within adjacent panels.

Estrada creates a pseudo-gestalt hinge between the fifth and six panels on her second page by arranging the lines of the snails' reflection in the water to seem to extend across the gutter. But for the lines in the sixth panel to appear less wavy, some amount of time must have passed between the two images, and so they cannot be temporally continuous. They are also not spatially continuous because the head of the snail is on the left and appears to connect to the body of the snail on the right.

Alagbé's sequence relies primarily on linguistic hinges. Lightman uses gestalt effects within her images (because we experience the entire image though she only draws fragments), but the sequence requires linguistic hinges to follow her purpose, as well as partially recurrent, temporal, and spatial hinges since we understand all of the drawings to be of a single photograph that itself depicts a single event. The four panels of Smyth's first two-page comic are numbered in each top left corner, but they would be similarly unhinged without the textual references to head and heart. Since the visual content is still ambiguous, viewers may also experience non-sensory hinges.

Continue to explore the anthology for more hinge effects.

3

Sequences

CHAPTER OUTLINE

Combine two or more images and you have a sequence. Or you do if the images are arranged and viewed in a specific order. In English-language comics, that order is usually from left to right, and so in that sense viewers "read" them. Though not all comics images are ordered, for now we're talking about the ones that are. And though comics can be abstract, we'll begin with representational sequences.

Since "graphic novel" and "graphic narrative" are synonyms for "comic book," it's not surprising that the majority of comics definitions include the word "story" or "narrative." But what is a narrative? The term is often used the same as plot, which, since Aristotle first defined it, requires a beginning, middle, and end. Since the alphabetical entries of dictionaries and encyclopedia are not plotted, plot involves more than just ordered parts. The parts need to be further connected—or sequenced. But before delving into the specifics of stories in the comics form, let's step back and think about plot more generally and so from the perspective of the story-world and the people inside it.

Character Goals

Look at the character you designed at the end of Chapter 1. In terms of plot, one question stands out: what does your character want? According to novelist Kurt Vonnegut, "Every character should want something, even if it is only a glass of water" (1999: 9). By some definitions, characters who don't have goals driving their behavior aren't character at all; they're just objects. Goals turn them into people.

Though a prose writer can (but really shouldn't) describe a goal in abstract terms, a comics artist has to visualize it physically, ideally as a prop that can be held since achieving the goal needs to be an observable (and so drawable) action too. If the goal isn't physical, you'll still want to use a prop or some other visual representation, one that is part of or a step toward or in some way stands in for the bigger goal.

If there's nothing preventing a character from achieving her goal, then her plot isn't much of a plot since it will end as soon as it begins. It needs conflict-producing obstacles. If the conflict is external, then something outside the character is physically preventing her from getting what she wants. It might be something in the setting (a locked door, a final exam, an earthquake). But, even better, if it's another character, the conflict becomes dramatic because, like the main character, the obstacle has motives and feelings too. Better still, the conflict might also be internal, something psychological that complicates the character's desire because of a competing concern or conflicting goal.

Only dramatic conflicts require second characters, or antagonists. Those include stereotypical villains, but the range is much wider. The antagonist could be:

1 an intentional obstacle whose goal is to oppose the protagonist's goal;
2 an accidental obstacle whose goal happens to conflict with the protagonist's goal;
3 an unaware obstacle who doesn't realize the protagonist has a goal;
4 a partial obstacle who opposes the protagonist's goal but with an internal conflict;
5 a partial helper who shares the protagonist's goal but with an internal conflict.

And the second character might simply be a helper who shares the goal and thus isn't an obstacle at all. The first and last are the simplest and so perhaps the least interesting. Ideally both characters appear to have complex inner lives. To create those complexities, add layers.

Why does the protagonist want the goal? What is the deeper motive under it? Expanding Vonnegut's "glass of water" example, maybe quenching her thirst is only a step toward something else, like avoiding heatstroke or surviving a zombie apocalypse. And maybe heatstroke and starvation are just obstacles on a still longer path, like completing a marathon or saving the human race.

Why does the antagonist oppose her goal? Is it personal? Is his deeper motive to thwart *anything* the protagonist does? Or is it about this one specific goal? Would he thwart *anyone* trying to get it? And what's his deeper motive for being an obstacle at all? Is he trying to win the same marathon or did he enter the race because he has a personal grudge against the protagonist? Is he trying to survive the zombie plague in order to find his family or does he just want to stay alive long enough to see her die first? And is winning the marathon a step toward something even bigger, like making the Olympic team and so winning his dead mother's approval? Does he want to stop the protagonist from saving the world because he thinks we deserve extinction—maybe because of that incompetent doctor who failed to save his only child decades ago? Every motive can be the surface of another deeper motive. So dig deep.

Even more fun, people don't always understand what they want or why they want it. It's like we have secret people inside us who only reveal themselves through our contradictory actions. It might take the whole story to reveal the secret motives driving your characters' internal conflicts. Maybe your main character is her own secret antagonist, working to save humanity because she wants to think of herself as a good person, while at the same time undermining her progress because a part of her wants to see the world get the punishment it deserves.

Characters are motivation machines. Wind them up and watch them careen against each other. If one gets stuck in a rut, teach them a new tactic. After trying and failing to overcome an obstacle, approach it from a different angle—metaphorically if not literally. Since she can't open the water bottle with her hands, she tries using her teeth. If she overcomes the obstacle, insert a new one. The lid comes off, but another runner grabs the bottle out of her hands. Or a new situation interrupts, putting the goal on hold while another temporarily replaces it. The marathon coach jogs up, and neither runner wants to be seen fighting over the bottle. Or maybe zombies attack.

If the goal is achieved, that's your chance to reveal a deeper goal under its surface and so the next step in the plot. She's quenched her thirst, but how is she going to get up that next steep hill—especially with all those zombies in the way? Or maybe when her goal is achieved, or about to be, she realizes something that redirects her. Maybe she didn't really want it after all. Forget winning, forget risking her life to save humanity, she's going to lie down and take a well-earned nap. And how does the antagonist feel about that? Maybe his goals change now too. If she gives up, he realizes that extinction might really happen, and so now he's the one urging and threatening her to keep going.

Extending Vonnegut's example, here are the basic story elements for developing characters and conflicts:

1 Surface goal (quench thirst)
2 Prop (water bottle) and action (drinking)
3 External obstacle (the cap won't unscrew)

4 Dramatic obstacle (someone else wants the bottle)
5 Internal obstacle (guilt for taking it)
6 Deep goal (win the race)
7 Deeper goal (win dead mother's approval)
8 Secret goal (feel mother's unconditional love as if she were still alive)
9 New tactic (use her teeth)
10 New obstacle (another runner grabs it)
11 Interrupting situation (enter the coach)
12 Next goal (the next hill)
13 Reversed goal (don't finish the race, since mom would love me anyway)

Since comics are visual, you also need to externalize each character's internal qualities. "Thirsty" is relatively easy to picture because of the water bottle, but "longs for dead mother's approval" is going to take more work. Invent more props. Maybe she is wearing something the mother gave her. Maybe she has a tattoo or scar that's linked to a defining memory of her mother. Settings can communicate key information, too. What if the mother ran this same race years ago? And what visuals from her childhood would evoke the unconditional love she wants most of all?

Benjamin Percy described a comics script at the beginning of Chapter 2—or the skeleton of a script, since he only indicated that a husband and wife are "talking." Using that as a prompt, here's a fourteen-line dialogue written in play form:

Wife You know it's empty, right?

Husband Oh, I bet there's something left.

Wife Not enough.

Husband What can I say? I'm an optimist.

Wife You just don't know when to quit.

Husband I like to get to the bottom of things.

Wife We haven't touched that bank account in decades. My sister probably cleared the money out the minute our mother died.

Husband Unless she didn't. Unless it's just sitting there waiting for someone to grab.

Wife I'm done with this, Carl.

Husband What if there's enough to pay off a credit card or two, get us on our feet?

Wife I want to walk away from this all.

Husband The bank is opening right now.

Wife I want a clean slate.

Husband One bus ride. That's all I'm asking you to do.

Wife I want out.

The husband has a surface goal: to check if there's money in his wife's old family bank account. He mentions credit card debt, so this is the first step in a deeper goal of fixing their financial problems. Getting to the bank requires a bus ride, a minor but useful external obstacle, but the wife is the real obstacle—a dramatic but partial one involving an internal conflict, since she doesn't want to check the account, but she does want to escape their financial situation too. There might be more layers, deeper reasons why she doesn't want anything to do with her family's money or her family generally. And she might not know it consciously, but she may want to escape not just money problems but her husband.

The husband's tactic is consistent verbally, but if the scene were developed in a comic, we might see him place his hand comfortingly on her arm while speaking his last line in a softer voice. For props, Percy mentions that the husband pours and drinks a glass of milk and the wife uses a plate for an ashtray as she smokes a cigarette—all potentially useful objects and actions that could take on greater significance in relation to the dialogue. Percy tells us that the couple bundles up and walks to the bus stop next, so the husband achieves his first goal—but how does their dynamic change as a result? The wife agreed to his surface goal, but does she now want something in return—and at what cost to the husband? And what happens when they get to the bank? If there's enough money to pay off their debt, will the husband maintain that goal, or be distracted by other ways to spend it? Will the wife change her mind too, deciding that she would rather suffer bankruptcy than spend her dead mother's money?

The character-driven possibilities can go on and on.

EXERCISE 3.1 *MOTIVATING STORY*

1 Look back at your character from Chapter 1 and write down at least one possibility for each of the twelve elements listed above in your sketchbook: Surface goal, Prop and action, External obstacle, Dramatic obstacle, Internal obstacle, Deep goal, Deeper goal, Secret goal, New tactic, New obstacle, Interrupting situation, Next goal, Reversed goal.

2 Keeping those details in mind, draft a dialogue between your main character and a second character, giving one or preferably both an internal conflict.

3 Knowing her surface, deep, and secret goals at the start of the story, describe the thoughts and emotions running through her head at the beginning of the story and invent visual cues (posture, facial expression, hair, clothing, behaviors, props) that suggest her internal state. Draw your character at the start of the story.

4 As her tactics, obstacles, and goals evolve, her internal state should evolve along with those visual markers. You don't know yet what all is going to happen and how she might turn out, but it can be helpful to have some ideas, even if you end up abandoning them later as new ideas evolve in your sketchbook. List internal and external descriptions for the middle and ending stages of her tentative story. That's another approach to plotting: the character arc. She begins in one state and ends in another. Or she begins in one state, attempts to change, but fails. Draw your character the way she might look at the middle and at end of the story.

5 What matters is the possibility and so the question: will she change? And that's yet another way to define plot: a question the audience is waiting to have answered. Sometimes it's simply: what happens next? List a range of questions you want your viewers to be asking when reading your comics story.

Visual Plots

Character-driven approaches to plot apply to any writing form: prose, stage, screen, and of course comics. Since what happens in comics is visual, now consider story structure in visual terms. Gustav Freytag's is the most common:

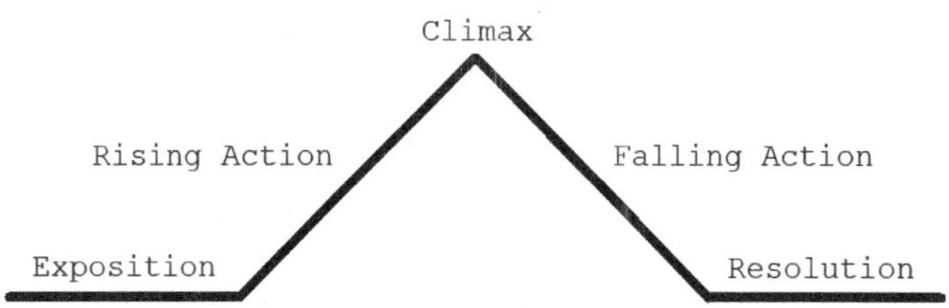

Freytag's Pyramid

Freytag had Tragedy in mind, with each part corresponding to an act. But that's not how his pyramid is usually understood today, since we would now call his climax the "turning point." So sometimes the pyramid is shortened:

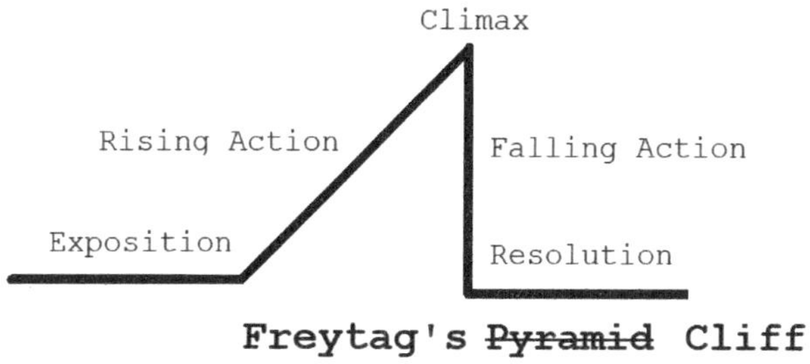

But not only are the "falling action" and "resolution" hard to differentiate, the status quo at the beginning and at the end shouldn't be identical because the new status quo is achieved through the ordeal of the story. So instead of a post-climax descent, imagine a plateau that restores order at a new, post-story elevation:

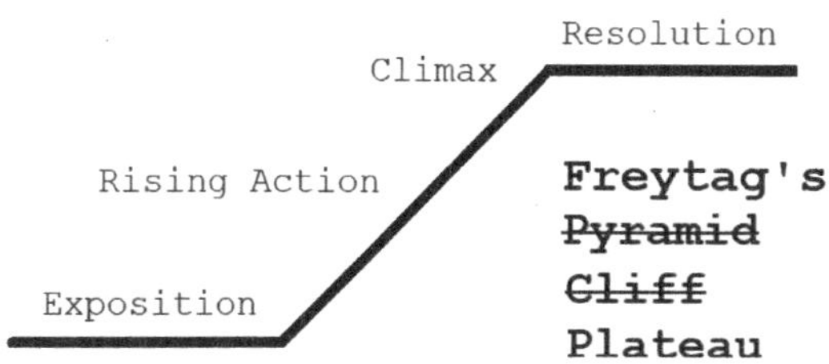

Contemporary versions of the cliff helpfully add "inciting incident" between exposition and rising action, but Tzvetan Todorov's (1969) terms are even better:

1 Equilibrium
2 Disruption of equilibrium
3 Recognition of disruption
4 Attempt to restore equilibrium
5 New equilibrium

For comics, Neil Cohn calls plots "arcs" defined by six types of narrative panels:

Orienter provides a superordinate information, such as setting

Establisher sets up an interaction without acting upon it

Initial initiates the tension of the narrative arc

Prolongation marks a medial state of extension, often the trajectory of a path

Peak marks the height of narrative tension and point of maximal event structure

Release releases the tension of the interaction.

2013: 70

Combining his first two panel types, Cohn's terms map onto Freytag:

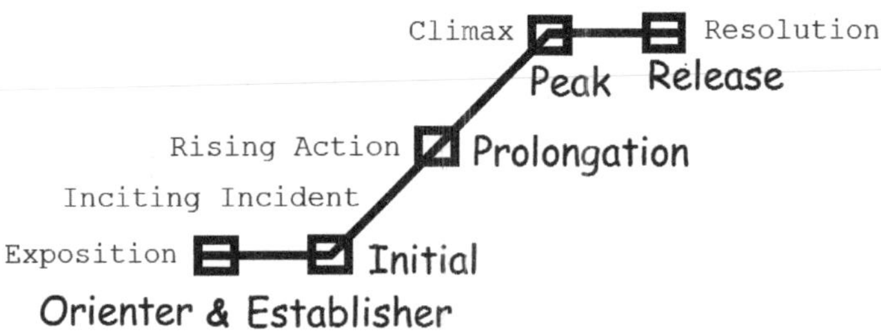

Combining Todorov's terms, we'll swap out "equilibrium" because "balance" is visually more precise (set a carpenter's balance inside the first and last panels and it would literally balance). The disequilibrium slope is imbalanced in the same sense. We'll use "climax" because it's such a ubiquitous term but keep Todorov's "disruption." Note how those two points visually mirror each other, just as they do conceptually: the first disrupts balance; the second restores it.

The combined comic strip version looks like this:

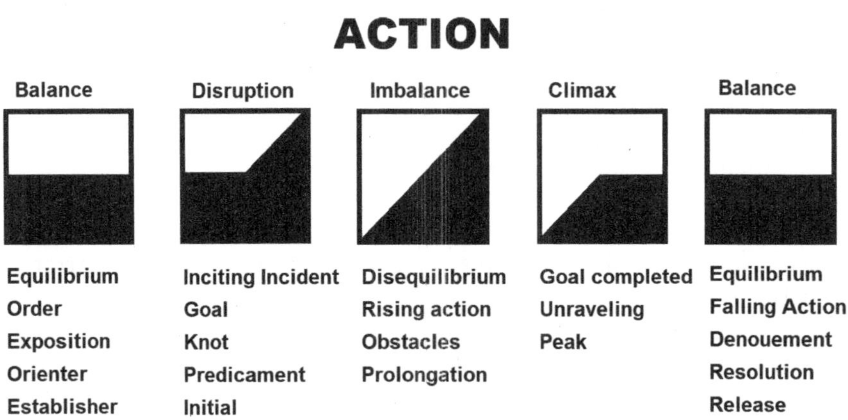

Though Freytag's began as a pyramid, Todorov's as a circle, and Cohn's as panels, this approach unifies them. Instead of plot or narrative, call this

an action sequence. A single action can also be a complete plot, but a plot might combine any number of actions—like opening a water bottle, fighting to get it back, smiling while the coach is there, drinking the water, running up the next hill. Breaking those actions into distinct snapshot-like parts is the key to creating a representational sequence.

A film breaks actions into still images too—usually twenty-four per second. Since that's far more than almost any comic can handle, creators draw just a few and leave the rest implied. Since a viewer imagines actions taking place in the story-world, a drawn sequence can skip over one or more action parts. Multiple images can also repeat the same part, so a single-action sequence can include more than five images—maybe many more since imbalance can be drawn out almost indefinitely. Chris's following six-panel comic strip is a single-action plot, with imbalance extended over two middle images. (It also illustrates the paradox of "blurgits," or blur-units, that cartoonists draw to suggest motion by duplicating part or all of an object.)

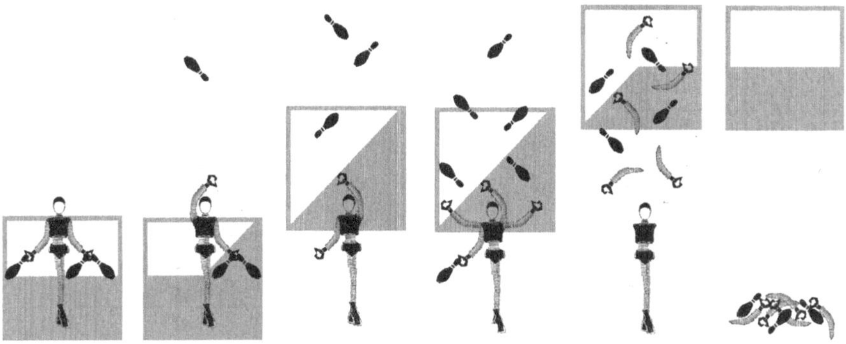

This next strip is a single-action sequence that opens with two balance images but then skips two parts by leaping from disruption to new balance, retroactively implying the undrawn imbalance and climax that a viewer understands as happening in the world of the story. Though we don't see the figure destroy the Modigliani paintings, we infer she did because of their condition in the fourth panel and the appearance of the scissors in her hand in the third panel (an expanded example of the causal hinges discussed in Chapter 2). The causal hinges between the first three panels also imply that the two figures walk from painting to painting.

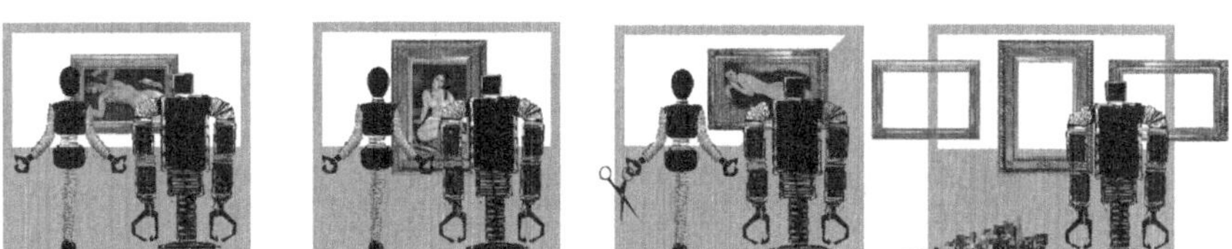

Many comic strips and probably all comic books include more than one action. Chris's next illustration, "If Only," is a one-page comic that combines multiple actions. To identify the actions, first categorize the images. Use each of the five action parts as many or as few times as feels right, noting that actions can overlap and so an image can have more than one function. We'll discuss the use of words in a later chapter, so for now just look at the visual content. How many actions do you see?

ILLUSTRATION 3.1 *"If Only."*

Some balance images suggest continuing stasis, so it can help to imagine them repeating. If the repetition seems natural, the image is probably a balance. We noticed this with panels one, five, and nine, ten, and the combined eleven and twelve. Here's nine repeated:

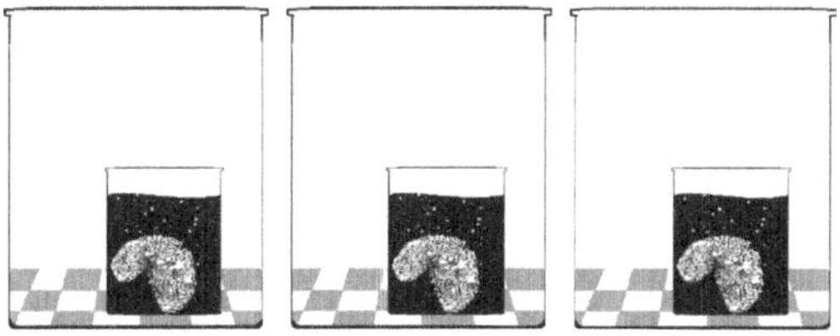

Unless you imagine an action sequence for those tiny bubbles, this is about as balanced as an image gets. Now look for a disruption in the next panel and, since it's within a multi-action sequence, a climax in the preceding one. Remaining images are probably imbalances. We doubt every viewer will agree about every category, especially since three (disruption, imbalance, climax) are all subtypes of Todorov's disequilibrium. But as long as you're examining how an image works in relation to its surrounding images, you're examining how sequences create stories.

We count seven actions. If you counted fewer, that's because the comics form is effective at implying content that viewers don't experience consciously. Here's one way to divide out two actions into shorter sequences:

"Exposing the Brain"

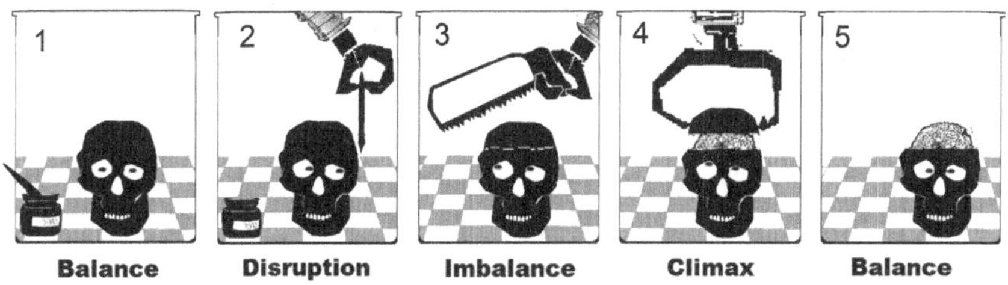

"Transferring the Brain"

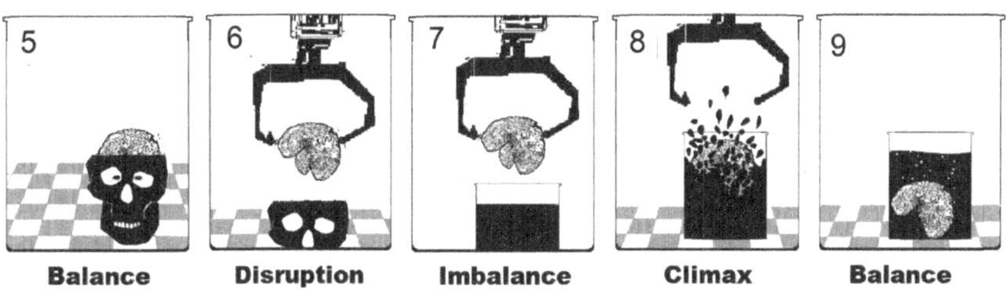

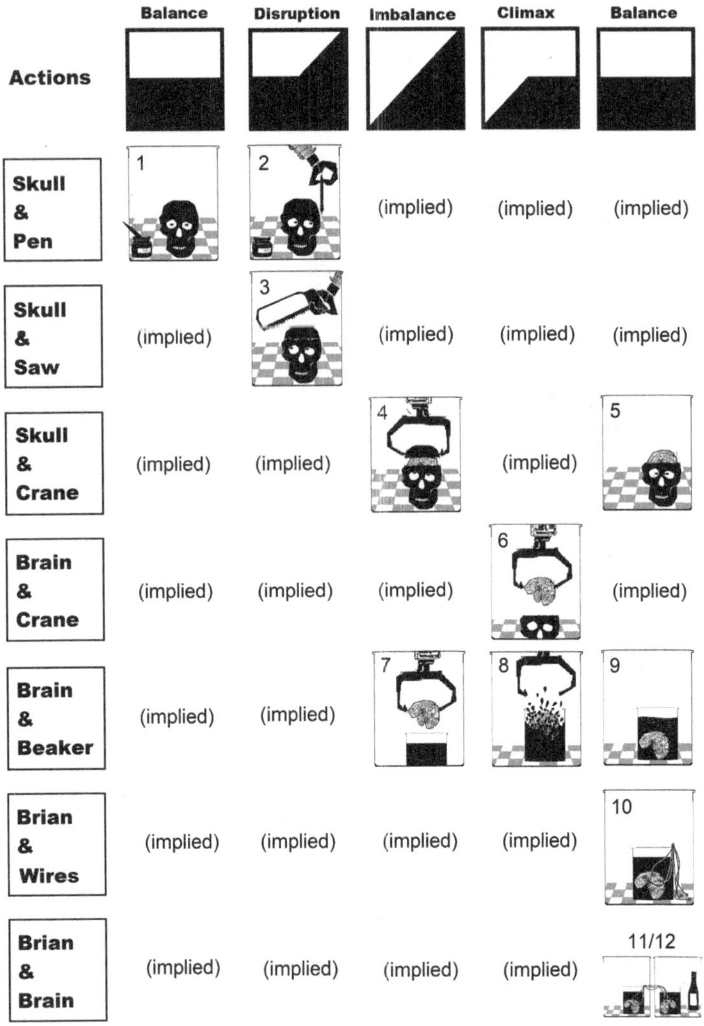

ILLUSTRATION 3.2 *Action chart.*

Notice that the ending balance of the first action is also the beginning balance of the next action. Both sequences can also be further divided into still smaller actions. "Transferring the Brain" includes lifting the brain out, carrying the brain across the table, and dropping the brain into the vat. "Exposing the Brain" includes at least three as well: drawing a line on the skull; sawing open the skull; and lifting off the skull top. Most of the action parts are implied:

"Skull & Pen" (now with deleted scenes!)

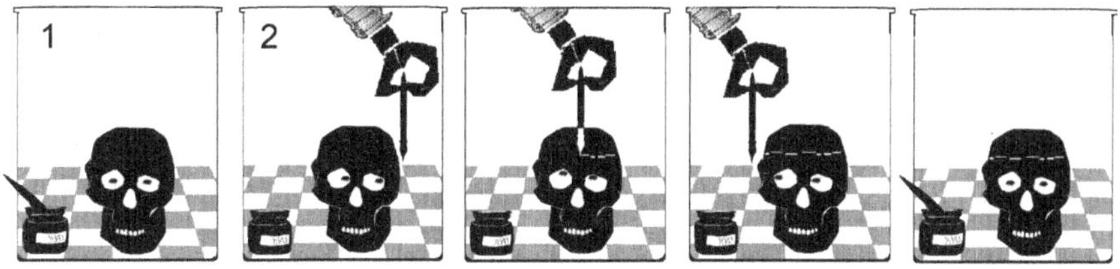

Balance **Disruption** **Imbalance** **Climax** **Balance**

We could also add "Removing the pen from the ink well," as well as literally an infinite number of imbalance images tracking the progress of the pen around the skull. The point is to recognize how much story content is implied. We chart all of the drawn and undrawn action parts in Illustration 3.2. Of the thirty-five, only eleven are on the page. The other twenty-four happen only in a viewer's head. The last two actions—attaching wires to the brain and then the wires to the second brain—are implied by just the ending balance image.

EXERCISES 3.2–3.10 *SEQUENCING CARDS*

Look back at your character drawings and descriptions from Chapter 1, your hinged panels from Chapter 2, and the goals you plotted at the beginning of this chapter, and decide on an action to develop.

1 Draw your character in an action sequence using all five segments: begin in a state of balance, introduce something that disrupts that balance, extend the imbalance, build the imbalance to its climax, and end with the tension ended because of the new balance. Don't assume that, just because the word "balance" has a positive connotation, an ending balance is positive too. If the climax is a bomb exploding, the final image could be a pile of rubble—a stasis-suggesting image that can be repeated without altering the story. Draw each image on a separate notecard or cut the images into separate pieces.

2 Place the cards in a row and take turns eliminating one at a time. What happens if you take out the middle imbalance? Can the sequence begin with the disruption, or can it leap over it? Can it end on the climax or skip it? When you eliminate an image, do you also eliminate its story content or do the other images imply the content so that a viewer still experiences it as happening in the story-world? Of the five possible four-image sequences, decide which you like best, and redraw it in your sketchbook.

3 Now eliminate two images at once. That creates ten possibilities:

Balance, disruption, imbalance
Balance disruption, climax
Balance, disruption, balance
Balance, imbalance, climax
Balance, imbalance, balance
Balance, climax, balance
Disruption, imbalance, climax
Disruption, imbalance, balance
Disruption, climax, balance
Imbalance, climax, balance

Do these shorter sequences imply the undrawn content clearly? Select and redraw your favorite three-image sequence.

4 What happens when there are only two images? There are again ten possibilities:

Balance, disruption
Balance, imbalance
Balance, climax
Balance, balance
Disruption, imbalance
Disruption, climax
Disruption, balance
Imbalance, climax
Imbalance balance
Climax, balance

Now there's more content undrawn than drawn. Do any of these versions leave out too much? Once again, pick your favorite and redraw it.

5 Continue the story by drawing another five-image action sequence that begins with the ending balance of your first sequence and adds four new images. Returning to the Vonnegut example, after opening the water bottle with her teeth, the marathon runner had at least three potential next actions: getting the bottle back from the antagonist who grabbed it; pretending not to be fighting over the bottle when the coach enters; and running up the next hill. Does your character's first action suggest a second? Start with some gestural sketches in your pad and then make cards again.

6 Repeat step two for your second action sequence and redraw your new favorite three-image sequence. Remember that the ending balance of your first sequence is now the new opening balance of your second.

7 Repeat step three for your second action sequence and redraw your two favorite two-image sequence.

8 Combine the two sequences by spreading out all nine cards in a row. Remove each card one at a time and choose your favorite eight-image sequence. Next remove two cards at a time and choose your favorite seven-image sequence. Continue removing different combinations, selecting your favorite six-, five-, four-, and three-image sequences. Look back at "If Only" and you'll see that its first two actions are communicated in just three images. Of all of these variously nine-to three-image sequences, pick your favorite and redraw it in your sketchbook.

9 Can you go down to just two images—or even one? According to some definitions, comics include single-image newspaper cartoons like *The Far Side* and *The Family Circus*. If you had to tell this story in just one image, which one would you choose? Redraw it, adding in details if it clarifies the story. If the image is a disruption, make it forecast its climax clearly enough that a viewer can experience it as happening. If it's a climax, help the viewer piece together the disruption that lead to it and the balance that follows. And if it's the ending balance, sometimes everything that led up to it can be implied too. The only image type that probably can't tell a story is an opening balance because there's no tension without introducing a disruption.

Abstract Plots

Though narrative comics and abstract comics might sound like opposites, all representational images are made of abstract marks and a sequence of abstract marks can be a kind of story. A comic can be abstract in two ways: the individual images don't represent anything, and the combination of images don't create a story. But even when they're abstract in the first sense, shapes and marks can still create a forward-moving rhythm that in some ways feels like a story arc. Just the fact that the images are divided into panels can make viewers look for and therefore find a narrative logic even in the most abstract of images.

Since some of the best-known abstract images are from 1950s abstract expressionism, imagine a row of Rothko field paintings or Pollock action paintings hanging in a gallery. Most viewers would experience connections between them, probably through the thematic recurrence created by similar color, shapes, and brushwork. And though different arrangements would produce different sequences, each would create a specific aesthetic progression and so a kind of story.

ILLUSTRATION 3.3 *Maddie's abstract comic.*

Look at the abstract comic by our student Maddie in Illustration 3.3. Though the two-page spread contains only abstract marks with no illusion of depth on the surface of the paper, the seven images appear not only related but arranged in a specific order: in a traditional 3 x 3 grid on the left side and a full-page panel on the right. If analyzed as an action sequence, the first panel is a balance image, the second a disruption, the next three imbalances, until the climax at the bottom of the first page resolves into the new balance of the second page. If Maddie added a page in the middle, its last panel would be the climax instead. But the first panel and the last panel would still be balances, and the second and penultimate would still be disruption and climax. That's true of most abstract plots. Since the images don't represent anything else, their positions determine their action parts. Unless they imply a missing image, abstract stories begin and end on balance—even if there are only two images in the entire sequence.

This might be straining what we usually mean by "story." Panels in comics are often experienced as windows into other worlds, and Maddie's panels instead draw attention to themselves as marks on paper representing nothing else. But even though the absence of a story-world peopled by characters performing actions in a setting might seem to preclude narrative, there's a way that a comic composed entirely of abstract marks can still have characters. Thierry Groensteen points out that:

> it is feasible for a line, a shape, a color, or of any kind of graphic entity, to have "adventures" in its own right, as Menu suggests is the case of Baldi's

> mini-album *Petit trait* [Little Line], given that the "story" recounted is that of the transformations undergone by the line in question, through a kind of *physics*, whereby each new image is generated by the preceding one.
>
> 2013: 12

For a viewer to understand that a line drawn in one panel and a line drawn in another panel both somehow represent the same line, "Little Line" is a recurrent character. And repetition and transformation are the basic building blocks of visual narrative. Place two identical images next to each other, change one element in the second image, and a viewer will likely understand the difference as a change that has occurred during a lapse of time between the images. Now imagine an explanation for the change, one that might even involve motivations if aspects of the image can be understood as a character who is transforming or two or more characters are changing due to their interactions.

Look at Maddie's abstract comic again. Are the hinges between each image pairings more than just thematic recurrence? Is this a kind of evolving character—one that begins small in its black surrounding but then expands in size and complexity? Since the existence of a recurrent character requires a stable reality, and transformations can only happen over time, there's a kind of story-world too. That means some action parts could be implied. If Maddie's images were on cards and we removed one, each would realign with its new position. The only way to change that norm of abstract plotting is to imply the existence of undrawn content—which is possible if the world is stable and time-driven. Look at the first two panels again. The flame-like shape is surrounded by black, and then it is larger with less surrounding black. If you understand that as the shape growing, then you might also understand the first panel as a disruption of an implied but undrawn image of total blackness. The shape's first appearance disrupts that balance. It was born.

Maddie's images have no foreground and background, no sense of depth, and so no three-dimensionality or apparent laws of physics either. That's not true of all abstract comics. Leigh Ann's twenty-four abstract panels in Illustration 3.4 depict a vividly three-dimensional world. Either the objects are floating past us or the narrative point of view zooms or both. Each pair of panels is hinged not only temporally but spatially, so the objects seem to continue to exist in the implied spaces beyond the edges of each frame. The "window" effect even includes a gestalt hinge between the last two panels of the fourth row. We are looking at not just a piece of paper but into another world.

Different viewers will likely categorize content differently, but we see at least three actions. Since the motion of the tentacle-like objects doesn't suggest plot tension, the first row begins with two balance images followed by the disruption of the first plug-like appendage detached in the third panel. The next three continue that imbalance, before the plot shifts with the movement of the viewer's perspective entering into the space of the plugs—or maybe the plugs are growing? Row four creates a double action: more tentacles emerge from the plug as the plug (or the viewer) floats past. Row

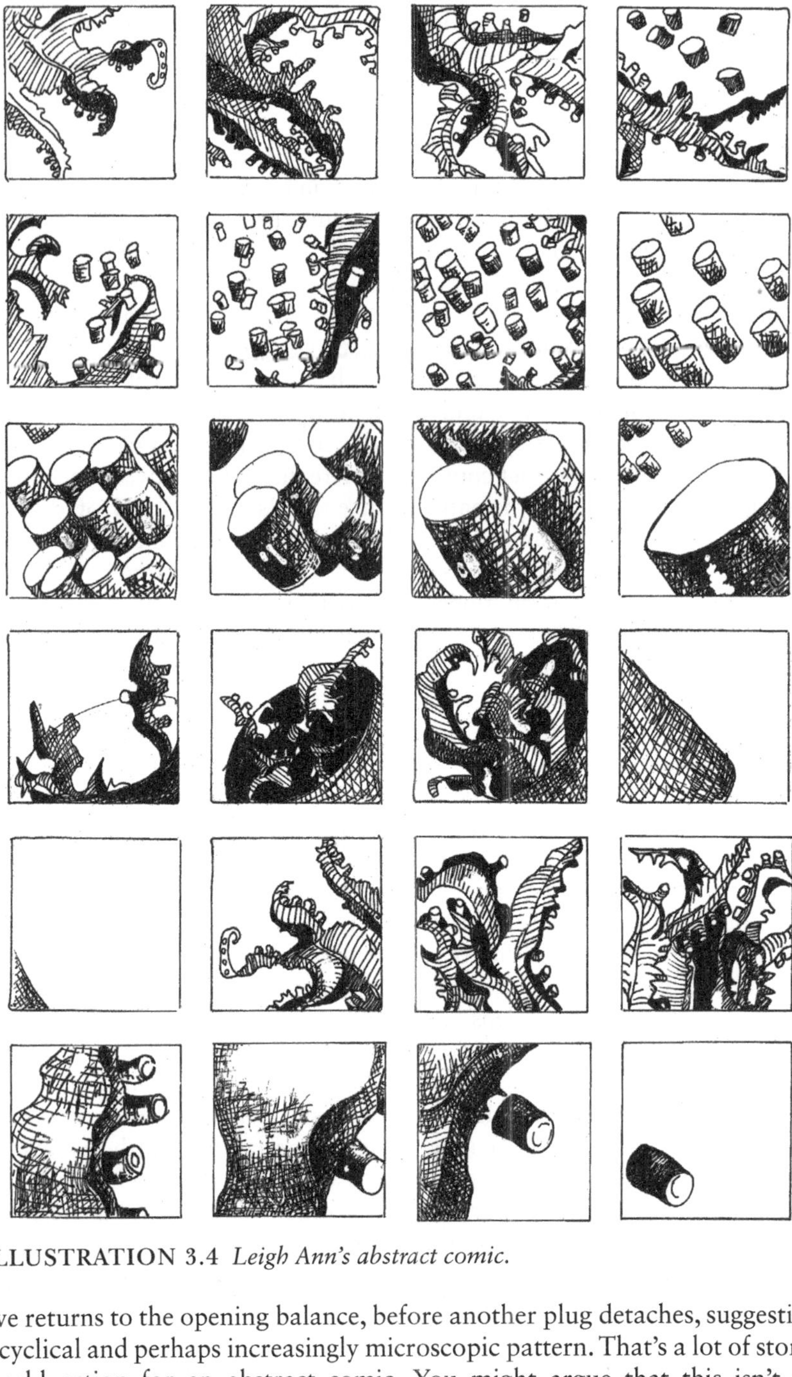

ILLUSTRATION 3.4 *Leigh Ann's abstract comic.*

five returns to the opening balance, before another plug detaches, suggesting a cyclical and perhaps increasingly microscopic pattern. That's a lot of story-world action for an abstract comic. You might argue that this isn't an abstract comic then, but if so, it's as "abstract" as many of the pages of Andrei Molotiu's anthology *Abstract Comics*.

EXERCISES 3.11–12 *TELLING ABSTRACT STORIES*

For the next two assignments, set aside your previous character and hinged and plotted images to create abstract comics—though you could still derive abstract qualities from your previous images. You have your own ways of making lines and shapes and value that you use when drawing representationally. Use those same techniques now, but let the stylized marks be the only content of the images.

1 Tell a multi-image action that includes no recognizable people, objects, or settings. Your character or characters are shapes and lines that don't resemble or represent anything in the real world. They have no world but the surface of your paper. But through image repetition and alteration, your characters and their abstract settings can still face conflicts and undergo transformations that a viewer can recognize and even empathize with. In terms of plot, your purely abstract images will move from balance to new balance, with any number of imbalance images between.

2 Create an abstract world that is three-dimensional and follows laws of physics—though not necessarily our laws. The panels are windows into an impossible world peopled by non-people-like characters that exist and change in unfamiliar ways. Since this world exists beyond its images, you can imply undrawn content and so multiple action segments. Tell a story that includes at least two actions, divided into as few or as many images as you like.

Unsequenced Sequences

If that sounds like a contradiction, that's because "sequence" has two different meanings. Sometimes a sequence is just the succession that something happens to follow—as in a sequence of randomly shuffled cards. Shuffle them again and you still have a sequence of randomly shuffled cards. Order doesn't matter. But comics images are usually in a very specific order. Shuffle the pages or panels and you change and most likely destroy the story. Order is everything. We'll call the first kind of sequence a "set" and save "sequence" for ordered images.

Though "images in a specific order" is a pretty good definition of a comic, it's still possible for an unordered set of images to be a comic and maybe even for it to include a story. If you remove the photos from a baby book and shuffle them, does the random set still contain the story of a growing baby? The content is the same as the baby book with its pages intact, and so if you define story by content, it's the same story. But if you define story by order, it's a completely different story—or no story at all. Entries in an encyclopedia have a specific order, but the content of each juxtaposed entry isn't otherwise related. That's why there's no plot. Which means "story" is a combination of both content and order: the events and the way those events, including their order, are revealed.

Almost all comics definitions include some variation on "narrative" or "sequence." That's because "narrative" and "sequence" are nearly the same. But not all comics are sequenced—and certainly not all pages within a comic are. The opening of Jim Steranko's *Captain America* #111 (1969) features thirteen unordered panels depicting an arcade. Since an actual arcade is designed to be wandered in no particular order, the unsequenced arrangement is an ideal form for the subject matter. When Tillie Walden visited our class, she had our students draw their worst fears; her version featured a dozen unpaneled cartoons arranged across her paper, perhaps suggesting that she fears them all equally. If she had instead placed the images in rows, that surface order would probably suggest a numbered ranking. So unsequenced sets are a perfect fit for certain content.

An entire comic can be unsequenced too. The images would still relate, but the hinges between juxtaposed images would be the same as those between distant images. The pages would be physically but not conceptually ordered, allowing a viewer to flip through them in any direction or manner. Manju Shandler's 2003 *Gesture* combines theme, form, and if not character then event, while avoiding sequence. Her work consists of 3,000 4" x 9" unframed paintings thumbtacked to exhibition walls, with the background of a white wall creating the effect of a grid of gutters. Such formal uniformity is already a connection, one heightened by each canvas shape evoking the World Trade Center towers and the number of canvasses referencing the number of victims. 9/11 unifies the images, and so may be enough to classify the art installation as not just a comic but as the telling of an event and so a story too.

Leigh Ann drew sixteen unframed whitethorn leaves in Illustration 3.5. A hinge of thematic recurrence connects all of the images equally and so produces no sequence. Though they are arranged in five rows of four, a viewer doesn't "read" the leaves in that order. If the images were experienced as a recurrent but altered representation of the same leaf, then order would matter as we followed the evolution of the character "Leaf." That's not the case. Like Steranko's arcade and Walden's fears, this is a representational set not a representational sequence.

The vast majority of comics are representational sequences. They're plotted stories with clear characters in a story-world. That's the kind of story we explored in the first section of this chapter and will be for the majority of the next chapters. In the second section, we explored a kind of abstract comic that we can now call an abstract sequence. The content may vary in its level of abstraction, but there's still a kind of plot involving character-like recurrence and progression.

ILLUSTRATION 3.5 *A representational set.*

And we can now identify a second kind of abstract comic. An abstract set still has character-like recurrence relating its images, but there's no order. Without additional hinges guiding a viewer down a sequenced path, the eye roams freely, taking in the similarities and variations randomly. Abstract sets might include a range of works by abstract painters. Robert Motherwell's *Elegy to The Spanish Republic*, a series of over one hundred paintings, and Barnett Newman's *Onement* series are potential examples. Look back at Illustration 1.3 in Chapter 1, and the 6 × 4 grid of line variations is an abstract set too. Since it lacks both representational content and image order, some might say this kind of comic isn't a comic at all. But if the unsequenced abstract images are drawn in rectangular panels with gutters between them, it probably *looks* like a comic. So call it what you like.

Like an abstract set, a representational set has no order, but its images are still related, and they may even contain a fragmented story that can only be understood fully after all the images are viewed. The randomly shuffled photos of a baby book are an example. Though a representational set contains story content, it doesn't create the kind of story experience triggered by the same content placed in chronological order.

EXERCISES 3.13–14 *DRAWING SETS*

For this chapter's final assignments, you'll create two sets, using elements of your earlier stories.

1 **Abstract set:** Look at the two abstract stories you drew in the previous section. Select one and cut the images into separate units (or redraw them on cards or photocopy and cut them up). Experiment with new arrangements that discourage a viewer's eye from following a sequenced path. That probably means placing previously hinged images further apart and suggesting new hinges in directions a comics reader isn't trained to go. When you've finalized an arrangement that's both unsequenced and interesting to wander, revise and redraw it on a new page in your sketchbook.

2 **Representational set:** Look at the nine cards you made in the first section of this chapter. Arrange them on a page-like surface in a way that prevents a viewer from following any logical path. After experimenting with different patterns, expand the set by drawing three new images that somehow relate to the original ones but that don't clearly follow or precede any of them. Next remove three of the original images and replace them with your three new ones. Rearrange to intensify the unsequenced effects. Once finalized, revise and redraw your final arrangement.

Anthology

Each of the comics we selected for the anthology present a complete scene, either created as a complete work or excerpted from a longer narrative or ongoing series. They range from one to GG's eight pages. All but Tamaki's second page (which is not continuous with her first) consist of multiple images. We included her one-page cartoon because it still presents a narrative. The marks in the snow reveal that two animals fought and the larger one won and that it then met an even larger animal and lost. In terms of sequence, the image is a new balance since the actions have already concluded. The arrival of the two women creates an additional plot since their walk is halted by their seeing and pausing over the marks, also producing new balance.

Both of Bick's *Street Ballets* are a single page, but each is composed of sixteen individual photographs that might be understood sequentially in more than one way. If in the first the interaction is between the walker and the archway he passes through, the first three panels are balances that establish the unobstructed view of the figure walking, and then the fourth panel introduces the archway which disrupts the status quo and so is a kind of plot tension that builds with the imbalances of the figure and the archway (which paradoxically is the mobile object in relation to the framing of each photograph) nearing each other, until the climax of the walker vanishing in the third panel of the third row, before the last row establishes a set of new balances roughly the same as the opening panels. The second *Street Ballet* is open to similar analysis, depending on which figures are understood to be interacting relative to each other or to the crooked grid of the pavement.

Unlike Bick, traditional comics creators typically limit the number of images and so avoid many instances of the same sequence types. Tomine's one-page "Drop" accomplishes its single action in four panels. After the first panel establishes the setting of a car at night, the next three divide a continuous action: the character raises his foot (a disruption of the implied balance of his standing with both feet on the ground), stumbles backwards (literally imbalance), and continues to fall (further imbalance). Though the climax is undrawn, we infer that he eventually stops falling, where he presumably remains after a fatal impact, implying a new balance.

Comeau's first page presents a single action too. After the first row establishes balance, the second row disrupts it by introducing the pliers, followed by the third-row climax of removing the tooth. The next page extends that new balance across four panels, before the character reacts to what he has done, creating a second action that climaxes with his two-page scream.

Instead of expanding actions across multiple pages, D'Salete's two pages include three consecutive visual plots: a woman delivers food to the hut (four panels), the chief eats the poisoned food (three panels), and the woman discovers he is dead (six panels of the second page). Johnson's four pages are more complex as they weave together a range of brief actions (the son enters house, removes tie, interacts with father, leaves house, gets into car, catches cigarettes). Johnson introduces the tie in the first and second panels of the first page, interrupts the action for the next four panels, and then restarts it at the top of the second page. Similarly, Johnson vacillates between two simultaneous scenes in two locations (son and his friend outside in the car, father inside at the kitchen table), making their content interact too. The last page ends with the father, continuing the visual plot of his interaction with the letter on the table that began in the second row of the first page.

Though dialogue and narration are not part of a visual plot, words and visuals interact in complex ways. Analyzed visually, the first appearance of the possibly non-literal mold in the second panel of Radtke's two-page excerpt disrupts the balance of the mold-less first panel and then extends imbalance across the next six panels without reaching a clear climax. The dialogue and narration parallel that escalation, intensifying it without directly commenting on it. Note also that visually the two figures are included in each panel, but their varying positions produce no clear visual plot.

Dhaliwal's two-page installment of an ongoing series relies heavily on dialogue, but visual plotting is still central to the combined effects. The first seven panels take place in water, and the last two by a fire, creating a balance to new balance progression. But the first two panels also feature both women together, before dividing them in the next four panels, and then reuniting them in the seventh, creating an additional kind of visual plot. The absence of speech in the seventh panel, regardless of the linguistic content of the speech, also contributes by visually emphasizing the unmarked white space around the floating figures. Now note how the dialogue interacts with the visuals, switching to a different tone in the final panels.

Not all of the excerpts produce visual plots. Without her accompanying narration, Lightman's excerpt would maintain a constant imbalance as the partially drawn fragments change without progressing any closer toward or further from a completed image. Hankiewicz's images are ambiguously representational, and their progression produces no clear visual plot either. Vallotton's ten-image *Intimacies* is an unsequenced set, as is Smyth's second, twelve-image comic. For Vallotton, we placed his woodcuts into a two-page arrangement. The arrangement of Smyth's second comic triggers no sequenced reading path either, in part because, like Vallotton, she includes no recurring characters. Ernst uses recurring image elements, but they don't combine into a visual plot. Barry's images are thematically related, but also not visually plotted.

These are just a few examples. All of the comics in the anthology can be studied closely for visual plots. Take your time with each page. When an image strikes you, pause to look at the surrounding images and their sequential relationships to each other. Look for patterns of your own, noting what kinds of images (balance, disruption, imbalance, climax, balance) especially draw your attention and why. When you notice an interesting visual plot, think of ways to apply its approach to your own story content.

4

Pages

CHAPTER OUTLINE

Until now, we've been discussing comics as if their images were either free-floating or arranged in lines like typeset words of prose. Every time your eye reaches the right margin, you jump to the next line at the left column. The number of lines and their breaks are random. No prose writer controls for them. But spatial arrangement is central to the comics form. And while a prose work can be published in different formats without affecting its content, comics are designed for specific page shapes and sizes.

The dimensions of mainstream comics, 6⅝" × 10¼", originated in the 1930s from a newspaper sheet folded into quarters and are still the format of the monthly comic books and trade paperbacks by publishers including Marvel, DC, and Image. The pages currently in your hands are likely 6" × 9". The size is a standard for prose-only texts, the non-comics traditions that Pantheon and Houghton Mifflin evoked by publishing Marjane Satrapi's *Persepolis* (2003) and Alison Bechdel's *Fun Home* (2006) in the same format. By using shapes and sizes that differ with each project, publishers including Drawn & Quarterly, Koyama, and Fantagraphics evoke the eclectic traditions of art books. Renée French's *micrographica* (2007) is only 4½" by 5". The squares pages of Michael Dumontier and Neil Farber's *Constructive Abandonment* (2011) measure 7" × 7". Brecht Evens' *Panther* (2016) is atypical because it's wider than tall, as is the much larger 12" × 9" collection of *The Eternaut* by Héctor Germán Oesterheld and Francisco Solano López (2015). The box holding the variously sized booklets and broadsheets of Chris Ware's *Building Stories* (2012) measures 11½" × 16½". Because art books are typically published in large formats—a 1985 printing of Henri Matisse's *Jazz* measures 8½" × 11" and Sally Mann's *What Remains* (2003) 11½" × 12½"—larger sizes call attention to those comics as works of visual art.

Comics, like books in general, typically assume a vertical spine, on the right for *manga*, on the left for European-language works. David Lasky and Mairead Case exploit that vertical flexibility in "Soixante Neuf" (2011), a story narrated from two perspectives, each upside down to the other; when the two meet at the center fold, the reader must turn the book upside down and begin again from the opposite edge to continue left-to-right reading. The wide pages of Alan Moore and J. H. Williams' *Promethea* #11 (2001) fold down from a horizontal spine in the style of a calendar—an approach also used by Art Spiegelman for *In the Shadow of No Towers* (2004), John Hankiewicz in *Asthma* (2006), Bryan Talbot's *Metronome* (2008) and Dash Daw in *Body World* (2010).

Regardless of size and orientation, the two-page spread of every pair of facing pages is comics' primary unit of composition. Early comic books were designed as individual pages so publishers could insert advertisements between any two pages, but that single-page norm ignores the physical construction of a book and so a reader's actual visual scope. Neal Adams introduced two of the first two-page spreads in *X-Men* #58 (July 1969) by drawing content that extended across the spine. Mariko Tamaki and Jillian Tamaki include six in *Skim* (2008) and twenty-two in *This One Summer* (2014). Spiegelman's *In the Shadow of No Towers* (2004), Lauren Redniss' *Radioactive* (2011) and Richard McGuire's *Here* (2014) consist entirely of two-page spreads. Even when an image does not overtly cross the page fold, facing pages can be composed so their content visually relates, as David Mazzucchelli typifies in *Asterios Polyp* (2009) and Dave McKean in *Black Dog* (2016).

Though the annual *Best American Comics* typically preserves facing page arrangements, excerpts of Jessica Abel's *La Perdida* (2006), Leela Corman's *Unterzakhn* (2013), and Adrian Tomine's "Translated, from the Japanese" (2014) feature different facing pages than in their original publications. When reproducing pages of his own novel *Life on Another Planet* (1980) in his *Comics and Sequential Art*, Will Eisner disregarded page spreads too, turning two formerly back-to-back pages into facing pages. The poetry comics journal *Ink Brick* reinforces a one-page norm by publishing in an e-book format that displays pages in a continuous column that eliminates two-page spreads entirely. Artists can also widen the spread. For the Nick Fury episode in *Strange Tales* #167 (1968), Jim Steranko drew a four-page pull-out, an approach Dianne Kornberg uses multiple times in *Madonna Comix* (2014), her poetry comic collaboration with poet Celia Bland.

Divisions

Pages are usually subdivided—though they don't have to be. The early twentieth century woodcut novels of Frans Masereel and Lynd Ward include only one image per page, as do Renée French's *h day* (2010) and Leanne Shapton's *Was She Pretty?* (2016). In mainstream comics, John Byrne's Hulk episode in *Marvel Fanfare* #29 (1986) consists entirely of twenty-two full-page panels. Viewed as a two-page spread, William Hogarth's 1751 *Beer Street* and *Gin Lane* divides two otherwise undivided pages into a contrasting diptych.

When subdivided, a page traditionally follows a blueprint-like layout of panels divided by the negative space of gutters. When gutters align horizontally and vertically, the layout creates a grid of rectangular panels; the grid is regular if panels are all the same size and irregular if they vary:

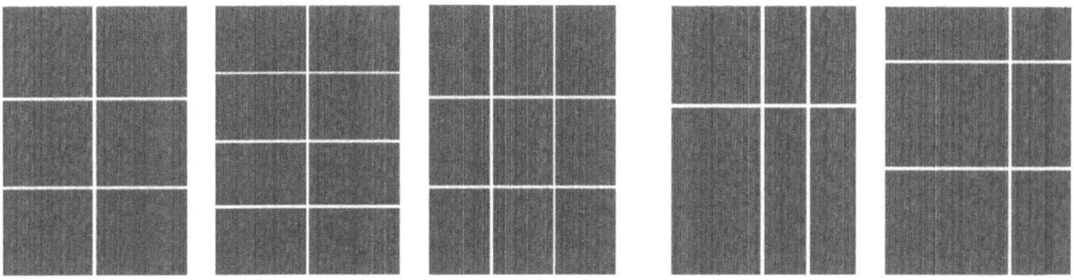

Though the number of panels per page can vary radically even with in a single comic book, Kaitlin Pederson and Neil Cohn document a steady decrease in mainstream comics from an average of six and a half panels in the 1940s to a little over four in the 2010s (2016: 13). Tillie Walden's *Spinning* (2017) includes pages with twenty-four panels divided into 6 × 4 regular grids, and for *Hawkeye* (2015), David Aja composed a page of twenty-four panels, but within an implied 7 × 5 regular grid suggesting thirty-five possible panels:

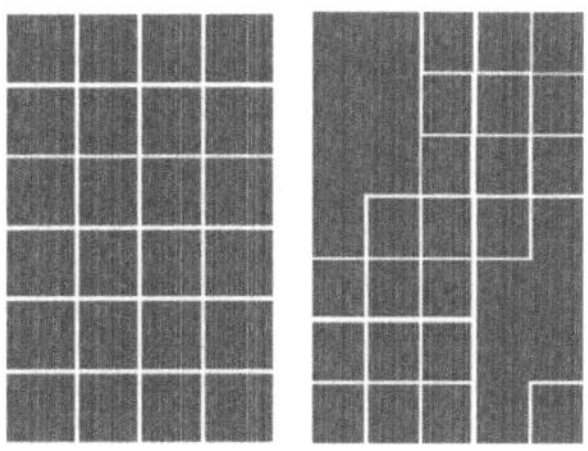

When not in grids, images are often arranged in rows of varying panel sizes, aligning horizontal but not vertical gutters. Though four-row layouts were common in the 30s, the mainstream comics in Pederson and Cohn's sample group averaged about two and two-thirds rows across decades (2016: 13). Three equally spaced rows of one to four panels is one of the oldest and most common layouts, popular with Jack Kirby and Steve Ditko in the 60s and still in use with Daniel Clowes, Seth, Clément Oubrerie, and many other artists.

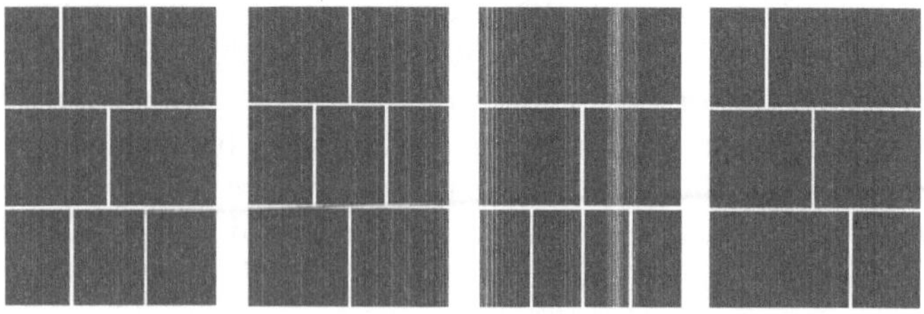

Other recent creators, including Howard Cruse, Charles Burn, Jessica Abel, and Noelle Stevenson, follow a three-row norm but with more variations. Pages vacillating between two, three, and four rows became a mainstream norm in the 70s and are still common with artists including David B., Carla Speed McNeil, and Craig Thompson, while Joe Sacco, Alison Bechdel, and Leela Corman fluctuate between two and three rows. Row heights can vary too, producing an even wider range of irregular layouts:

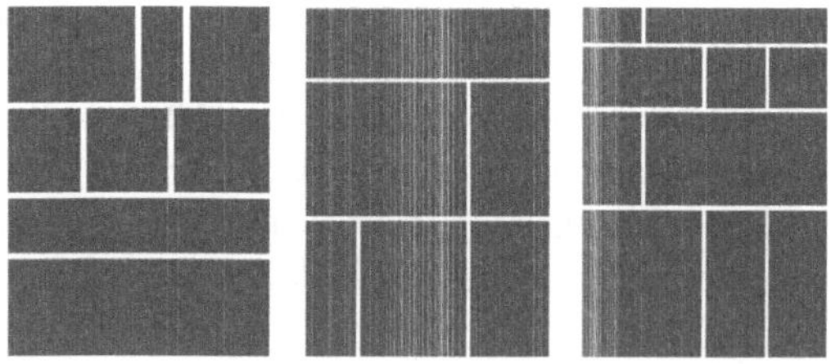

Though rows tend to be the default form, many comics pages use columns instead:

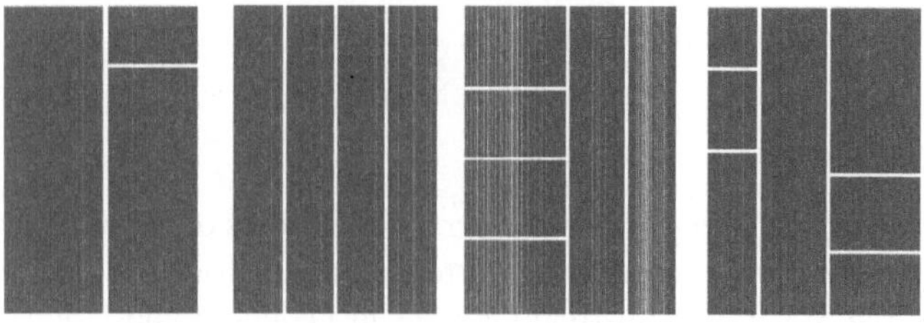

Layouts can also combine rows and columns:

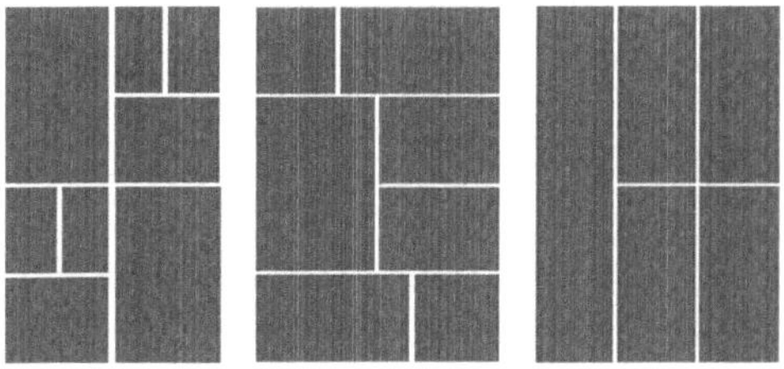

Or they can avoid rectangular norms entirely:

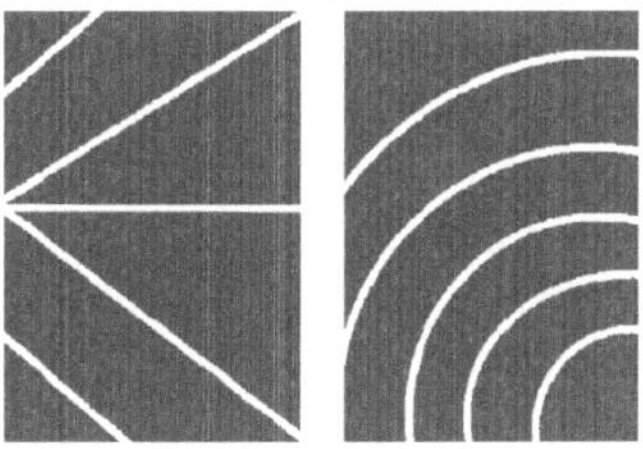

Whatever the layout, Abel and Madden warn against drawing frames too closely together "because panels will tend to run together and be hard to read" (2008: 83, 80), but the thin gutters of Adrian Alphona's *Ms. Marvel: No Normal* (2014) resembles their "too narrow" example. Chris Ware's gutters are even thinner, while Guido Crepax, Dash Daw, and Sophie Goldstein sometimes eliminate gutters entirely, creating "grids" in the sense defined by Barbara Postema: "panels that are separated by lines only, not by gutter space between the lines" (2013: 40). GG sometimes eliminates even these shared frame lines, drawing no divisions between unframed panel content. Abel and Madden also warn against "too wide" gutters "because the panels will tend to visually fall apart from one another and not look like a unified page" (80), but Manuele Fior's *5,000 Kilometers Per Second* (2013) and Daishu Ma's *Leaf* (2015) use wide gutters that evoke characters' isolation. Widths can also vary on the same page. When Bianca Stone draws panels and gutters, they are skewed and composed of uneven lines, an effect Roz Chast increases in *Can We Talk About Something More PLEASANT?* (2014) with slight misalignments and unframed panels with rounded edges that fade partly into the white of the page.

Gutters also don't have to be the undrawn negative space between panels, but instead the drawn space that creates the panels. In *Knights of the Living Dead* (2011), Dusty Higgins divides panel content with interconnected frames drawn to resemble the physical frames of hung paintings. For his adaptation of *Moby Dick* (1990), Bill Sienkiewicz paints stick-like lines and jagged whale-tooth motifs for his gutters. For the nonfiction *Threads* (2017), Kate Evans uses digitally manipulated strips of lace.

Dividing a page into panels reinforces an assumption that gutters should be the only undrawn areas of a page—an attitude inherited from newspaper publishing where space is sold by the inch. Other visual arts commonly use white or unmarked areas of a page or canvas or poster as compositional elements. In *M* (1990), Jon J. Muth leaves areas of white space that traditional layouts fill, a style Michael Gaydos expands in *Jessica Jones: Alias* (2015). A page of unframed images will also produce more white space with ambiguous divisions between the white of an image's background and the non-representational white surrounding it. Move two unframed images closer and they become each other's frames or appear to touch or overlap, eliminating all white space and so gutters entirely.

Layouts aren't neutral. Each composes a page according to a visual aesthetic. Rectangular gutters evoke the solidity and immobility of pillars and crossbeams, with panels resting like boxes on shelves. To counter that effect, Ditko emphasized diagonal and curved lines in the action-focused content of his *Amazing Spider-Man* panels, often skewing ground lines and windowpanes to contradict the paradoxical calm of his layouts. Diagonal panels and gutters instead communicate movement and volatility, as Neal Adams achieves on roughly half of his *X-Men* pages and J. H. Williams in the action sequences of *Batwoman: Elegy* (2010). Though the 1947 French

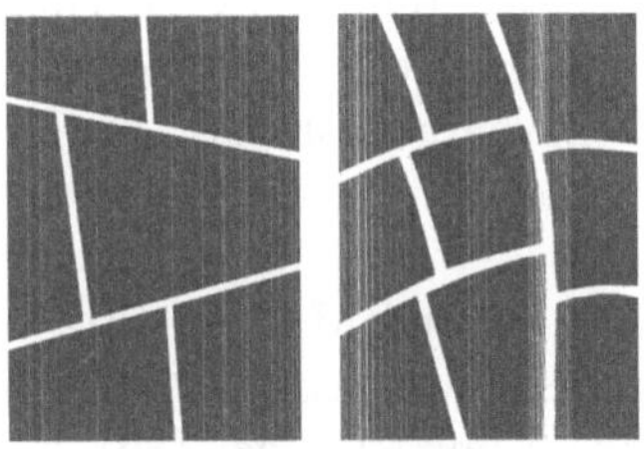

superhero newspaper series *Atomas* follows a 3 × 3 structure, artist Pellos undermines the grid effect with non-rectangular panel shapes, some with aligned curves to create wave effects across the page.

While still creating a predominantly horizontal effect, Emma Rios' *I.D.* (2016) offsets traditional rows by using multiple, small insets. Richard McGuire uses insets in *Here* (2014), but none line-up horizontally or vertically to suggest either rows or columns.

Student Examples

Illustration 4.1 includes eight layouts by our students:

1. Emily draws a 5 × 3 regular grid. The square panels and rigid form echo the repeated image content of the cube on the bookshelf.

2. Mims' 2 × 2 grid includes such loose framing lines that it doesn't have the feel of a regular grid, even though the four panels are roughly identical.

3. Henry draws an irregular 2 × 3 grid, with the second panel of each row roughly twice the size of the first. Also notice how the gestalt effect of the descending staircase in the second panels effectively hinges them into their own column despite the Z-path layout.

4. Daisy's layout is irregular, with three rows of varying heights and unframed image content and words in the horizontal gutters. The first two rows are divided into panels, including an overlapping, circular one, while the single frame of the third row encloses three images.

5. Maddie's regular three-row layout consists of a full-width panel at the top and bottom and a middle row of three equally sized panels. Rather than creating gutters, Maddie uses a single frame line between images, pulling the underwater content closer together.

6. Though Katie's images are all unframed, they suggest a four-row layout divided into two and three panels each. The absence of frames parallels the absence of a definite reading path since the top caption suggests a thematic but not necessarily sequenced connection between the images. The character may have experienced the story content in any order, and so the viewer can too.

7. Coleman draws a regular four-row, with two panels divided equally in half, and the two full-width panels feature vertical caption boxes at opposite edges. The four other horizontal caption boxes mirror each other too, creating an orderly quality to the overall layout—a sharp contrast to the disorder of the family trauma building in the story.

8. Anna's two-page spread was inspired by the center fold of Alan Moore and Dave Gibbon's "Fearful Symmetry" in *Watchmen* #5 (1987), with their four irregular columns creating an N-path. Although the juxtaposed images of the firing gun appear to take place within a second of each other, the middle gutter actually hinges two different races months apart, making the two arms only thematically recurrent since they presumably belong to two different people.

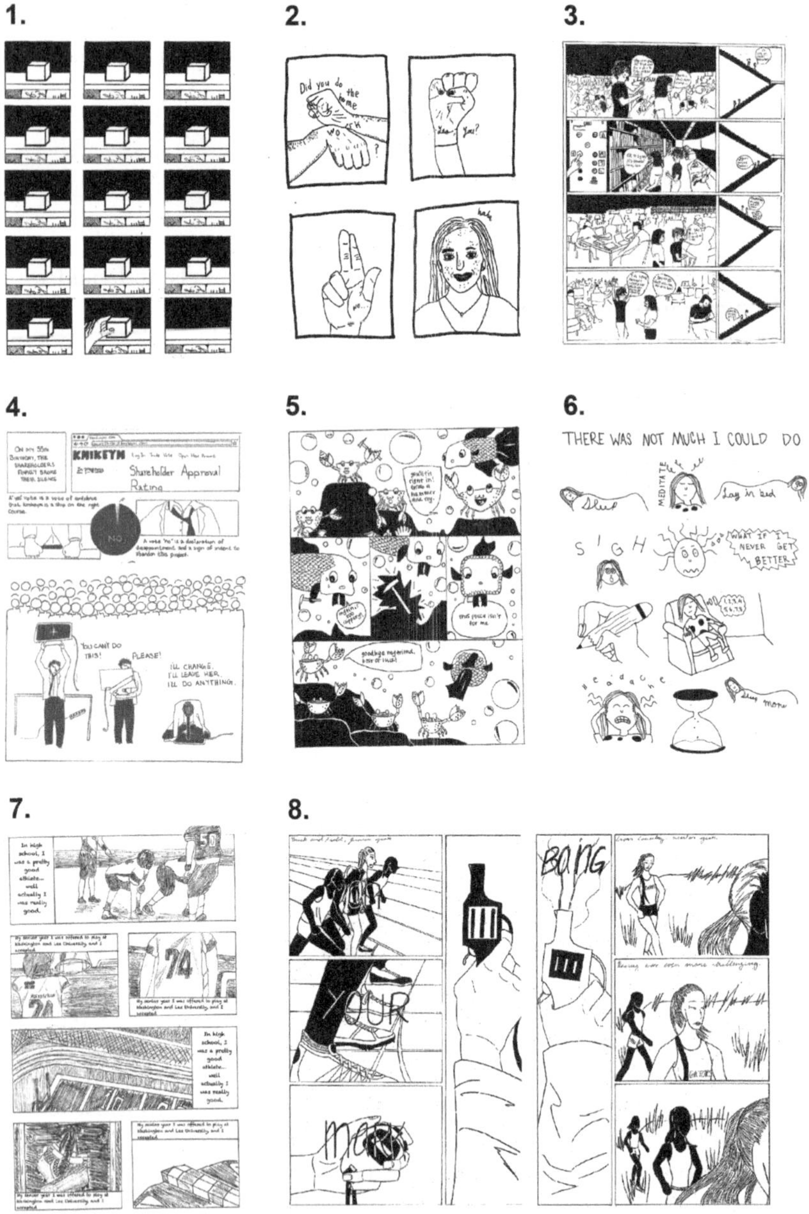

ILLUSTRATION 4.1 *Eight layouts.*

Paths

Layouts also produce reading paths. If images are in rows, they follow a Z-path, which viewers "read" left to right or (as noted above), for manga, right to left, while also descending top to bottom. If arranged in columns, images are first viewed top to bottom in an N-path:

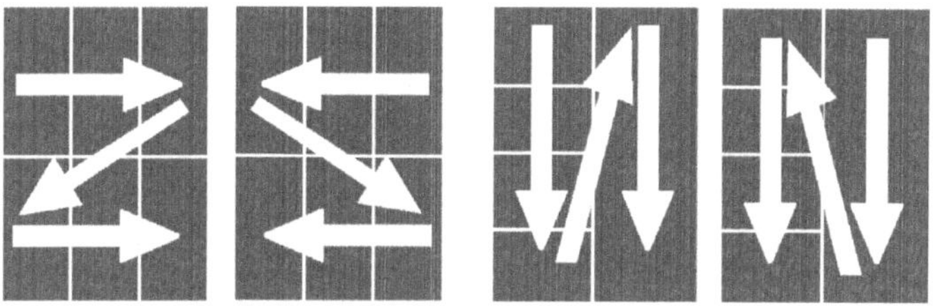

As discussed above, layouts can combine rows and columns, which then produce mixed reading paths, represented here by panel numbering:

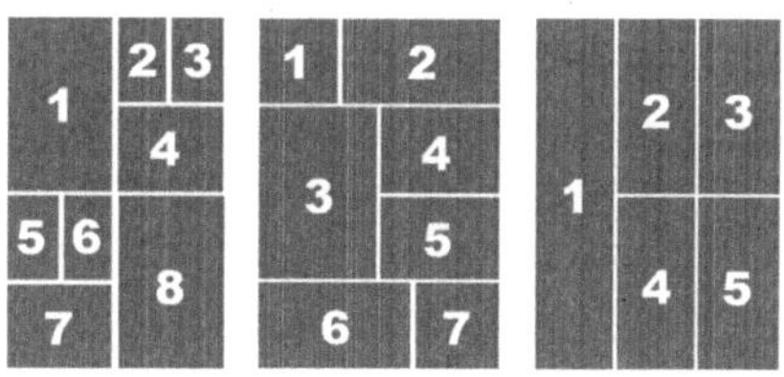

Some pages feature unsequenced sets that can be viewed in any order and so any path, such as Steranko's arcade page from *Captain America* #111 discussed in the previous chapter:

Steranko avoids confusion by establishing quickly that his panels have no single correct reading path. Unless there's a reason related to story content, you probably don't want your viewers spending much if any time testing possible paths before settling on a right one. Since most layouts are rectangular, most confusion occurs when a viewer has an option between following rowed panels in a Z-path or columned panels in an N-path. Notice how the following four layouts each have two possible reading paths:

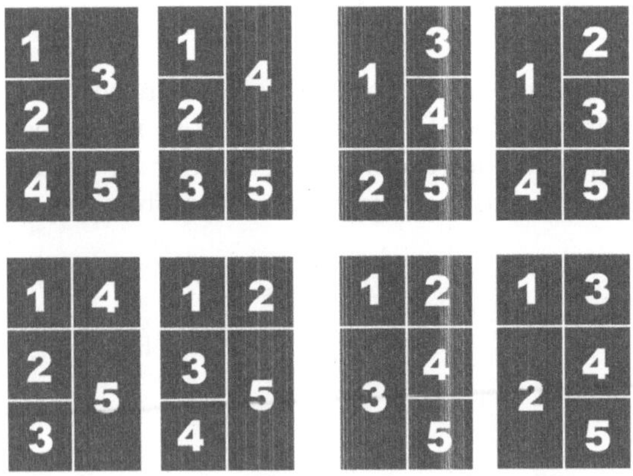

Most English-speaking comics readers are trained to expect a Z-path and so they see panels arranged along a shared horizontal gutter as a row. The first two layouts lack that row-establishing gutter, so once a viewer begins down a column, she has to decide whether to continue until she does hit a shared horizontal gutter or until she hits the bottom of the page. The second two examples begin with a shared vertical gutter, but the presence of the columns underneath it can still trigger an N-path.

The next examples avoid those potential confusions through three different strategies: 1) eliminate a panel in order to create a full-height column and so an unambiguous N-path; 2) stagger the horizontal gutters so they don't line up; and 3) widen the lower horizontal gutter to create two separate areas (what we'll call "visual phrases" later in this chapter).

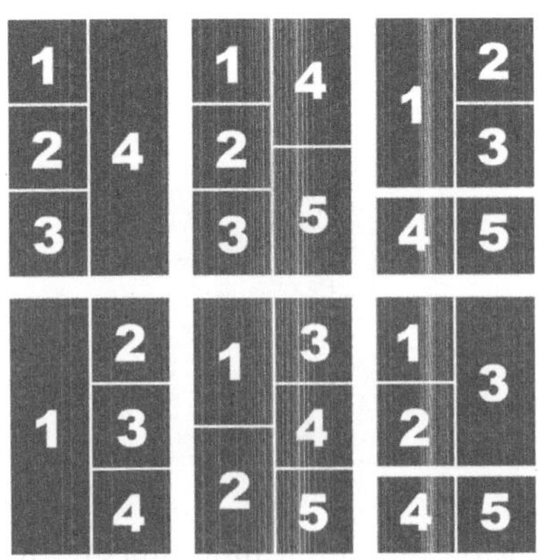

Paths can also be constructed by story content—and so the kinds of hinges discussed in Chapter 2. Gestalt hinges are especially effective at moving a viewer's eye along a preferred path, but stylistic similarities of almost any kind can too. Notice how in the next two examples, the 3 × 3 grids produce N-paths despite a default expectation of row reading:

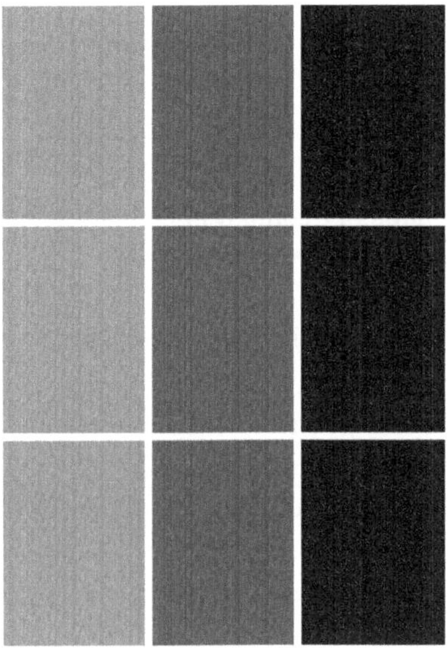

Illustration 4.2 features four pages with reading paths that avoid standard Z- and N-paths. Although the first page features a regular 5 × 3 grid, Grace avoids a Z-path by using gestalt hinges to pull the eye along an alternating path created by the abstract leaf shapes that move first left to right but then right to left as they descend the page. The second page could be read as three rows, but Leigh Ann's image content produces no hinges, allowing the eye instead to wander freely and so in no set order. The third page has no path either, but instead of panels Katie draws a set of unframed images that makes the absence of an order immediately apparent. Readers will likely attempt to find a reading path for Leigh Ann's images in the fourth page, but Chris's seemingly three-dimensional layout also resists any clear order.

Whatever layout and path you choose for a particular page, consider how that approach relates to your subject matter. Can the layout reflect visual elements from the story-world—windows, bookshelves, prison bars, tree branches, tumbled bricks? Can it create thematic connections through formal connotations—stability or rigidity, freedom or chaos, intimacy or compression?

EXERCISE 4.1 *TELLING STORIES THROUGH LAYOUT*

For each of the following prompts, sketch three layouts and list three story ideas either using characters and material from earlier chapters or inventing new material now.

1 Regular grids. What content might suit these identically sized and uniformly spaced panels?
2 Irregular grids. What story content might suit horizontal and vertical gutters that line-up but not uniformly?
3 Regular rows with irregular panels. What story content might suit these identical rows containing different numbers and shapes of panels?
4 Irregular rows and panels. What story content might suit these rows of differing heights?
5 Regular or irregular columns with regular or irregular panels. What story content might suit these N-paths?
6 Combined rows and columns. What story content might suit these mixtures of Z- and N-paths?
7 Non-rectangular layouts. What story content might suit these non-traditional panels and gutters?
8 Wide, thin, and single-line gutters. What story content might suit these different gutter spacings?
9 Drawn gutters. What story content might suit gutters that instead of being empty spaces between panels create the empty spaces of the panels.
10 No reading paths. What story content might suit unsequenced sets that prevent Z-, N- or mixed reading paths?
11 Two-page spread with a horizontal spine. Connect any two layouts, but rotate them ninety degrees like a calendar. What story content might suit these horizontal shapes and the physical gutters of the spine?

Accents

Ivan Brunetti calls a grid "democratic" because panels "are all exactly the same size . . . from which we can infer their equal weight and value in the 'grand scheme' of the page" (2011: 45). But Joseph Witek warns that "highly regular grids tend inevitably toward both visual monotony and flatness in narrative action" (2009: 153). Abel and Madden recommend a middle position, working with "a basic grid of equal-sized panels" but also varying from it "by introducing a tilted panel, to name one variation, the effect is much more powerful because the tilted panel jumps out at the reader to emphasize a mood, plot point, or dynamic motion" (2008: 71). We call these variations "accents."

ILLUSTRATION 4.2 *Non-standard reading paths.*

Creators have a range of techniques for accenting images. Illustration 4.3 identifies nine. The key is scarcity. A page can include one and sometimes two accented images before the layout becomes so irregular that nothing stands out because there is no underlying norm. While accents prevent visual monotony, they also give greater attention to the story content of the accented image.

1. **Size** is the most obvious means for establishing a panel's importance over other panels on the same page. The larger the panel, the greater the implied significance of its content. In *SuperMutant Magic Academy* (2015), Jillian Tamaki draws a three-panel page beginning with a top panel four times larger than the two panels below it. The large panel contains the most visually dramatic image: a character triumphantly kicking open a set of double doors to celebrate surviving and now leaving her high school. Evie Wyld and Joe Sumner in *Everything Is Teeth* (2015) include two facing pages, each with a top row depicting characters fishing on a boat and below it an image of a shark swimming underwater. Each shark image occupies the equivalent of three rows, communicating the power of the shark over the human characters.

2. If frames are rectangular and aligned with page edges, frame **tilt** is a visual accent mark, drawing attention to an otherwise identical panel. In film, tilting a frame means tilting only the content of the frame while the frame itself must remain unchanged. In comics, an artist instead has three tilt options: 1) tilt the frame and the content; 2) tilt the frame but not the content; or 3) tilt the content but not the frame. All three work as accents. In *Unflattening* (2015), Nick Sousanis begins a bottom row with a nearly square panel perpendicular to the page in order to follow it with two similar panels drawn at increasing tilts; the panel images show a pair of feet lifting into flight, so the content parallels the implied movement of the frames as they seem to lunge forward. In *Maus II* (1991), Art Spiegelman draws five tilted photographs as if placed across an eight-panel grid. The tilt creates the illusion that the image are actually resting on top of the layout of other panels and so blocking the other content.

3. Because perpendicular rectangles are the overwhelming norm, individual images may be accented by any variation in **shape**. The first eight-page episode of Matt Baker's *Phantom Lady* #14 (1947) include one circle or half-circle on each page of rectangular panels. Though Baker appears to have been interested only in visual variety, the panels also create a narrative rhythm in which one moment is always literally circled. On a page of *The Finder Library* (2011) that contains other tall panels, Carla Speed McNeil draws two twice as thin as the page norm, accenting them even though each occupies only half as much space; as a result, the image content—a climactic moment when an enraged character is about to strike out but then suddenly calms down—is highlighted too.

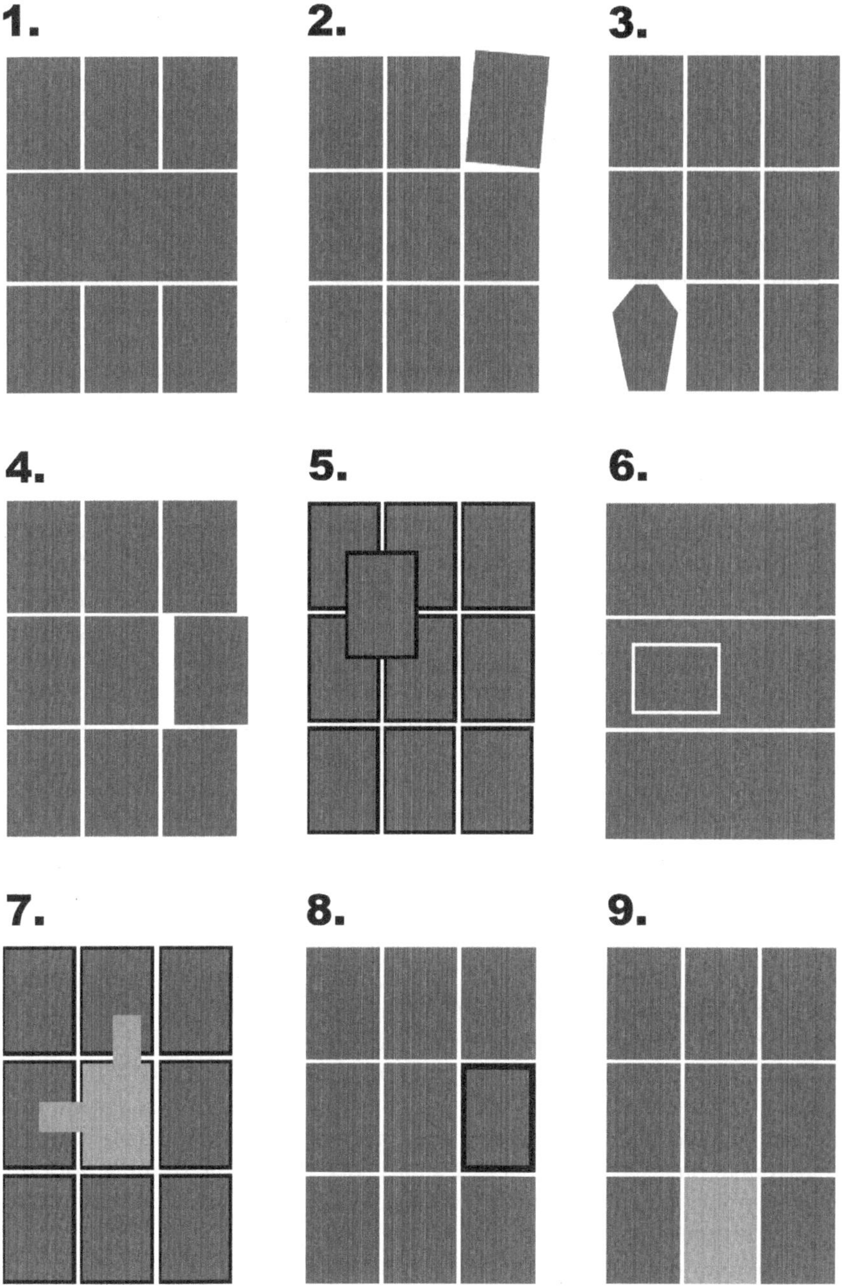

ILLUSTRATION 4.3 *Nine ways to accent panels.*

4. As discussed above, if gutters are otherwise parallel, individual panels may be highlighted by differences in **spacing**. Julie Maroh widens horizontal gutters in *Blue Is the Warmest Color* (2010) to indicate scene changes. In *Omega: The Unknown* (2007), Farel Dalrymple draws increasingly wider spaced panels as a character wanders deeper into a maze.

5. A reverse technique to spacing, images can draw attention by appearing to be placed overtop other images, creating the effect of playing cards arranged with their corners or edges **overlapping**. Though now a norm of mainstream comics, the approach is as old as the comics tradition, with an example by Raymond de la Nézière from 1886 on display in the Le Musée de la Bande Dessinée in Angoulême, France. If the overlapping image is unframed, it can also interact with the content of the other images—an effect Brian Stelfreeze creates for the opening page of *Black Panther* #1 (2016) in which the main character crouches in front of three different background images, each representing a different memory in his thoughts at that moment.

6. **Insets**, which appear as if placed entirely within the borders of a larger image, are a variation of overlapping. In *Bitch Planet* #4 (2015), Valentine De Landro uses insets for a self-consciously erotic and semi-parodic sexploitation shower scene. Drawing panels as insets over a full-page panel can also emphasize the background image as the page's foundation. As Luc Sante explains in the Foreward of *Madonna Comix*, Dianne Kornberg uses Marjorie Henderson Buell's 1930s comic strip *Little Lulu* as the "backing scrim" of each page, and "Atop the strips, half-effacing them, Kornberg draws and paints" (2014).

7. Even if images are similarly sized, shaped and arranged, the drawn quality of **frames** can highlight content. In *Elektra: Assassin* (1986), Bill Sienkiewicz draws choppy black lines around images that represent events currently taking place in a psychiatric asylum and no frames between images and white gutters for past events. When a choppy, black frame appears on a page of unframed panels, the framed image is highlighted and identified as representing either a time shift to the present or a thematically related moment, as when the frame appears around a teenaged Elektra attempting suicide. In *Batwoman: Elegy* (2010), J. H. Williams III draws sharp-edged frames around Batwoman and ornately curving frames around her antagonist; when ornate elements first appear around Batwoman on a page of otherwise sharp-edge panels, the framing not only distinguishes the content but also formally communicates the antagonist's power over her.

8. Frames can also accent image content if elements of the content are drawn as if breaking the frames and entering the negative space of the gutter and possibly the space of other images—and so another form of overlapping. **Broken frames** are often used to depict movement and violence, as if the frame is unable to contain the image due to the subject's speed and power,

as Sana Takeda demonstrates in *Monstress* (2016), depicting a splash of blood, the swinging of long hair, a head thrown backwards, a bird in flight, and two figures in full combat—though when broken frames become a page norm, they no longer accent content. In *A Chinese Life* (2012), Li Kunwu draws a figure falling from a windowsill so that his arm and shoulder break into the next two panels framing the shocked faces of two characters watching.

9. If images contrast other images through differences in **style**, they may stand out in the page composition too. In *Age of Bronze* (2013), Eric Shanower draws highly detailed, almost photorealistic panels and so is able to accentuate an image with an abrupt drop in line density, one that also signifies a shift to a character's childhood memories, ones rendered in a contrastingly cartoonish style. In *CancerVixen* (2006), Marisa Acocella Marchetto highlights the image of a restaurant receipt by using a photocopy that starkly contrasts the cartoon style of the surrounding images.

Marchetto also tilts the receipt and reproduces the receipt at more than twice the size of other images—showing that accent approaches can be combined. In *Maui: Legends of the Outcast* (1996), Chris Slane centers a pair of tall, overlapping, single-color panels on a page of primarily wide and square, multi-color panels, combining the accenting strategies of shape, overlap, and position. By placing the image at the center of the page, Slane also reveals one more tool for accenting content, one that involves no visual differentiation because not all areas of a pages are created equal. Groensteen writes: "panels find themselves 'automatically' reinforced by the fact that they occupy one of the places on the page that enjoys a natural privilege, like the upper left hand, the geometric center or the lower right—and also, to a lesser degree, the upper right and the lower left" (2007: 29). If grids were "democratic" as Brunetti claims, panels would have the same value; Groensteen instead argues for shades of importance.

Now consider how layouts and accents can interact with the plot sequences discussed in the previous chapter. Recall the five parts of an action sequence: balance, disruption, imbalance, climax, and new balance. How might they map onto a page layout? If you didn't want to emphasize one of the parts, you could draw five, evenly sized and evenly spaced, full-width panels. Or you could accent one by leaving it unframed. You might instead draw a three-row layout, dividing two rows in half and leaving the third as an accented full-width panel. If it were the first row, the opening panel would be accented; if the middle, then the imbalance; and if the last, the new balance. Tilts and shape accents can be applied to any panel, though since they work better in grids, you might add an additional imbalance panel to create a 3 × 2 layout. Whatever your preferred accenting technique, what happens when each action segment is highlighted? Disruption and climax are often the most dramatic moments—but does that mean they should be accented or not? The choices you make will affect how a viewer experiences the content.

Student Examples

Illustration 4.4 includes four pages, each with a different layout, different accent techniques, and accents on different action parts:

1. Hung begins with three rows of slightly irregular heights. Although the first two are divided into two panels each, the bottom full-width panel is less accented by size because the middle panels are taller. The primary accent is instead the overlapping panel positioned in the center of the top four panels. It is also tilted, and its black background with white letters stylistically contrasts the rest of the page.

The page details Hung's main character's acceptance into a soccer team, with images of him performing multiple actions: getting the news on the phone, jumping for joy afterwards, flying in an airplane, and arriving at the team's city. There's also a panel of a sign with the team logo and the accented caption panel with the words he presumably says to his parents after the first phone call. In terms of sequences, the accented panel is its own one-panel action, since nothing else on the page depicts that phone conversation. The news he delivers to his parents shakes up the status quo and so is both disruption and climax.

2. Grace begins with an irregular four-row layout, progressing from two to four to three panels in each row, before the final accented panel. While the circular shape clearly breaks the rectangular norm, Grace further accents it with wide areas of white space on both sides. And though the gutters are a consistent width above it, the gutter shapes create an additional overlap effect, suggesting that the last panel occupies the space that would otherwise belong to the third row.

Grace's page also tells a complete story that combines at least three actions. The first row disrupts the character's walk home; the second depicts the emergence of the cat from the garbage; the third depicts their first interaction; and the final, accented image skips a range of implied actions—walking the rest of the way home, putting away groceries, etc.—to end on a new balance that resolves the combined plot of the whole page. The wide white margins of the final spacing also seem to relate to the narrative leap to that much later moment in a different location, as if additional gutter space is needed conceptually too.

3. Henry draws a regular 3 × 2 grid with every panel identical in size, shape, frame, tilt, and spacing, with no overlapping or frame-breaking elements and no insets. Henry instead accents the bottom left panel through a stylistic difference. The background of the fifth panel is heavily shaded in black, a sharp contrast to the white and uncrosshatched backgrounds of the five other panels.

The page continues an action sequence from a previous page, with the narrator being electrocuted in an attempt to trigger his mutant powers. The first three panels complete that action, followed by a one-panel action of the guards untying him and giving him water, before the torture continues

1.

2.

3.

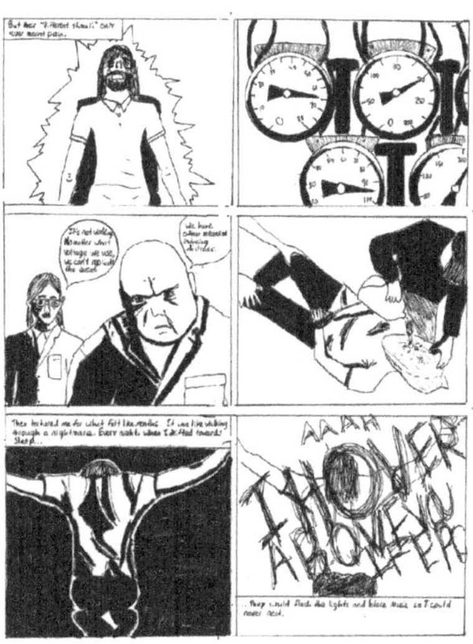

4.

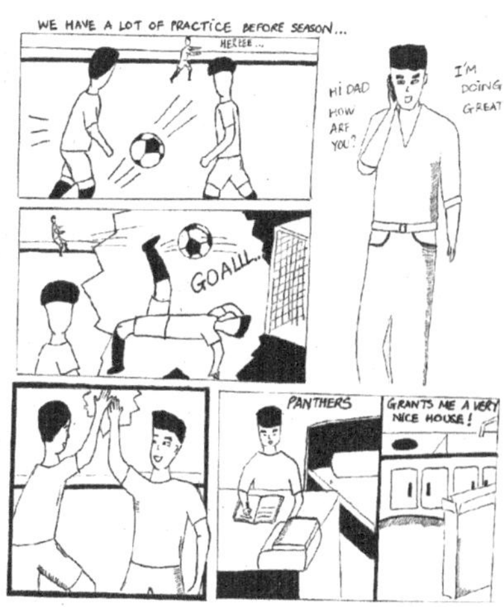

ILLUSTRATION 4.4 *Accent examples.*

in the last row. The accented panel includes captioned narration explaining that every time he nearly falls asleep he is jolted awake as shown in the last panel. The last row then is a two-panel action sequence, beginning in balance and ending in disruption, with the climax and new imbalance left implied as well as cyclical. By accenting the first balance panel, Henry highlights the character's moment of near peace.

4. For his second layout, Hung uses a mixed path approach, beginning with a two-panel column paired with an unframed second column, and ending with a bottom row of three panels. The lack of a frame around the second column accents it through contrast with the other framed panel, while also effectively expanding the image content by merging its background with the white of the page and so accenting it by size too. To a lesser degree, Hung also accents the first panel in the bottom row with a contrastingly thicker frame.

Like Hung's previous page, this one includes the narrator performing at least three actions, each condensed to one or two images: receiving a pass and then scoring; speaking to his father on the phone; and reading in his new home. Again, Hung accents the phone conversation to a parent, establishing a link between pages that creates a suggestive pattern about the main character. If the panel of him scoring was accented instead, it would appear that wining was more important than connection to family. The secondary accent is also on the high five between players, further emphasizing relationships over the sport itself.

EXERCISE 4.2 *ACCENTING PANELS*

Select one of your previous or invent a new one-action sequence that is divided into at least five parts.

1 Decide which part to accent and sketch three different page layouts, each using a different accenting technique.

2 Select a different image to accent and sketch three more layouts that use three different techniques.

3 When you've sketched the sequence six times, look them over and pick a favorite. Revise it by drawing it larger and in more detail.

Phrases

When the French paper *Adventures* published Siegel and Shuster's *Superman* dailies in 1939, editors converted the four-panel strips into five-panel rows in order to publish six dailies in a weekly 5 × 5 grid:

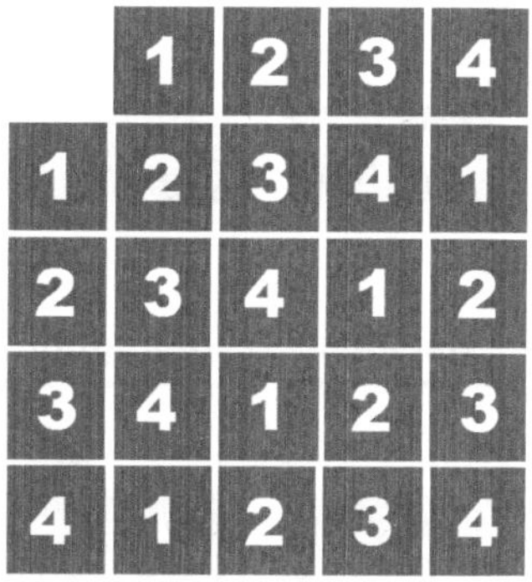

In poetry, this would be the equivalent of reformatting a haiku—a three-line stanza of five, seven, and five syllables—into a quatrain with lines of mostly four syllables. The editors were thinking like prose writers not like poets. In prose, it's up to a typesetter to determine where a line happens to break. In poetry, line breaks are carefully determined by the author. And since artists not typesetters control the arrangement of images on a comics page, phrasing matters. The most common phrase is a row, though columns and other kinds of clustering can create the same visual effects. Like the words in a line of poetry, the images in a comics phrase are viewed for individual meaning but also together as a sub-unit within the larger compositional unit of the page.

That means related sets of images should be arranged together—or not. Breaking related images apart can be effective too. Weigh your choices and select what feels best. Again, identifying images by the parts of their action sequences can be helpful. If a one-action sequence consists of three images, it should fit easily into a row or column or other visual phrase, so that the physical unit and the story-world action combine. If the sequence is too long to fit into a phrase—or if you don't like the effect of sequestering a sequence into a single page area—then you have to decide where to divide it.

Enjambed

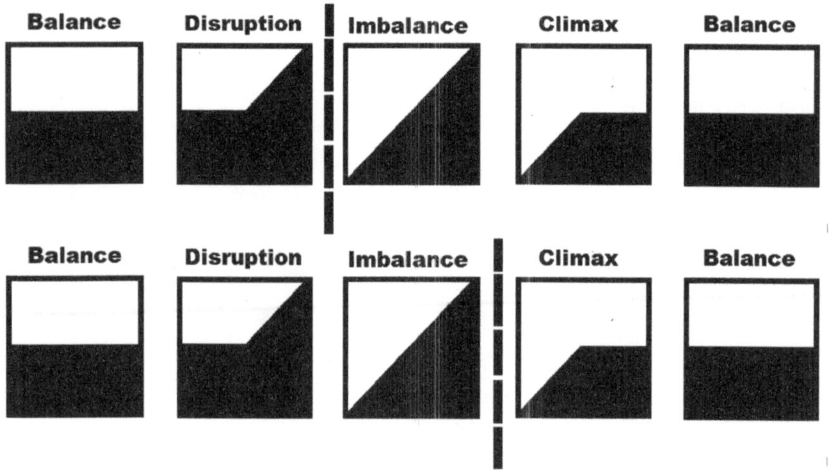

End-stopped

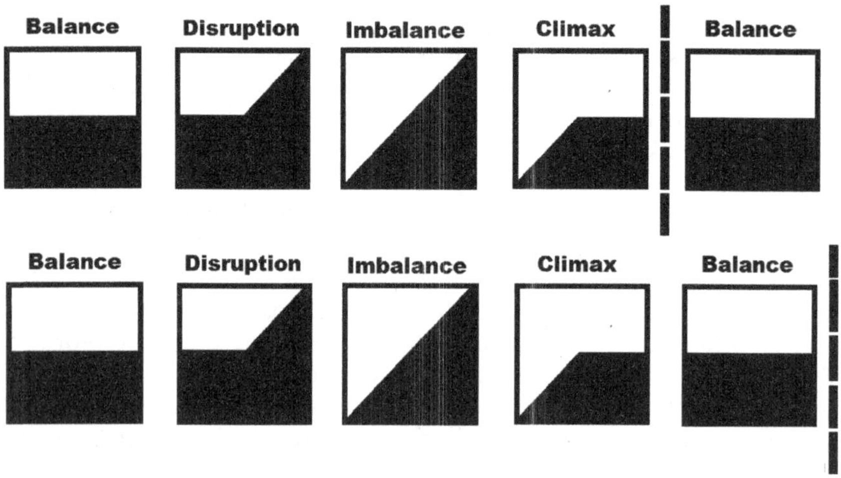

Returning to a poetry parallel, you have two basic choices: end-stops, which in poetry include lines that end on natural pauses and so usually on punctuation; or enjambment, lines that break in less obvious and less comfortable places, usually creating a mini-cliffhanger as a reader rushes to the next line to complete the meaning. An end-stopped comics phrase ends with a similar sense of completion and so on a climax or ending balance. An enjambed phrase instead ends on imbalance or disruption. The last image of a page can be enjambed too, pushing the viewer not just to the next area of the same page but to the following page. For the most extreme effect, the

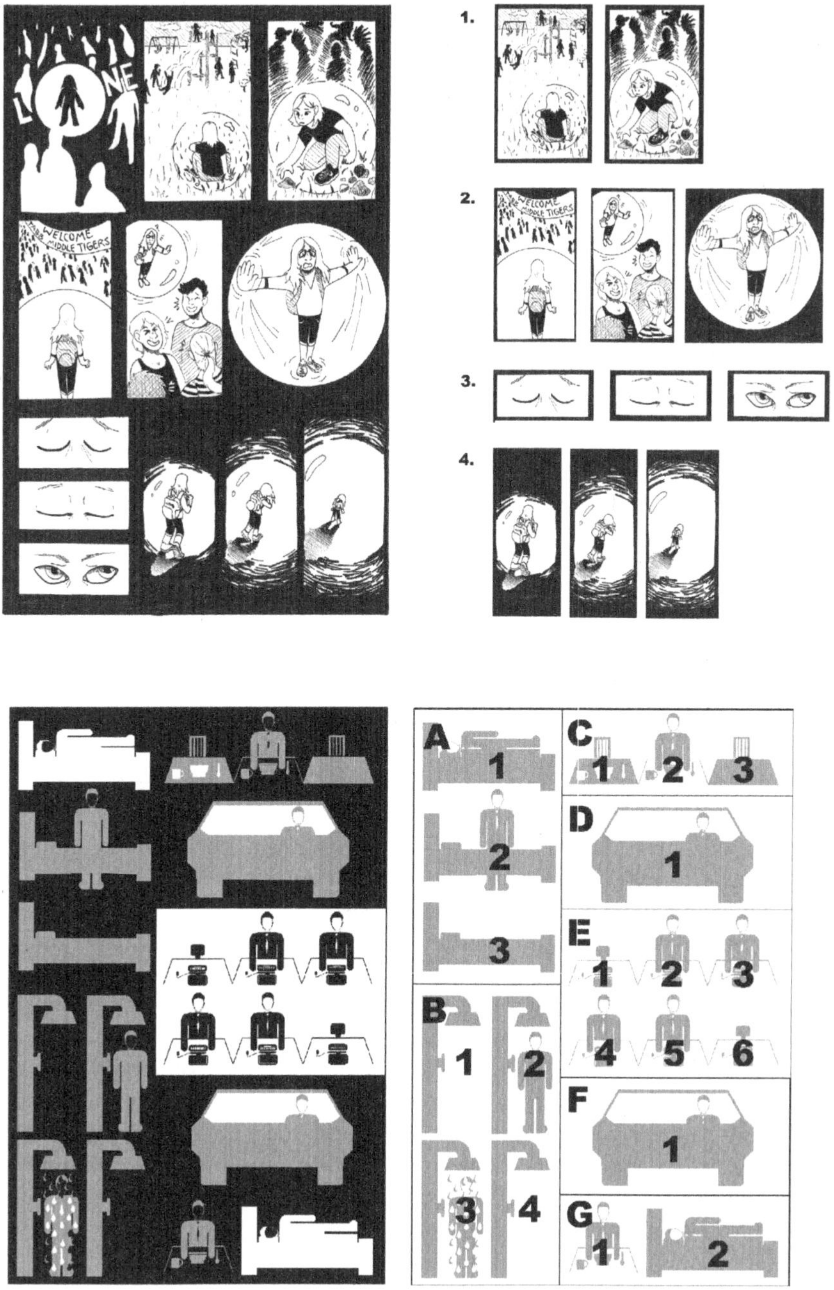

ILLUSTRATION 4.5 *Phrases.*

enjambment will involve a physical page turn and so a blocked view of the coming climax. Benjamin Percy recommends using a cliffhanger at "the end of every scene," of which a mainstream comic of twenty to twenty-two pages contains "five to seven" (2016: 26–7). Alan Moore recommends the opposite approach: "all that's needed to accomplish a good transition is to write in basic units of a single page, so that the reader's action in turning the page becomes the beat in which I change scene without disturbing the rhythm of the story" (2008: 17). You might find that each approach is useful at different moments.

Illustration 4.5 provides two examples of phrases. In the top half, Grace draws the first page of a two-page comic. The twelve panels divide into one title panel and four connected action sequences of two and three panels each. The shortest shares the first row with the title panel, creating a split phrase; the spacing is uniform, but the title panel is unframed and its figures are silhouettes, stylistic elements that help to visually divide it from the two-panel action of the main character playing alone in the grass. Row two forms the next phrase, which contains the complete second action: she attempts to interact with others but can't break through her bubble. Row three includes two phrases. The first is a panel-sized column of the narrator's eyes as she appears to sadly accept her situation. The second is the three unframed bubbles which she descends into. Both phrases contain complete actions and so the page consists entirely of end-stops. Although the larger story doesn't end here, it could since no cliffhanger propels the page turn.

In the bottom half, Chris draws a twenty-image sequence that divides into seven phrases. Though none of the individual images have separate panels, the first phrase opens the page with a three-image column. The second phrase continues the column but with internal 2 × 2 rows. The remaining five phrases then produce consistent rows, with the middle and longest separated in a phrase-defining panel. Each phrase is complete and so end-stopped.

In Chapter 3, you drew a two-action sequence of nine panels. Consider different ways to arrange those images. Do they belong on a single page or do you need two? If two, should it be a two-page spread, or should the page break involve a page turn? Do the two actions belong in separate visual phrases—perhaps with a wider gutter dividing the panels in the top half of the page from the panels in the bottom half? Or should each action have its own column? Changing the dimensions of the images widens the range of possibilities—maybe one action is drawn as tall images and the other as wide ones? If you avoid rectangular frames, what different kinds of arrangements does the visual content suggest?

EXERCISE 4.3 *DRAWING PHRASES*

Look back at your previous drawings, including your hinged panels and your action sequences, and select some combination to appear on a single page, inventing as much new material as you like. Decide which groups of panels will be your phrases.

1 Sketch four layouts that vary the arrangement of the phrases. Experiment with different enjambments and end-stops. Isolate phrases by changing reading paths or visually dividing them in other ways.
2 Look over the four sketches, select a favorite, and revise it by drawing it larger and in more detail, researching any new content.

Canvas

Combining layout, accents, and phrasing with action parts and other storyworld content is a lot, but it doesn't include the most important quality of a comics page: it has to look good. An effective layout is effective partly because it divides a page in a visually compelling way. Approaching the page as a canvas also means appreciating what is normally viewed as multiple images as a single image.

Though not an artist himself, Stan Lee acknowledges that "you've got to put your pictures together so that it's pleasing to the eye" with "the flow of the design" creating "a pleasant, unified mass" and a "feeling of movement"—which for Lee meant panels that "are not evenly centered" and vary in "different sizes" (Lee & Buscema 1984: 110–21). Whatever your particular aesthetic preferences, treating the page as a unified space is treating it as a canvas. It should be developed as a whole, the way a graphic designer composes a poster or an advertising team designs a magazine ad. Do the shapes and values work together? Does it all balance? Sometimes it helps to take a literal step back and squint.

In Illustration 4.6, Leigh Ann draws four variations of the same page. The first consists entirely of contour shapes, and the next three are variations on value balancing. Note what objects are filled in each example. While all four are viable as compositions, all have their strengths and weaknesses.

Page 1 is purely linear. The read is swift, legibility is definite and clean. Depth is constructed by overlap and size of shapes. The lack of value causes the shapes to have no three-dimensionality and therefore no mass. The overall aspect is flat.

Page 2 has one value only, black with white as a default. The panels are flat, large shapes are perceptible as definite shapes, but there is no information as to top, sides and bottom. Detail is an impossibility. The viewer's eye can

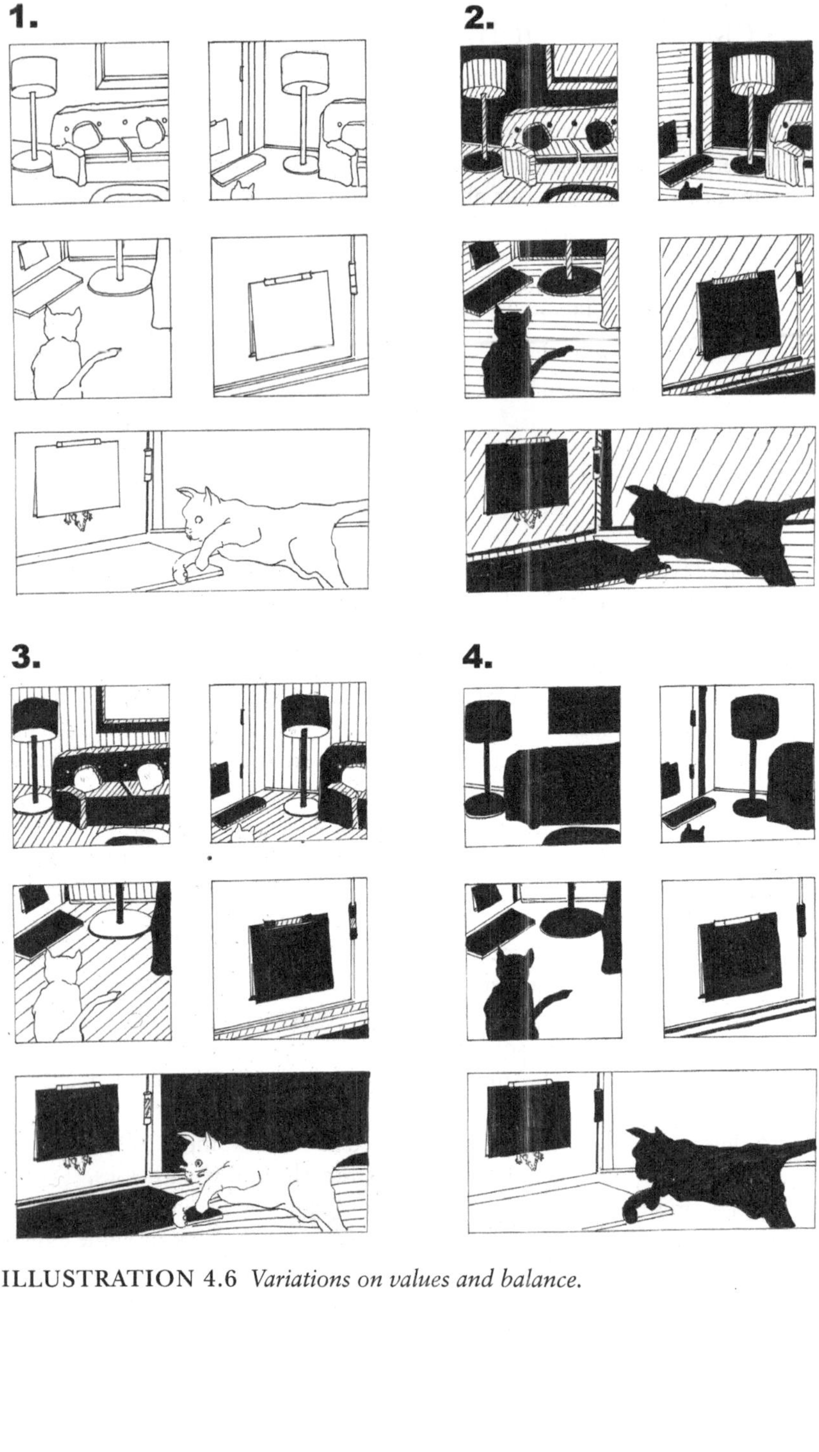

ILLUSTRATION 4.6 *Variations on values and balance.*

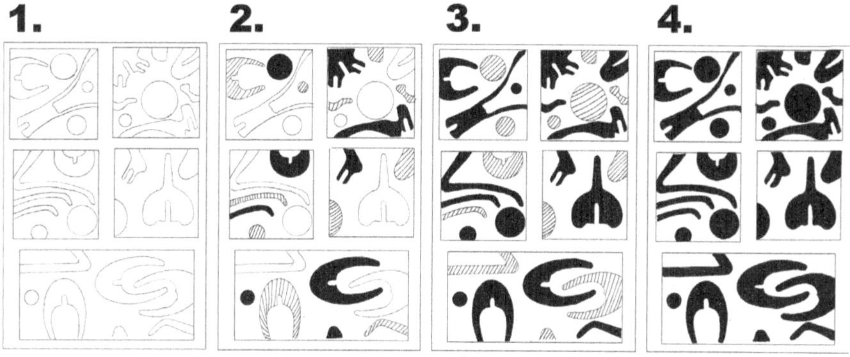

ILLUSTRATION 4.7 *Abstract shapes.*

make out large shapes—a cat, a lamp, a door flap and a mouse—but all of this is a quick read with no detail or mass to catch the eye. Panels with multiple shapes (zoomed out panels) are confusing and claustrophobic. Panels with small amounts of information (zoomed in panels) are much more legible.

Page 3 has two values, black and grey, with no opportunity for a highlight. Depth is achieved with overlap, size of shapes *and* the direction of the contour hatch marks in the grey. The aspect is monotonous. A lot of information is communicated with directional hatching and proximity of lines. There is little opportunity for detail but even for that, there is much opportunity for pleasing, readable shapes.

Page 4 has the most opportunity for depth, detail and image legibility. The use of three values allows for three dimensional shapes. The direction of the hatch marks and the proximity of those hatch marks to each other gives lots of potential for depth and varying degrees of value. The read is slightly longer but not too long and is ultimately satisfying (a win-win in any drawing).

Illustration 4.7, four pages of six panels of free-floating positive forms on a white ground, is similar to the earlier set of pages with one striking difference—the background acts as a set negative shape, heightening the importance of the positive shapes. All of the objects or figures act as the positive, and the background or ground is the negative. This simplifies options and, for better or worse, takes away most options for creating depth. Because the shapes are varied in size and configuration, they are visually appealing in any configuration, as linear shapes or variously valued shapes.

The first is the calmest option with low contrast and transparent, insubstantial shapes. The second has the advantage of high contrast. The positive/negative shape relationships are complicated and eye-catching. The negative shapes are as interesting as the positive shapes, something every artist strives for. The third is every bit as interesting with added eye attraction of a bit more depth. The black shapes appear to come forward, in front of the hatched shapes. A little bit of movement (eye interest) is achieved by hatching—diagonals are exciting! The fourth is somehow quieter than the third and a bit more complicated to read. The three differently valued shapes on a white background begin to take on a bit more character, inching toward narrative. The shapes are more evocative of real-life shapes, and the shapes and their relationships to each other evoke more meaning.

Finally, note that all of the compositions appear to be floating into and off of the panel frame. This is achieved by the shapes stopping mid shape as they hit the frame. Remember that if a shape's edge touches the frame and acknowledges the edge, the conceit of this scene as a snapshot of floating abstract objects stops.

EXERCISE 4.4 *VALUE VARIATIONS*

Look back at your previous work and select or create content for a multi-panel page. Draw the page using only contour lines. The drawings should be simple shapes. Photocopy the page four times. This may require experimentation so extra copies may be necessary. The objective is to make a pleasing composition with value shapes, and this will take practice.

1. No values: line. The first copy is only line. Leave it be.
2. Two values: black and half tone. Draw hatch lines for the half tone and fill in other shapes to make the solid black.
3. Three values: black, half tone, and white. Leave some shapes without value (white), fill in others with half tone hatch marks, and completely blacken other shapes.
4. Two values: black and white. Fill in some shapes completely with black and leave all others white.

Anthology

As seen in the anthology excerpts, maintaining consistent grids and varying layout page-by-page are both common. Though not considered a comics artist by curators or herself, Bick's two photographic sequences both form familiar 4 × 4 grids. Barry, Lightman, Radtke, and Tomine (in his first comic) use 2 × 2 grids, and Estrada, Roberts, Smyth, Tamaki, and Tomine (in his second comic) use 3 × 2 grids. Siciliano uses both. Ma's grid is 3 × 3, and

Finck's is a 4 × 3 grid before she breaks from it on her final page. Alagbé begins with a full-page panel and then divides his following pages into two full-widths. Ott begins and ends with full-width panels, as variations on his baseline 2 × 2 grids. Davis begins with a 3 × 2 grid, before replacing panels with white space and then returning with full-width panels that imply a union in the marriage relationship by physically combining the pairs of square panels. GG uses a four-row grid of full-width panels, varying it by combining panels. While Hernandez and Johnson each draw one 3 × 2 grid, their other pages vary, creating no baseline norm. Libicki and Comeau vary even more, by drawing non-rectangular panels. For Libicki, that also encourages viewing the center images on her first page as a column, despite the Z-path of the caption boxes.

The most common reading paths in the anthology, and comics generally, are three-row Z-paths. Because the content of Barry's 2 × 2 grid does not produce definitive hinges that determine a reading path, it could be read either as two rows or as two columns. While Alagbé and Hankiewicz work in columns, other artists vary their layouts with brief N-path instances within predominately Z-path layouts. Bechdel, D'Salete, Dubai, Johnson, Katin, Satrapi, and Tsai create these kinds of mixed reading paths by inserting a sub-column within a row. While such moments are not necessarily significant narratively, isolated Z-reading can be used as a form of accent. Bechdel, however, uses the strategy five times in six pages, making mixed paths her norm, producing no accent effect.

The most common form of accent is size. Dabai's one column is also her largest panel, giving its content double emphasis. Johnson's largest panel (at the bottom of his first page) emphasizes the distance between his characters, making that emotional fact the underlying thematic quality of the four-page scene. D'Salete's final panel is his largest, a reaction shot implying the undrawn content of the tribal leader's poisoned corpse. Estrada, Comeau, and Powell also end their sequences on full-page images. Finck's final page features a single image too, but the accent is produced primarily by the spacing of the extremely wide margins that isolate the image. Tobocman accents the column of words on his last page with a similar spacing accent. Though the first panel of Nickerson's third page is accented by size, it stands out more than the equally sized second panel of her second page because of the image content. The image of the person sleeping inside the dumpster uses a darker background, white marks, and a comparatively realistic style. Roberts accents her second panel similarly by shading it with realistic crosshatching absent from the other panels.

Other artists accent by altering their frames. Tsai's two pages both begin and end with his Zhuangzi cartoon addressing the viewer, but he leaves the first panel of the first page and the last panel of the second page unframed, emphasizing those moments and balancing the two-spread page. Dhaliwal leaves the middle panel of her second page unframed, creating a panel of mostly undrawn white space that gives it further emphasis. Though the bottom right image on Thompson's first page is equal in size to the one to the left and only half the size of the image above it, the tilted accent of the frame overwhelms those other visual elements. Katin breaks her frame multiple times, but the final instance is most accented because the breaks occur in two directions (the head of the bottom image protrudes into the frame above it, and the foot from the top image protrudes into the panel below it) within a sub-column that alters the reading path.

Although Corman changes frame style on her fourth page, she repeats the new style five times, reducing any accent effect and instead grouping the darkened bedroom scene into a visual phrase. Varying layouts also allow artists to create visual phrases that separate short visual sequences from surrounding content. Satrapi eliminates gutters with single frame lines that turn the three panels in the bottom row of her second page into a phrase focused on the narrator and her grandmother; the effect is deepened by the shift to N-path reading. D'Salete uses a similar combination, placing the three images of the tribal leader eating his poisoned meal into a three-panel column. While Libicki maintains Z-paths, the bottom row of her second page is an even row of squares, separating it from the curving shapes preceding it; both the repeated image angle and the single sentence subdivided across the row reinforce the phrase affect. While Powell varies the tilt and spacing of his panels in ways that prevent accenting any single image, the frame angles and spacing of the bottom four panels on his first page create a phrase that isolates the middle panels of a character's eyes surrounded by cropped police in the left and right panels.

Some phrases fill entire pages or extend across more than one page. While Abel's shift in layout from three-panel rows to two-panel rows divides her second page into two phrases, her next pages are each a visual phrase: page three eliminates frames as the point of view moves closer to the expanding blood stain, and page four is a three-panel scene of increasing panel sizes, echoed by the architecture of the drawn room. Davis' first two pages feature square panels, and her second feature two full-width panels, creating phrases linked to each two-page spread.

These are just some of the layout effects we noticed. Keep looking through the anthology pages to find more.

5

Words

CHAPTER OUTLINE

Words are characters.

Characters are printed symbols that exist as ink on paper or pixels on screen. In this sense, words are images, no different from any other kind of image. The fact is easy to overlook when reading a prose-only book where letters are typeset in a single font and color with uniform margins. Chapter titles might be larger, bolder, and isolated within a larger area of white space, but then the typesetting reverts back to its undifferentiated norms. That uniformity tells readers that word rendering doesn't matter. And since it communicates no meaning, it becomes invisible.

Words are also characters in the sense that Little Line discussed in Chapter 3 is a character. Though Little Line is represented by specific lines in a sequence of panels, Little Line also exists beyond those images as a concept or cluster of ideas in a reader's head. That's how we typically understand words, as free-floating definitions and connotations that are triggered when an image of a word appears on a page.

Because prose writers focus on words as concepts and ignore words as images, they lack the range of possibilities open to comics creators. "What we are looking at when we read," explains Mendelsund, "*are* words, made up letterforms, but we are trained to see past them—to look at what the words and letterforms point toward. Words are like arrows—they *are* something, and they point *toward* something" (2014: 322). Prose-only writers attend only to what words point *toward*, the network of meanings that a word's history of usage accrues. Since they leave word rendering to typesetters and printers, word rendering doesn't matter. Comics script writers don't render words either, and so they sometimes adopt a similar attitude. "Lettering," insists Brian Michael Bendis, "should be invisible. You shouldn't notice it unless it is a determined piece of storytelling in graphic design" (2014: 43). Bendis is right, but only because words in a comic are always a determined piece of graphic design.

Words on comics pages tend to fall into six conventions: character speech, character thought, narration, sound effects, titles, and words drawn as elements of the story-world. Traditionally, the first three are typeset (or uniformly hand-lettered) and placed in category-identifying graphic containers: talk balloons, thought balloons, and caption boxes. While the last three tend be drawn as overt elements of the artwork, it's important to understand that all words in a comic are always part of the art. So comics creators must attend to their three visual aspects: word rendering, word containers, and word placement.

Word Rendering

The appearance of a word affects how a reader understands its meaning. Even typeset fonts aren't neutral. Each differs in line thickness, shape, and ornamentation, evoking an overall tone or personality. If the words are character speech, font is voice, whether in dialogue, thought, or narration. Even if words are not linked to a character, their style still communicates information. A caption box that includes only a time stamp and a location has to be rendered in a certain style and so with certain visual connotations. The most generic, no-frills, corporate-looking font communicates exactly those qualities. Retype that same information in **Bauhaus** or **Broadway** or *Brush Script* and feel the differences.

Comics creators select or create a font style that relates to the story content. For *Wonder Woman* #20 (1988), George Pérez draws his narrator's text in a font similar to courier news, because the narrator is a reporter seated at a typewriter in an opening panel. Dialogue and third-person narration still appear in standard hand-lettered style, differentiated from the character's first-person narration as he types. When a character in *Can't We Talk About Something More PLEASANT?* (2014) reads aloud the ingredients listed on a bottle, Roz Chast switches from curving lines of hand-drawn letters to typeset words arranged in choppy lines.

Comics lettering, whether hand-drawn or mechanical, typically features letterforms with no serifs and consistent line thickness. While sizing and spacing are usually uniform, typesetters can add bolding and italics to suggest the rhythms and emphases of speech. Comics lettering tend to use bolding more often, and letter sizes vary—as an inevitable aspect of hand-drawn imprecision, but for targeted emphases as well. Typesetting creates the impression of invisible lines holding the evenly-spaced words and letters in uniform rows, an effect that can clash on a page that otherwise consists of hand-drawn images. Unless you have a targeted aesthetic reason to typeset, draw your letters. If you do typeset, try creating your own font (Google "create your own font" for advice), as Mira Jacobs did for her graphic memoir *Good Talk* (2019), especially after her publisher tried to convince her to use a font associated with a YA wizard series.

In *Skim* (2008), Mariko and Jillian Tamaki's main character passes a road sign announcing a town named "Scarborough," and her narrating-self respells it "Scarberia" in a gothic font unlike any other word in the graphic novel. Word rendering can vary for a range of such story reasons. Whispered words can be smaller, shouted words larger, mumbled words illegible. Should a narrating character "speak" to the reader in the same font as she does in her dialogue with other characters? Should characters' words differ, echoing their visual qualities, so that the lines of their bodies and the lines of their words visually relate? Or if characters share a single font, perhaps their words differ in color or sizing or some other characteristic?

Mainstream comics traditionally include sound effects, usually onomatopoeia words drawn in expressive lines, shapes and sizes that visually suggest the quality of the sounds they're evoking: Ka-Pow! ZAP! Even when there's a separate lettering artist, these words are drawn as part of the initial artwork. In *Walking Dead* #1 (2003), Tony Moore renders the words of his sound effects BOOM! and WHUMP! in sharp lines and shapes that contrast the looser style of his other images, a difference that parallels their physical difference in the story-world. Mariko and Jillian Tamaki play with the sound effect convention by placing drawn words within images even though the verbs aren't always sound-related: "clench" beside toes, "stir," and "stab" beside a straw, and even "apply" beside a bar of deodorant a character rubs in her armpit. In their *This One Summer* (2014), the words "Slut. Slut. Slut. Slut." trail behind a character's flip-flops as she walks. The insult is in her thoughts after hearing older boys use it to flirt with older girls, so rather than a sound identical to all listeners, it's filtered through just one character's unmarked consciousness.

Sounds effects, like most letters on a comics page, are paradoxical because from the perspective of a character they don't exist. A character can't "see" a "BOOM!" even though the lines of its letters might overlap with the lines of her own body. But she can see words tattooed on her arm or glowing on a computer screen because they are part of the story-world. The division isn't always clear. Will Eisner established a splash-page norm of words that playfully merge with the story-world. The letters of *The Spirit* might be blocked by a passing ship, or form from the smoke spewed from chimneys, or appear on a card held by a character, or provide an object for characters to climb.

Because it breaks the baseline naturalism of most mainstream genres, such effects are usually limited to opening titles—but not always. After a young woman agrees to go out with the main character in *American Born Chinese* (2006), Gene Luen Yang draws the repeating word "YES." in a column above the narrator's bed, with the last "YES." shaped to the contours of his bed. In Hannah K. Lee's *Language Barrier* (2017), the letters of the one-page "You Don't Owe Anyone Anything" consist of variously stretched, yellow smiley faces; and in "Student Loans," the letters of the second word are darker, thicker, and drawn in front of and blocking the letters of the first word. The artistic potential of words has been explored outside of comics too. Glenn Ligon's *How It Feels to be Colored Me* (1989) and Kay Rosen's *The Ed Prints* (1998) are paintings that consist entirely of rendered words.

However you choose to render a word, evaluate how that style relates to the word's meaning. Does the style support the meaning or does it contrast it? Imagine the word "thin" drawn in thin letters and then in thick ones. Imagine the word "red" in red ink and then in blue ink. Comics titles are often drawn in letterforms that reflect the title character: Bob Wiacek and Todd McFarlane's design for *The Incredible Hulk* #340 (1988) appears to be constructed from blocks of stone; Bernie Wrightson and Gaspar Saladino's letters for *Swamp Thing* #1 (1972) might have grown from an actual swamp. The title design for the film *Hulk* instead uses metallic lettering, and after the character Swamp Thing is revealed to a be kind of god, the lettering changed accordingly. The appearance of letterforms can contradict word meaning too, as with this dilapidated billboard:

Browse magazine ads and cover designs for other examples of word rendering outside of comics. *Lolita: The Story of a Cover Girl* (2013) includes over a hundred variations on Nabokov's novel, many consisting only of letters. Beginning with its January 2018 issue, the covers of *Poetry* magazine include only the six letters of the word "poetry" arranged in a 3 × 2 grid and rendered in a different style each month. Of course, any word can be designed in different styles:

EXERCISE 5.1 *RENDERING WORDS*

1 Look at the dialogue you drafted in the first section of Chapter 3 and select one sentence. What letterform style suits the character speaking? Try three different pre-made fonts, and then draw the statement in three different styles of your own.
2 Draw an image that involves a sound. Add the letters of a corresponding onomatopoeiac word. Draw the image again, this time with a related but less expected word. Draw it a third time with a completely unexpected word.
3 Draw an image that includes a variety of story-world words in the background, the foreground, or both.
4 Choose a word or phrase taken from or inspired by one of your previous drawings or story ideas and design it in three different title-like styles.
5 Select your favorite word design and incorporate it into an image that partially merges with a story-world. The words are both separate from the drawn world and yet paradoxically interacting with it.

Word Containers

Conventionally, words of speech are arranged inside circular talk balloons, thought inside cloud-like thought bubbles, and narration inside rectangular caption boxes. Thought bubbles fell out of popular use in mainstream comics in the early 1980s, and so character thought also often appears in caption boxes. Speech containers date to at least medieval manuscripts that include "speech scrolls" arranged near figures' mouths. Talk balloons usually have tails or pointers directed at the speaking character. For *Doonesbury*, Garry Trudeau draws only single-line pointers with no container around the spoken words. Words of any kind might be unframed, so that the lines of the words are integrated into the artwork.

No word containers are necessary, but mainstream comics included them in part to make revision easier and so speed production. 1960s' Marvel artists Steve Ditko and Jack Kirby would draw a large number of word containers per page, with only a general sense of the dialogue, thoughts, and narration that Stan Lee would later compose for a letterer to add. If Lee composed less than the containers implied, the letterer could draw the words larger, creating the impression that a character was shouting. That's because the containers, unlike the words, are an integral part of the artwork. Like sound effects, they are a drawn element to be balanced in each panel composition. Speech bubbles rarely contain more than thirty-eight words. While entire comics and certainly sections of comics are wordless, a word-heavy page might include as many as 230—though under 200 is more common.

Like word rendering, the lines and shapes of a word container are expressive. Jagged, smooth, rounded, angular—the visual qualities imply aural qualities, especially of speech. Dotted lines often indicate whispering, and thick jagged lines shouting. In 1925, Soviet graphic designer Aleksandr Rodchenko produced a now-iconic poster for a publishing house that featured a woman in profile cupping her hand to her mouth and shouting the Russian word for book, with the letters contained and shaped by a bullhorn-like triangle extending from her open mouth. Since speech is a character-defining quality, just the shape of a talk balloon can establish personality. The speech of Marvel's android character The Vision first appeared in white, oval talk balloons in 1968, but by 1972 later artists and colorists converted them to yellow, round-edged rectangles to suggest a robotic voice.

When designing your own text containers, consider whether the lines of the container match or contrast the lines of the words. Does the container have a background color or texture that carries a connotation too? Is the container simply a framing line, leaving the background image visible—or does the container appear to be cut out of the image, exposing the white of the page beneath? And do all containers follow the same design, or do they vary according to type or character or situation or mood?

For *Elektra: Assassin* (1987), Sienkiewicz and Miller place the title character's narration in white rectangles with sharp corners and her partner's in blue rectangles with flattened corners. When Elektra assumes the persona of an innocent romantic, her rectangles are pink with bubbly corners. In *Red Winter* (2018), Anneli Furmark contrasts her typical oval talk balloons with rectangular ones and zigzag lines for voices on the phone. The talk balloon around a voice on the television is oval, but its frame cuts off parts of the words, making the container into a kind of window into a different plane.

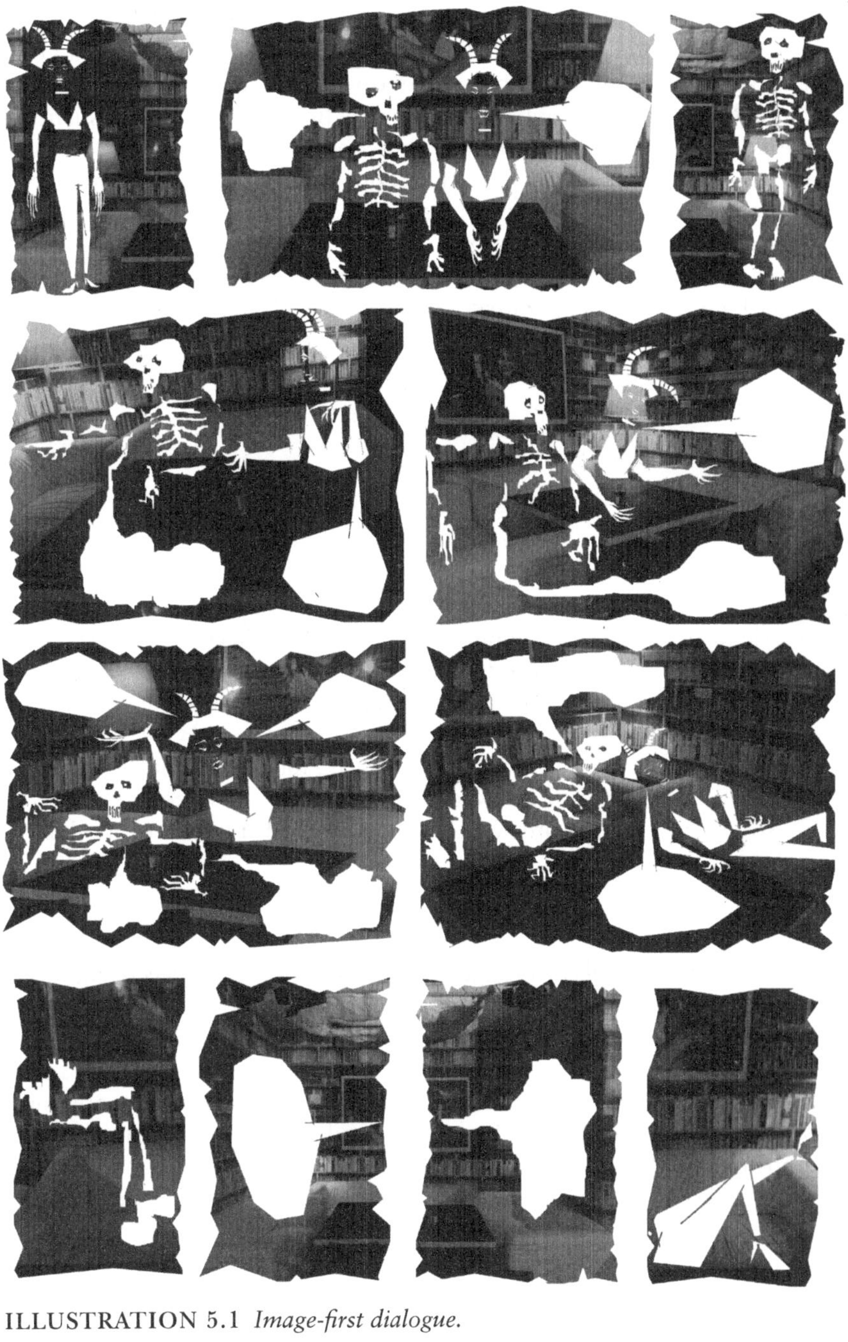

ILLUSTRATION 5.1 *Image-first dialogue.*

When two characters speak the same words simultaneously in *Asterios Polyp* (2009), David Mazzucchelli draws their two talk containers, an oval and a square, overlapping with the shared words in their centers.

Though they are not composed and set as lines of poetry, words lettered inside containers resemble stanzas. The containers function like pages in prose texts, forcing arbitrary line breaks, but the units are brief compared to a page of prose, so the containers also create units distinct from sentences and paragraphs or lines and stanzas. They create rhythms unique to comics, and so a writer needs to weigh how to group words into container phrases. Jennifer Egan's short story "Great Rock and Roll Pauses" in *A Visit from the Goon Squad* (2011) was composed in PowerPoint and consists of typeset words and word containers—and so might be considered a comic.

EXERCISE 5.3 *WRITING IMAGE-FIRST DIALOGUE*

Illustration 5.1 includes fourteen empty speech containers drawn in the style of the figures they point toward. Based on the containers' shapes and sizes, the background setting, and the characters' various postures and expressions, draft dialogue suited to the image. Where are these two characters? What is their relationship to each other? What does the sequence of images suggest about the subject, tone, and content of their speech? Is there a plot here? Note that the size of the speech containers constrains how many words you can use and whether sentences are short or broken up.

Illustration 5.2 displays a range of ways that fonts and speech containers combine for different effects. Typically, speech appears in images with facial expressions that influence how readers understand the words, but here the robot's face is blank, placing all significance on the other elements. In the first row, the "words" are identical, and so the speech containers are doing all of the work of implying volume, tone, and other sound qualities. In the second row, the "words" are in the same containers but they now vary in size and placement, creating new effects. In the third row, the "words" vary only by font, with a range of further possibilities suggested in the last row.

In Illustration 5.3, Chris uses human figures as word containers for three different types of text: thought ("You don't know what I'm thinking"); narration ("You have the right to remain silent"); and speech ("SHUT UP!"). Leigh Ann merges word containers and story content by writing words inside falling boulders as they urge hikers to safety out of frame, and

ILLUSTRATION 5.2 *Fonts and speech containers.*

ILLUSTRATION 5.3 *Non-traditional word containers.*

in the last image Leigh Ann draws words as they appear on bulletin board flyers, creating a story situation through what looks like coincidental juxtapositions.

EXERCISE 5.4 *CONTAINING WORDS*

Select your favorite word style from the previous section and draw your dialogue in a container with shape and line qualities:

1 that suggests a tone and volume that matches the word content;
2 that suggests a tone and volume that contrasts with the word content;
3 derived from the character's physical appearance;
4 derived from the word content.

Using the same words or developing new ones, invent your own ways of visually indicating that the words in an image are:

1 being spoken by a character;
2 being thought by a character;
3 being narrated distantly.

Word Placement

Page compositions typically group words within panels and between subjects foregrounded in the artwork. Words or word containers can also be superimposed over images or, if they match the qualities of the page background, appear to be cut out of them. Words can also appear in gutters, making the other panel frames their containers. Containers, especially talk balloons, often break panel borders, even in a comic that otherwise keeps all other images enclosed in frames. The distance between speech containers can suggest time durations. Dividing a character's words between two talk balloons creates a pause, especially if the balloons are on opposite sides of the figure. Overlapping containers between two characters implies they are speaking simultaneously, with the foregrounded container interrupting.

Image content can also frame and shape words. In *You Don't Have to Fuck People Over to Survive* (1989), Seth Tobocman places unframed white words in the black negative space between white figures, using their extended limbs to angle the words into rows or wrapping words directly around the figures' contours. The placement makes the words an inseparable aspect of the artwork. In *Phonograph: The Singles Club* (2013), Jamie McKelvie draws six words of song lyrics that dominate the page and also serve as panel frames for the cropped images of a sex scene drawn inside them.

The placement of words within panels creates a viewing rhythm by controlling how a viewer's eye absorbs the vacillating visual and linguistic content. For *One! Hundred! Demons!* (2017), Lynda Barry always partitions words in the top half of each panel, maintaining a words-then-image, words-then-image pattern. Eleanor Davis' two-page "The Emotion Room" (2016) works similarly until the final panel which includes both a top text caption and a bottom caption—giving words literally the final word. Yvan Alagbé uses a range of approaches in *Yellow Negroes and Other Imaginary Creatures* (2018). One story positions words in the gutters between each page's two panels. Other pages place caption boxes near the bottom of panels, until the end of sequences where final captions appear instead at the top or the centers of panels. Wide panels offer similar possibilities since whatever words or images appear in the left half will be absorbed first. Whatever choices you make, evaluate how word and word container placement affects content rhythm:

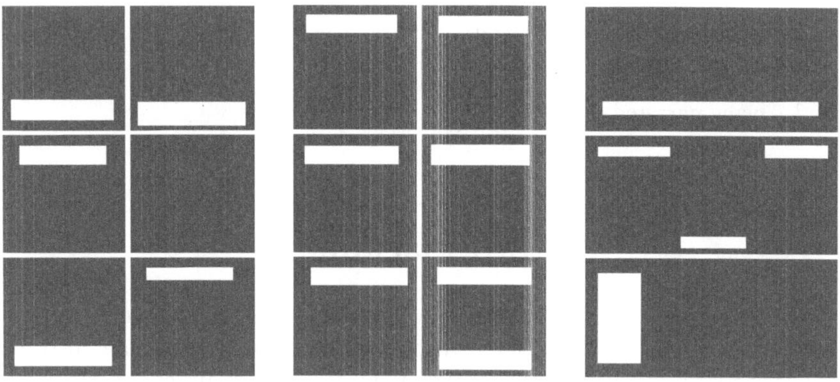

Some readers privilege words and so their eyes travel to text first, regardless of placement. If so, the images directly surrounding words or word containers receive greater attention than more distant content. Word placement then can be another way of accenting images—a strategy to add to the ones discussed in Chapter 4. A words-first viewing approach can also alter reading paths, since a viewer can ignore frames and gutters while leaping from word container to word container regardless of the directions implied by the layout. As a result, panel areas that fall outside of an initial reading path may be viewed afterwards or while a viewer's eye vacillates between image and words or not at all.

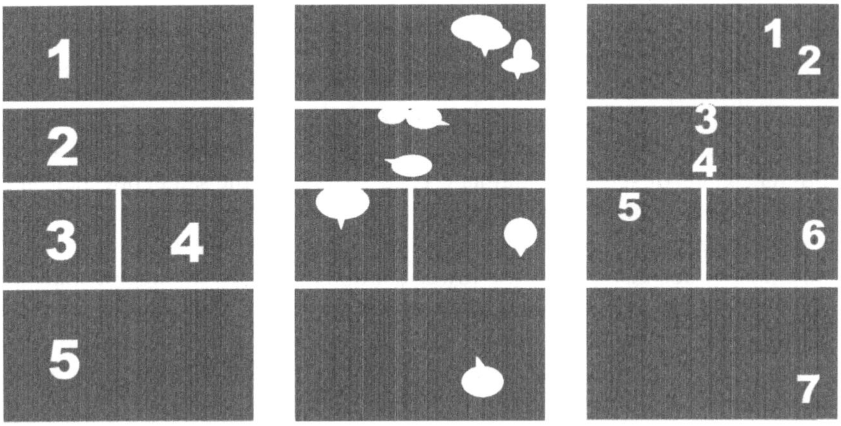

Look back at the one-page comic "If Only" in Chapter 3. Without the images and typeset as free verse, the comic would look like this:

If only
        there were
                some way
to be   together.

Though the loosely arranged 4 × 3 grid produces a Z-path, your eye may first move along the path created by the words before going back and attending to the surrounding images. If so, the page has two viewing paths—or possibly three since the final word "together" is black instead of gray, your eye may move to it immediately after "some way" and then travel left to read "to be," making grammatical sense of the arrangement only retroactively:

Student Examples

Illustration 5.4 shows a range of our students' approaches to combining word rendering, word containers, and word placement:

1. While drawing all words in the same style, Grace gives her two characters different kinds of speech containers. Their shapes are the same, but their line qualities differ. This would allow a reader to recognize who was speaking even if the speech tail pointed out of frame or the panel was black to indicate darkness. Grace also leaves the lower containers empty to suggest that the two characters continue talking—but it's not really the content of their conversation that matters. The gestalt hinge connecting the panels also adds to the plot tension of their growing closeness, especially since the reading path crosses back and forth over the gutter to follow dialogue.

2. Mims' two characters are speaking in sign language as they sit next to each other in math class. While their hand arrangements communicate words, Mims also draws accompanying English words in the spaces both outside and inside their hands and arms. The hands and arms then are word containers, and they provide the contour lines that the words follow. The word content also combines three different types: they are like speech, but since they indicate no sound, they could be understood as the characters' thoughts or as third-person narration translating their conversation for the reader.

3. Anna's panel is the second in a three-panel sequence and includes the middle word in the phrase "ON YOUR MARK" shouted at a track meet. Though it's speech, there is no talk balloon and no pointer indicating from whom or what direction the words are heard. While the capitalization and size of the letters suggest volume, the vacillating use of black and white lines against the contrasting background integrates the letters into the image to a degree usually associated with comics titles or other graphic design.

4. Henry's character is chained while forced to listen to blaring music—the words of which are scribbled over his body. Letter style, size, and placement all suggest the overpowering sound of the lyrics. The words are difficult to understand, which matches the situation. Henry also placed the "O" in the word "HOVER" so that it circles the character's head like an internal frame near the center of the panel, drawing the viewer's eye first.

5. Coleman's memoir narration appears in a caption box at the top of the panel. The box is made of the same lines that create the panel and so suggests a deeper level of connection than a word container drawn as if placed over the image content. After completing the artwork, Coleman scanned it and digitally inserted his narration in a pre-made font with a hand-drawn quality that matches the style of the drawing.

6. Grace draws the title of her comic "LONE" in white letters against a black panel, while also merging the letter "O" into the story-world by isolating a single figure inside it. The angle of the letters also add to the literally off-balance feel of the one-panel scene.

7. For her essay about gender in *Dracula* films, Anna draws a three-row layout with irregular panels that contain either images or words. If Groensteen is correct that the first, center, and final panels of a page are visually privileged, the layout accents the word containers. The containers and panels also share the same curving and fringed frame style, suggesting that words and images are essentially alike. Grace also includes white words and arrows in the black margins that link to and comment on the image content. Because the gutter words are not in containers or rows that create a rigid reading path, viewers may read them in different orders. The gutter words may also lead a viewer to the last image in the second row before the middle image, further disrupting the layout's expected Z-path.

8. Grace draws the onomatopoeia sound effect "BAM" next to the jagged emanata lines around the mouth of an overturned trash can. The letters also follow and are shaped by the triangular path the main character is walking in the background, creating a kind of word container that is also part of the story-world and that the bottom of the letters break as they reverse color. Because the word is read left to right, it also works as a kind of arrow leading the viewer's eye to the main character who is turning her head. Though drawn as a single moment of time, the image actually includes at least two moments: the can falls and makes a noise, and the character turns to look in reaction.

9. Daisy draws words and numbers inside the rectangular container created by the combination of the panel frame and the lines dividing the bedroom wall within the image. Though the writing could be part of the story-world if the character had decorated his apartment with them, they instead represent his thoughts as he lies in bed. Despite not existing visually in the story-world, the words and numbers appear to be blocked by the bed and table as they would be if actually written on the wall. Also notice how the white space around the lamp creates the effect of a glow because the writing is a kind of crosshatching.

EXERCISE: 5.5 *PLACING DIALOGUE*

Sketch a comics page using the dialogue you drafted in the first section. Incorporate words and word containers into the composition of each image, noting the order and path viewers might view the visual and textual content. Words placed in the top-left corner of a panel will likely be read before the rest of the image, while the same words placed in the bottom-right corner will likely be read afterwards. Sketch the page again placing the words and containers in different locations. Which do you prefer and why?

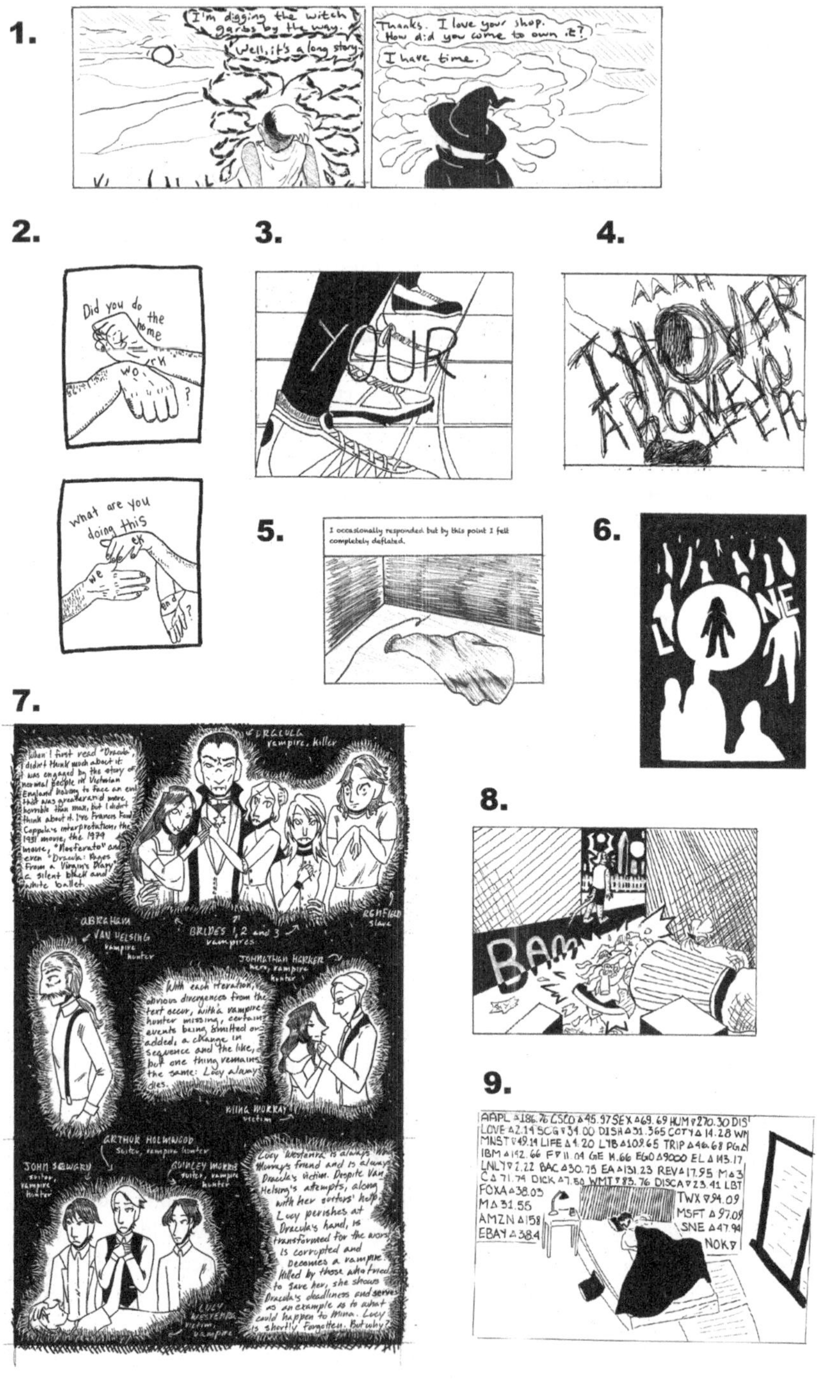

ILLUSTRATION 5.4 *Combining word rendering, containers, and placement.*

Word Relationships

Words are also affected by the images surrounding them. McCloud categorizes seven ways word and pictures can combine to produce meanings that words or pictures alone can't. We instead focus on just four broader categories. Do the words and images duplicate, compliment, contrast, or diverge?

If they duplicate, the two are in sync to communicate the same content in unison. Sound effects are an obvious example: the word "BANG" drawn inside the jagged lines of an emanata burst at the end of a gun barrel. McCloud might call that picture-specific, since removing the word doesn't change much, but not word-specific, since "BANG" without the image of the gun could be ambiguous. He might also call it duo-specific if the image and words are just duplicating each other. Early superhero comic books were heavily duo-specific. In Batman's first episode in *Detective Comics* #22 (1939), Bill Finger scripts caption box narration: "He grabs his second adversary in a deadly headlock . . . and with a mighty heave . . . sends the burly criminal flying through space," which Bob Kane's drawings visually repeat. While there may be specific aesthetic reasons to have words and images duplicate at times, redundancy is generally a bad idea. Avoid it. If words and images convey the same content, the easiest solution is to cut the words. In fact, if words don't add something unique and essential, always cut them. They're crutches—or training wheels, a useful step in the creative process, but don't let them get in the way later. Comics are first and foremost image-based. Trust the images.

Words and images can also have complimentary or contrasting meanings. In *Sex Fantasy* (2017), Sophia Foster-Dimino draws the words "I water the plants" beside a figure in a space suit and jet pack hovering above a row of plants as she waters them from a device attached by a hose to her suit. While the image doesn't contrast the words, it doesn't match any of the expected images the words suggest on their own. In *Was She Pretty?* (2016), Leanne Shapton writes: "Joel's ex-girlfriend was a concert pianist. He described her hands as 'quick and deft.' Her nails were painted with dark red Chanel varnish." The accompanying image is a woman's head looking over her shoulder in profile—presumably this is Joel's ex, who we see has long hair and bangs. McCloud might call this combination word-specific, since the image adds less than the words do, but the partial overlap is intriguing. In contrast to the words, the image includes no hands and so no fingernails and no piano or anything else indicating a connection to music. The image might be understood as quietly disagreeing with the words, a visual counterpoint suggesting that Joel was focusing on the wrong qualities.

Other contrast combinations are sharper. In *The Epic of Gilgamesh* (2018), next to Kent Dixon's translation: "they went down to the Euphrates; they washed their hands," Kevin Dixon draws only Gilgamesh washing his hands but Enkidu diving into the water head first—implying that the text is so incomplete that it's essentially wrong. In "Thomas the Leader" from *How to Be Happy* (2014), Eleanor Davis draws the main character angrily pinning and crushing the breath out of his best friend, before pulling back and saying, "I was just kidding, Davey. It was a joke." In *Anya's Ghost* (2011), Vera Brosgol writes "See you, buddy" in a talk balloon above a frowning character who doesn't seem to consider the other character a "buddy" at all.

Sometimes contrasts are ambiguous. *The Defenders* #16 (1974) concludes after the supervillain Magneto and his allies have been transformed into infants by a god-like entity. Scripter Len Wein gives Doctor Strange the concluding dialogue: "A godling passed among us today and, in passing, left behind a most precious gift! After all, how many lost souls are there who receive a second chance at life?" Penciller Sal Buscema, however, draws not just any children, but temperamental ones, their frowning, tear-dripping faces repeating the geometry of the adult Magneto's shouting mouth from earlier panels. Because the images imply that the supervillains were always toddler-like in their immaturity, the babies appear innately bad, their inner characters unchanged by their outer transformations. The image contrasts Doctor Strange's hopeful conclusion, creating a dilemma for the reader: which is right, the text or the image? The ambiguity may be a result of the creative process involving a separate writer and artist, but it occurs in single-author comics too. In Alison Bechdel's *Fun Home* (2006), a caption box includes the text: "Maybe he didn't notice the truck coming because he was preoccupied with the divorce. People often have accidents when they're distraught." The image underneath depicts Bechdel's father crossing a road while carrying branch cuttings on his shoulder. Not only do his blank expression and relaxed posture not communicate "distraught," the cuttings are blocking his view of the oncoming truck and so they, not his preoccupation with his divorce, are the visually implied reason for his not noticing the truck. Bechdel's text stated earlier that her father "didn't kill himself until I was nearly twenty," the first reference to the memoir's core event, and yet one undermined by the image five pages later. Again, who should we believe: Bechdel the prose writer or Bechdel the artist?

In the last possibility, words and images diverge as if down unrelated tracks. The text of Chris Ware's six-page "I Guess" (1991) reads like a childhood memoir about personal incidents involving the narrator's mother, grandparents, best friend, and stepfather—while the images depict a superhero story in the style of a Golden Age comic. Robert Sikoryak's book-length *Terms and Conditions* (2017) arranges the complete iTunes user agreement into word containers on pages based on other artists' iconic work—Osamu Tezuka's *Astro Boy*, Frank Miller's *The Dark Knight Returns*, Allie Brosh's *Hyperbole and a Half*, etc.

Diverging combinations can also eventually connect. In *It's A Good Life, If You Don't Weaken* (2004), Seth divides words and images for the first three pages. The seventeen panels depict the main character walking down a city street, entering a book store, browsing, finding a book, buying it, and walking down the street again. The text in black rectangles at the top of each panel describes how important cartoons have been to the narrator, with a detailed description of a specific Charlie Brown strip. If the words and images duplicated each other, the book the main character is looking at would be a *Peanuts* collection. Instead, the narration reveals in the middle of the third page that "it was on this day that I happened upon a little book . . . by Whitney Darrow Jr. I picked it up on an impulse"—a description that retroactively applies to the preceding dozen panels.

Diverging combinations can also create double referents when words and images at first appear to reference the same subject before retroactively revealing a division. In Fábio Moon and Gabriel Bá's *Daytripper* (2011), the main character who has just turned down treatments for cancer stands in a jungle-like setting gazing toward an undrawn but brightly colored horizon—while circular word containers ask: "Did you have enough? Are you satisfied?" The page resolves with the realization that the containers are his son's talk balloons, and he's asking if his father would like more coffee as they sit at a backyard patio. Alan Moore is especially well known for double referents. He creates them through a film-like technique of cross-cutting two simultaneous scenes taking place in different locations and drawn in alternating panels with dialogue from one location placed within the panels of the other. In his and Dave Gibbons' *Watchmen* #2 (1986), an opening panel shows a female statue in a cemetery with the words in caption boxes: "Aw, willya look at her? Pretty as a picture an' still keepin' her figure! So honey, what brings you to the city of the dead?" The word "her" appears to reference the statue, and "city of the dead" the cemetery, but in the next panel, the dialogue continues in talk balloons pointed at a woman addressing her mother in a retirement home—retroactively establishing the intentionally obscured references to the first set of words.

Student Examples

Illustration 5.5 shows our students' word–image combinations:

1. Coleman's three panels all compliment or contrast. The first includes the narration, "I was very alone, and very tired, but I could not sleep," with the image of a ceiling fan. It's up to a viewer to connect the two by inferring that the image is the narrator's view while lying on his back in his bed. Without that inference, the words and image are non-sequiturs. The second caption box contains: "She then ran into the kitchen while my brother and father were distracted." The image of a cutting knife block is presumably an aspect of the kitchen, so not a contrast—except the text doesn't mention that the mother ran into the kitchen in order to get a knife. That's implied only by the empty knife slot. The third caption reads: "I met up with my brother and friend Dan down the street." The hand lighting a joint is

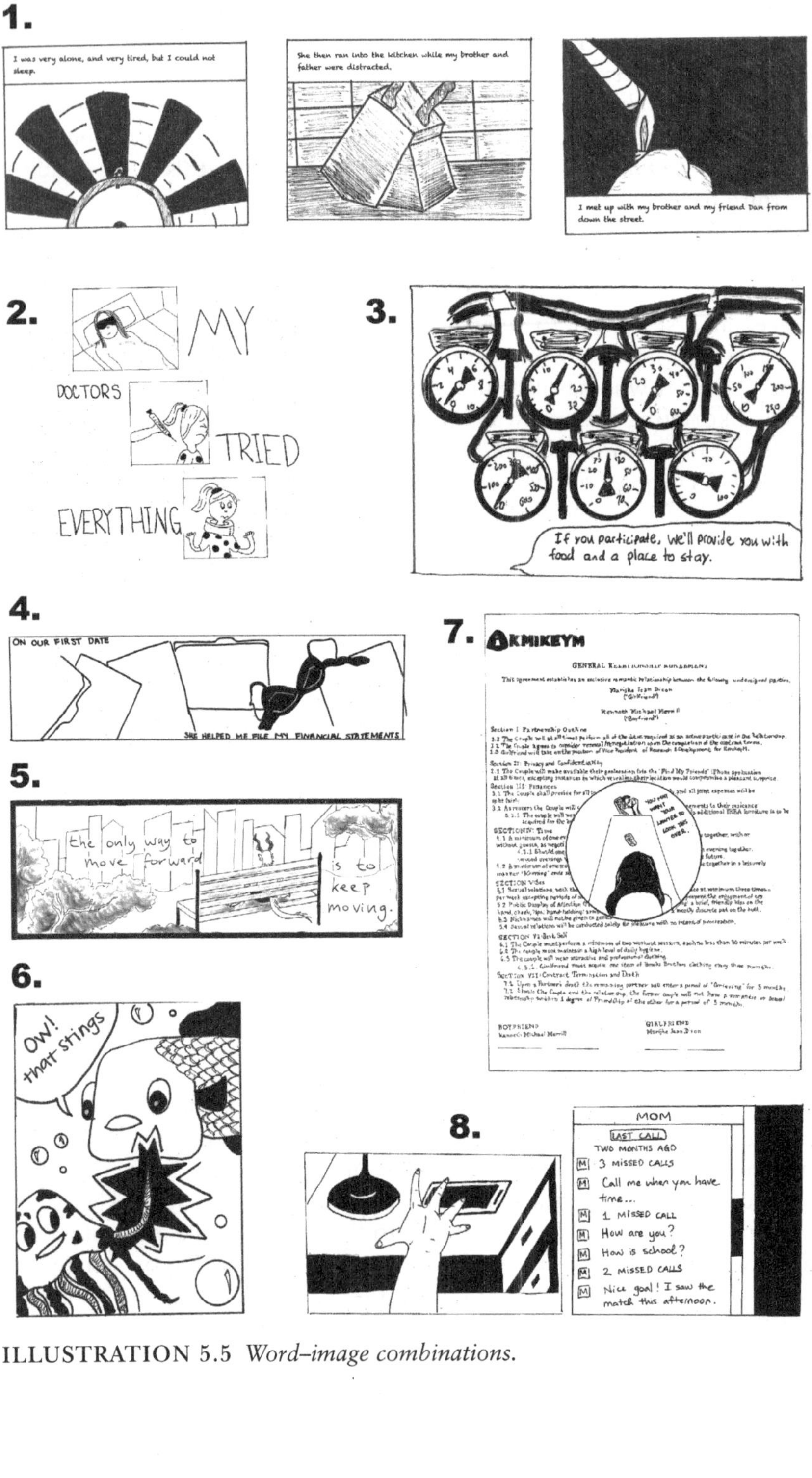

ILLUSTRATION 5.5 *Word–image combinations.*

presumably one of the three characters, adding key information excluded from the verbal narration, and so the image turns the words into a kind of lie of omission.

2. Katie mixes the unframed words "My doctors tried everything" with three images of her cartoon-self lying in bed with an eye mask, receiving a shot in the neck, and wearing a neck brace. Though the words don't mention those three actions directly, they appear to be specific examples of things the doctors tried. The images partly duplicate the words, while still providing additional, complimentary information. While it's possible that the images alone might communicate the content of the words, the combination also suggests that the list of things the doctors tried is longer than just the three included on the page.

3. Henry combines an image of pressure valves with the words: "If you participate, we'll provide you with food and a place to stay." Taken in context, a viewer would know that a corporate researcher is addressing a homeless man. Because the words are in a talk balloon pointing out of frame, we know the two characters are in the same room as the valves. A viewer will also likely assume the close-up isn't a random aspect of the setting but one related to the request. The combination is contrasting because the connotation of the valves is nothing like the researcher's positive assurances.

4. Daisy places the phrase "On our first date" in the top left corner of her panel and "she helped me file my financial statements" at the bottom right. Under the first phrase she draws manila folders, and above the second she adds a black bra—implying visually that the narrator and his date had sex. The words either omit this significant fact, or the image turns the statement into a metaphor for sex. Either way, the contrasting combination is effective.

5. Grace's contrast is more extreme. Though the unframed words state "The only way forward is to keep moving," the character in the image is seated on a bench and so not moving at all. If the words are the character's thoughts at that moment, the character becomes a kind of faulty narrator, apparently unaware of the contradiction. If the words are a third-person narrator's or the pictured character's narration looking back from another point in time, the words may read as an intentional critique of the character's inaction.

6. Maddie draws her fish protagonist being accidentally stung by a jellyfish and exclaiming in a speech balloon, "Ow! That stings." The words clarify the image content by duplicating it. This level of redundancy is usually unnecessary and unaesthetic—except in children's books, the genre Maddie's comic is working in.

7. A later page of Daisy's comic consists mostly of words. Before the couple introduced in the fourth example begins officially dating, the narrator hands her a contract to sign, saying in the circular, center panel: "You may want your lawyer to look this over." The content of the contract legible in the background page panel is complex: "The Couple will make available

their geolocation via the 'Find My Friend' iPhone application at all times, excepting instances in which revealing their location would compromise a pleasant surprise . . ." The extreme detail either compliments the narrator's advice or makes his advice a contrasting understatement. Also, his posture as he leans back in his chair at the opposite end of the table echoes the anti-romantic effect of the contract.

8. In Hung's first panel, his main character's hand reaches for a phone on a bedside table, and the second is a close-up of the phone screen, showing that the character's mother has been calling and texting him for the past month without his responding. The words are both part of the story-world and essential narrative content.

Illustration 5.6 includes four pages from Chris' poetry comic "Expected Outcomes," which uses diverging word and image combinations. The background of each page is a painting of his mother's college graduation portrait divided into a 4 × 3 grid and superimposed with figures climbing, diving, swimming, and floating. The words are taken from a document produced by the nursing staff on the Alzheimer's floor of his mother's assisted living facility as she entered hospice care. Though "Resident" refers to the same woman in the background image, there is a roughly fifty-year time gap, and the actions of the superimposed figures have no direct relationship with the list of numbered outcomes.

The next two-page comic is based on Benjamin Percy's sample script introduced in Chapter 2 and includes a range of double referents in the dialogue because the word-image combinations diverge. The words appear to refer to some drawn content, but they actually refer to undrawn content that the couple is discussing. First Chris expanded the script to include stage directions, and then Leigh Ann adapted the script (a process we will discuss in the next chapter):

Wife (*sitting at a table, tapping cigarette ash onto a plate*) You know it's empty, right?

Husband (*pulling out milk container*) Oh, I bet there's something left.

Wife Not enough.

Husband (*sitting at table, head in his hands, full glass of milk in front of him*) What can I say? I'm an optimist.

Wife (*inhaling the last of the cigarette*) You just don't know when to quit.

Husband (*glass now empty with white suds at bottom*) I like to get to the bottom of things.

Wife (*other hand on nearly empty pack of cigarettes, wristwatch visible above sleeve*) We haven't touched that bank account in decades. My sister probably cleared the money out the minute our mother died.

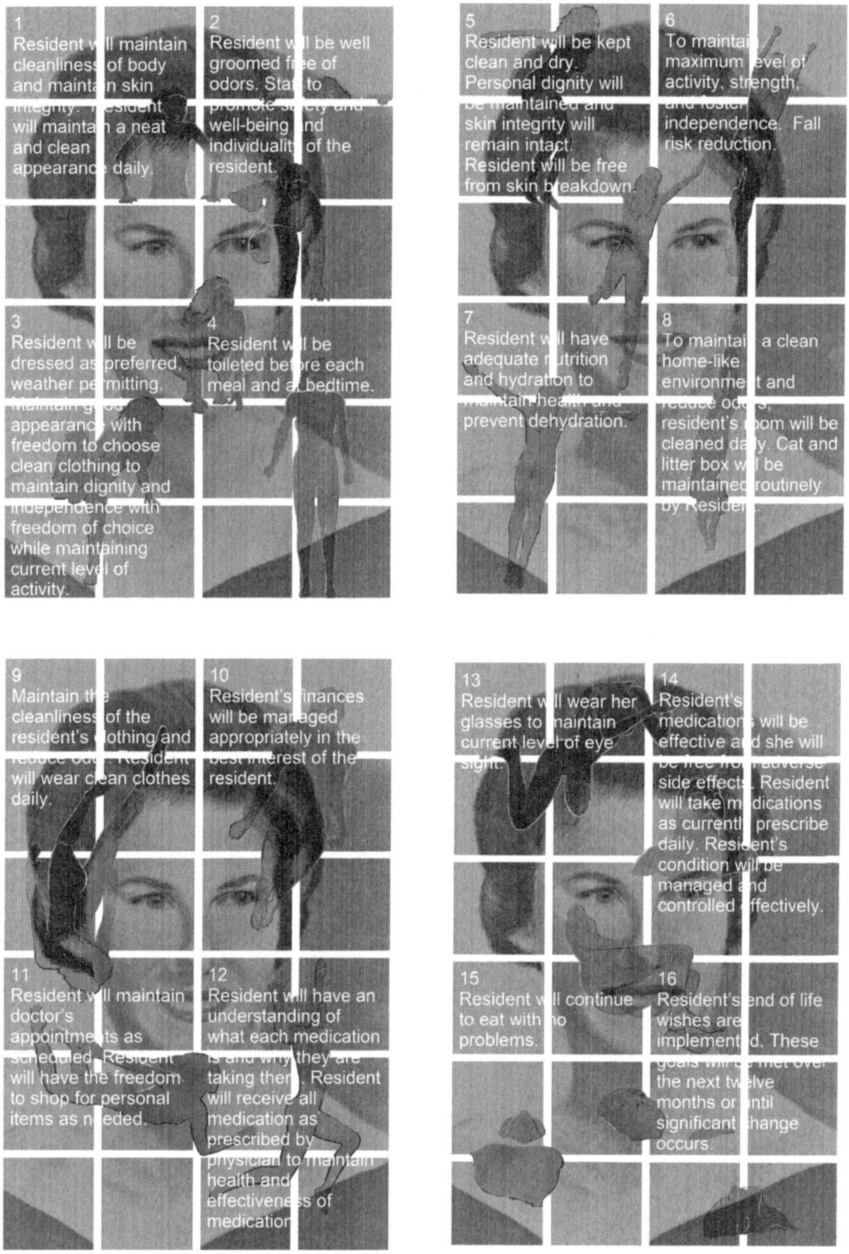

ILLUSTRATION 5.6 *Four pages from "Expected Outcomes."*

MILK
YOU KNOW IT'S EMPTY RIGHT?
OH I BET THERE'S SOMETHING LEFT.
NOT ENOUGH.
MILK
WHAT CAN I SAY? I'M AN OPTIMIST.
YOU JUST DON'T KNOW WHEN TO QUIT.
WE HAVEN'T TOUCHED THAT BANK ACCOUNT IN DECADES. MY SISTER PROBABLY CLEARED THE MONEY OUT THE MINUTE OUR MOTHER DIED.
MARLB
UNLESS SHE DIDN'T. UNLESS IT'S JUST SITTING THERE WAITING FOR SOMEONE TO GRAB.

I'M DONE WITH THIS, CARL.
WHAT IF THERE'S ENOUGH TO PAY OFF A CREDIT CARD OR TWO, GET US ON OUR FEET?
THE BANK IS OPENING RIGHT NOW.
MILK
I WANT TO WALK AWAY FROM THIS ALL.
ONE BUS RIDE
THATS ALL IM ASKING YOU TO DO.
I WANT A CLEAN SLATE.
I WANT OUT.

Husband (*picking up empty glass*) Unless she didn't. Unless it's just sitting there waiting for someone to grab.

Wife (*stubbing out cigarette on plate*) I'm done with this, Carl.

Husband (*tilting back in chair, only toes touching the floor*) What if there's enough to pay off a credit card or two, get us on our feet?

Wife (*pushing away from the table and standing*) I want to walk away from this all.

Husband (*putting milk container back in frig*) The bank is opening right now.

Wife (*washing plate in the sink*) I want a clean slate.

Husband (*handing her his glass to clean*) One bus ride. That's all I'm asking you to do.

Wife (*viewed from outside through kitchen window*) I want out.

EXERCISE 5.6 *RELATING WORDS AND IMAGES*

Selecting story content from your previous drawings or creating new content, draw an image that includes words either as speech, thought, narration, or as part of the story-world. Redraw the image six times, changing the words, the image content, or both so that the words and images:

1. convey essentially the same content,
2. convey different but related content,
3. convey contrasting content,
4. completely contradict each other,
5. seem unrelated,
6. at first seem to duplicate or compliment but actually diverge through double referents.

Multi-Image Interactions

Images and words interact not only when immediately juxtaposed, but also across the length of multi-image sequences. Consider this two-panel script:

Panel 1. Amara and her father stand in front of a tombstone. Her hands are in her pockets. His hands are in his pockets.

Panel 2. Same, except now his hand is on her arm.

Now reverse the panel content:

Panel 1. Amara and her father stand in front of a tombstone. Her hands are in her pockets. One of his hands is on her arm.

Panel 2. Same, except now both of his hands are in his pockets.

The first version ends positively with a gesture of connection between the two characters. The second is a micro-tragedy, moving from connection to comparative isolation. In terms of action sequences discussed in Chapter 3, both versions are two-image stories, starting in balance and ending in a new balance. Since neither involves words, both convey their story through images only. Now consider this text-only script of dialogue:

Panel 1.

Daughter I can't believe she cheated on you.

Father It was a long time ago.

Daughter Obviously.

Panel 2.

Father You're eighteen. You're old enough to know.

Daughter That my mother was an asshole?

Father That I'm not your father.

The words reveal information that the images can't, but the images would still communicate key emotional information about the characters that shapes what their words mean in context.

Illustration 5.7 shows the same dialogue and the same two images but the image order is reversed. What happens when the dialogue in the first panel is juxtaposed with the image of the father's hand on Amara's arm? What happens when the same words appear with the image of both characters with their hands in their pockets? And even more importantly, how are the words of the second panel, especially the statement, "That I'm not your father," altered by the placement of the father's hand? In the first version, he reaches out to her as he delivers the upsetting news, establishing a physical connection that contradicts the lack of biological connection communicated by the words. In the second version, he breaks contact, so that his gesture and his words echo each other, increasing the emotional distance. Both show how image narration and text narration combine.

ILLUSTRATION 5.7 *Two versions of a cemetery scene.*

EXERCISE 5.7 ALTERING MEANINGS

Words change meaning according to context, and in a comic the context is the drawn images. Look again at your dialogue from the beginning of this chapter.

1 Sketch a page that uses some or all of the dialogue. Draw characters and their actions in ways that alter the sense of the words as you originally intended them when the words were standing alone. The alterations may be subtle or they may be radical or anywhere between.
2 Draw the same page a second time looking for new ways to alter word meanings through context. Feel free to change the layout too.
3 When you're done, look over the two versions. What do you like about each? Is there a way to combine them into a third sequence that develops their best aspects? Redraw the sequence, researching and revising as needed to create a final version.

Anthology

The majority of artists in the anthology section use conventional word containers for speech: ovals with tails pointing at speaking characters. They also offer a range of variations. Katin uses sharp-cornered rectangles for all of her speech containers. Nickerson's containers merge with her ovals to form a unified drop-shape. Smyth's similarly shaped speech containers also appear to have three-dimensional depth because of lower shadow lines. Dhaliwal omits containers and draws a single line for tails (though sometimes a speaker is suggested only by the words' proximity to the character). Finck omits containers except for laughter, filling a panel with "HA" thirty times to dwarf the image of the bullied child underneath them. Comeau includes four speech containers, two oval and two splash-shaped with reversed white on dark gray lettering to suggest the volume and tonal quality of the character's pained sounds. Powell draws rectangles with Z-shapes in corners and connecting tails to indicate a voice heard over a radio. Thompson uses a similar Z-shape in a speech tail for a voice heard over a phone; he also arranges a gutter as if it were overlapping or cutting apart a speech container to emphasize the two characters' division. GG places all speech in uniform strips at the bottom of panels with no tails. Tsai follows the oval and tail convention but also includes drawn content inside his speech ovals, sometimes replacing words entirely.

Narrated voices, meaning words that do not appear to emanate from a drawn source, are conventionally arranged inside rectangular word containers called caption boxes. Again, the majority of artists follow the convention, while still offering variations. Libicki's narration fits tightly into scallop-edged containers. Abel and Bechdel sometimes create rectangular shapes in gutters that resemble and serve the same function as caption boxes. Alagbé places all of his narrated text outside of panel frames, usually between them. Lightman also places narration outside of images, but the effect is different because her images are unframed. Several artists, including Tsai, Finck, Roberts, and Powell, omit caption boxes and place words unframed within panels. Without the caption boxes, *Found Forest Floor* might not register as a comic, though even in this abstract context Hopkins sometimes arranges words unframed around the artwork.

Dabaie omits containers too and draws words for a range of expressive effects that are as visually significant as the images. Barry's hand-drawn letters vary between script and print, evoking the same line qualities as the images. Tobocman's narrated words are a dominating element of the artwork, filling spaces between figures and controlling the final page entirely. Characters in Finck's scene shout letters that she places as the primary, emenata-surrounded, graphic content of panels within a checkered grid. Smyth's unframed words in her fourth panel are so integrated into the artwork it is ambiguous whether they are spoken by the drawn characters, narrated by an otherwise absent narrator, or are in some other way linked to the content. Hernandez goes even further in his third page, exploring the divisions between images and words before breaking them down entirely. Conventionally that level of integrating words into artwork is reserved for sound effects, as Muñoz models.

While hand-drawn letters are the most overt way to integrate words into artwork, many creators employ fonts inserted digitally. The range is wide. Lightman chooses a font that imitates handwriting; Comeau's mechanical-looking all-caps create the opposite effect, and Dhaliwal's and Alagbé's fonts produce a hand-drawn effect. To further emphasize that quality, Finck letters her words in very loose lines that avoid the consistency of typesetting as used by Satrapi and Tomine. Doucet's hand-drawn words evolve to evoke sound qualities: first, the reversed letters suggest the speaker's drunkenness, and then various mechanical fonts show her eloquence and verbal mastery of different kinds of text, including scientific and poetic. Bechdel's word-heavy pages include three kinds of lettering: fonts for spoken and narrated words; hand-drawn words for images of physical objects that include words; and hand-drawn words in a different style for sound effects (KER-CLUNK! Shoont, SMEK), including actions that technically are not sounds (YANK! flick). There are also representations of words that are understood to be too small to be read. Nickerson draws similarly small word-like lines and dots inside speech containers to suggest inaudibly low volume. She also places a lone exclamation point in a speech container, which violates the expectation of spoken sound but obeys a parallel convention as a kind of framed emanata. Satrapi does the same with a question mark.

Next consider word and image relationships. Do they duplicate, compliment, contradict, or diverge? The text from Satrapi's first panel—"I was very religious but as a family we were very modern and avante-garde"—echoes the split image of the narrator surrounded half by tools and gears and half by ornate embroidery. The words and images also complement each other since both create their own connotative impressions that avoid full redundancy. Tsai's "the crows and vultures will eat" fully echoes an image illustrating the same content, and vice versa, but then in the final panel, the image of Zhuangzi's skeleton creates a more complex relationship because the speech container indicates that the *skeleton* is speaking, contradicting its visual appearance. Is his decomposed corpse still able to speak? Does the image show the future while the words remain in the present?

Nickerson complements the narration "Most of the time, we find what you might expect" with an image of garbage. If she had actually used the word "garbage," it and the image would duplicate redundantly, but the word is only linguistically implied and then visually supplied. Other artists use complimentary or contrasting relationships to create visual metaphors. Corman draws an image of fish scraps on a cutting board as a character describes an abortion. Within the story-world, the action and dialogue are only coincidentally related because the character just happens to be cutting up a fish at this moment, but for the viewer the juxtaposition is an associative overlap creating a metaphorical connection. Dabaie's visual metaphor is more direct; her statement "The Palestinians need another Hanthala" paired with the previous panel's "SILENCE" and the image of sewn lips turn the scissors into a symbol of free speech with no additional meaning derived from a story-world context. Smyth draws a similarly non-literal visual metaphor of a head inside of a box with the ornately lettered "BOXED" inside a speech container. Because the story-world is ambiguously surreal, the primary meaning of "boxed" is the linguistic sense of being emotionally cut off rather than the visual meaning of decapitated and placed in an actual box.

GG contrasts the mother's dialogue "She's doing so well in everything. When will you be successful?" with the preceding images of the daughter preparing, serving, and cleaning up their dinner, visually implying the mother's blindness to her younger daughter. Johnson's parent–child scene is more complex, providing contrasting images of the son and father at the current moment as well as years earlier when the son was an infant in his parents' arms. Johnson places the framed photograph between the current figures drawn at opposite edges of the full-width panel so that the images of the son contrast with the meaning of the father's "Be safe."

Lightman's images are understood to be drawings of a photograph in a sketchbook, allowing her narration to produce double referents when she writes "constructing yourself," meaning both psychologically and more literally constructing a self-portrait; the phrases "I still needed propping up" and "I still squashed Esther a bit" work similarly because of the diverging relationships. Bechdel's last page diverges further by superimposing the projection of her lover's dildo over her face as she critiques her own comics for their potentially reductive portrayal of lesbian culture. Though the scene implies that the image juxtaposition is merely coincidental, the drawn Bechdel narrates from an imaginary location, emphasizing the artificiality of the visual situation. How precisely the dildo affects the meanings of the words "Conventional" and "BORING!" is debatable, but the debate is only possible because of the diverging relationship.

Hankiewicz uses words and images that seem to completely diverge, producing no clear relationship between them. Hopkins and Blagsvedt pair their abstract language and images for even greater ambiguity, resulting in no clear meanings of any kind.

6

Processes

CHAPTER OUTLINE

While all of *Creating Comics* is about the creative process, previous chapters have segmented comics into parts that build conceptually but may or may not reflect the order an individual creator follows when developing a comic. So this final chapter combines approaches. Unless it's abstract, a comic always merges story and form. That means choosing what comes first and shapes what follows. And since a comic includes more than one image, those images need to develop in relation to each other. We see four main choices: image first, story first, layout first, and canvas first.

Image First

Begin with image content, drawing elements in whatever shape they would have in the story-world when viewed from whatever angle is most interesting to you. Instead of drawing a figure inside a frame, draw the figure and then see what frame goes around it. If the figure turns out wide, the frame will be wide; if the figure is tall, the frame is tall—even if you leave the image unframed and so the frame shape is only implied.

An image-first approach is especially helpful in early stages, allowing a creator to develop story ideas from drawn content rather than concepts expressed in words. A first image can also serve as a starting point for shaping and sizing other images on the same page. If you use your first image as a template for other panels, your page will develop into a grid, unless spacing or overlap prevents even gutters. Or you might instead develop the page in contrast to the first image, creating panels that differ in shape or size. You might even combine independently drawn images as if they were puzzle pieces, adjusting their sizes, shapes, and overlaps as needed.

A first image also doesn't need to be the first viewed on the page. Instead of a top-left panel, it might work better near the center or bottom—especially in relation to its plot position in an action sequence. It might help to physically or digitally cut out the image so you can experiment. Since all choices are revisable, a first image is a good way to start a first draft, sketching and resketching arrangements until one emerges as a favorite. And if you develop each page as a semi-independent unit in a larger sequence, you can use an image-first approach every time, allowing arrangements and even larger plot elements to develop unit by unit.

Illustration 6.1 demonstrates an image-first process:

1) Chris designed a figure with no consideration for page positioning or even story situation and setting. He just started drawing on his computer screen.

2) He developed variations of the figure while adding more plot parts in the same action sequence both before and after the initial image. After sketching each figure individually, he combined them in rows on a single page, ending each row and the page when he ran out of room. Because a new angle revealed the figure's chest, he added a chest emblem—something about the figure's pose suggested an exclamation point to him.

3) Because the poses also suggested it, he added emanata building in the figure's hands and then projecting from the arms, basing the shapes on the exclamation point on the figure's chest. The expanded image required eliminating some of the other figures, so he ended the page on the largest image, which also completed the action sequence, leaving the remaining images for him to develop on a second page later.

4) After experimenting with different layouts, he settled on two angled phrases of implied, overlapping frames, with the sequence beginning atypically in the top-right corner and descending right to left. He also altered the chest emblem so it changes from a period to an exclamation point to a question mark, making the chest a kind of word container. When everything else was in place, he added white edges to give the figures additional depth. Finally, he incorporated the words "SHINE A LIGHT" in Ariel Black font, reinterpreting the sideways exclamation point as kind of superpower spotlight.

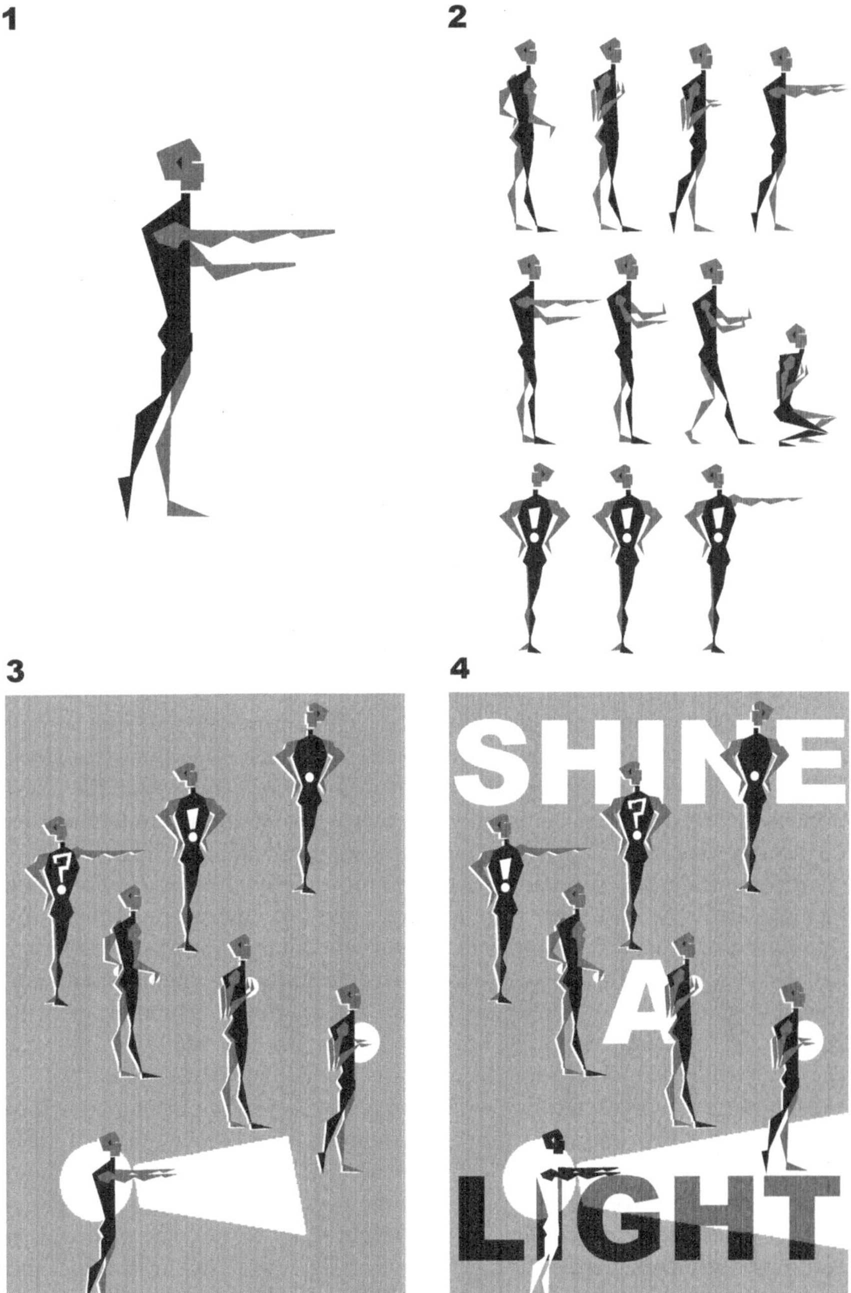

ILLUSTRATION 6.1 *An image-first process.*

EXERCISE 6.1 *DRAWING IMAGE FIRST*

Create a one-page comic by first drawing an image and then allowing the image to suggest ways for the story content to develop. This is similar to how you created your first character in Chapter 1, except now the character's actions and larger story are emerging too. Feel free to select images from any of your previous drawings and develop a story from them. This may involve starting more than once as you test different directions in which the story could evolve. Backtracking is part of the process, so do it as often as you like. Also note that the first image you draw isn't necessarily the first image in the sequence that eventually emerges. What if the first image turns out to be the final image on the page, or the middle one? You could even end up cutting the first image entirely if others emerge that you like better. Once you have a full one-page sketch that you're satisfied with, revise and redraw it into a complete comic.

Story First

Begin with story events and let them guide page arrangement. When an artist receives a script from a collaborating writer, the process emphasizes story. Standard scripts divide page content into numbered panels, but the artist decides their layout. Less commonly, a writer will describe all content and let the artist decide how to divide it and into how many images. Single creators sometimes use this approach too. Miriam Libicki drafted her ongoing memoir series *Jobnik!* in page-by-page textual descriptions, returning sometimes years later to adapt each into visuals. All memoirs involve a story-first approach since the story content is predetermined—though not entirely. Selecting and shaping nonfiction details offers almost as many creative choices as inventing details. The story-first approach begins with those details, letting them determine the elements of the page that follow.

Story-first can pre-determine which images to accent by placing important story moments in prominent frames. Big moments in the story can be literally bigger, overlapping the edges of less important moments or extending behind them as the foundation of the page. But the page's reading paths and visual phrases come second. Vertical action might lead to phrases grouped in columns and so N-path reading. Story-first can also lead to frames and gutters that reflect the story-world.

Recall Benjamin Percy's sample script in Chapter 2. He describes thirteen panels, which are usually too many for a single page, especially if each includes dialogue. So the content must be divided. Since the page is the unit of composition, make the break meaningful by coordinating it with story content. In this case, consider the locations: the kitchen where they drink and smoke, the hall where they put on their coats, the stoop where they step outside, the street where they walk, the bus stop where they wait, and the bus where they sit. Maybe page one takes place entirely in the kitchen, and page two everywhere else. Or page one includes the interior images, and page two the exterior. And why not place the opening refrigerator in the first panel and the opening house door in the last? Whatever the specific choices, the content isn't arbitrary, because each page is both a physical and a conceptual unit shaped by the story content.

The one-page comic "If Only" in Chapter 3 began story-first, as an adaptation of a thought experiment by philosopher Hilary Putnam:

> a human being (you can imagine this to be yourself) has been subjected to an operation by an evil scientist. The person's brain (your brain) has been removed from the body and placed in a vat of nutrients which keeps the brain alive. The nerve endings have been connected to a super-scientific computer which causes the person whose brain it is to have the illusion that everything is perfectly normal.
>
> 1981: 62

But even though it may initiate the process, story content can still evolve significantly. Instead of a "super-scientific computer," another brain is connected—an idea that emerged while Chris was drawing. He then inserted the wine bottle and checkered tablecloth afterwards and the words last, altering Putnam's ideas so much that the comic is no longer an adaptation. So a story-first approach still allows a comic to evolve significantly through the drawing process.

Illustration 6.2 is a one-page comic that Leigh Ann developed from her own following story-first description:

> When I was three, I liked to catch fireflies on our farm in Virginia. I caught them out of the air and put them in a jar. I liked to watch them up close from the top of the jar—I couldn't get enough of how their abdomens lit up slowly, slowly, slowly until there was a full glow. One night at dinner, after a session of firefly-catching, I smelled fireflies so strongly that I said it over and over again. My father looked and laughed to see that there was a firefly blinking far up in my nose. He tried to get it out with tweezers but couldn't. We went to the hospital where they took it out with longer tweezers. My father always remembered that I said, "Don't hurt it!"

Leigh Ann then developed a script based on the story idea:

Panel 1: Small hand reaching up into dark sky. Sky is sparkling with fireflies.

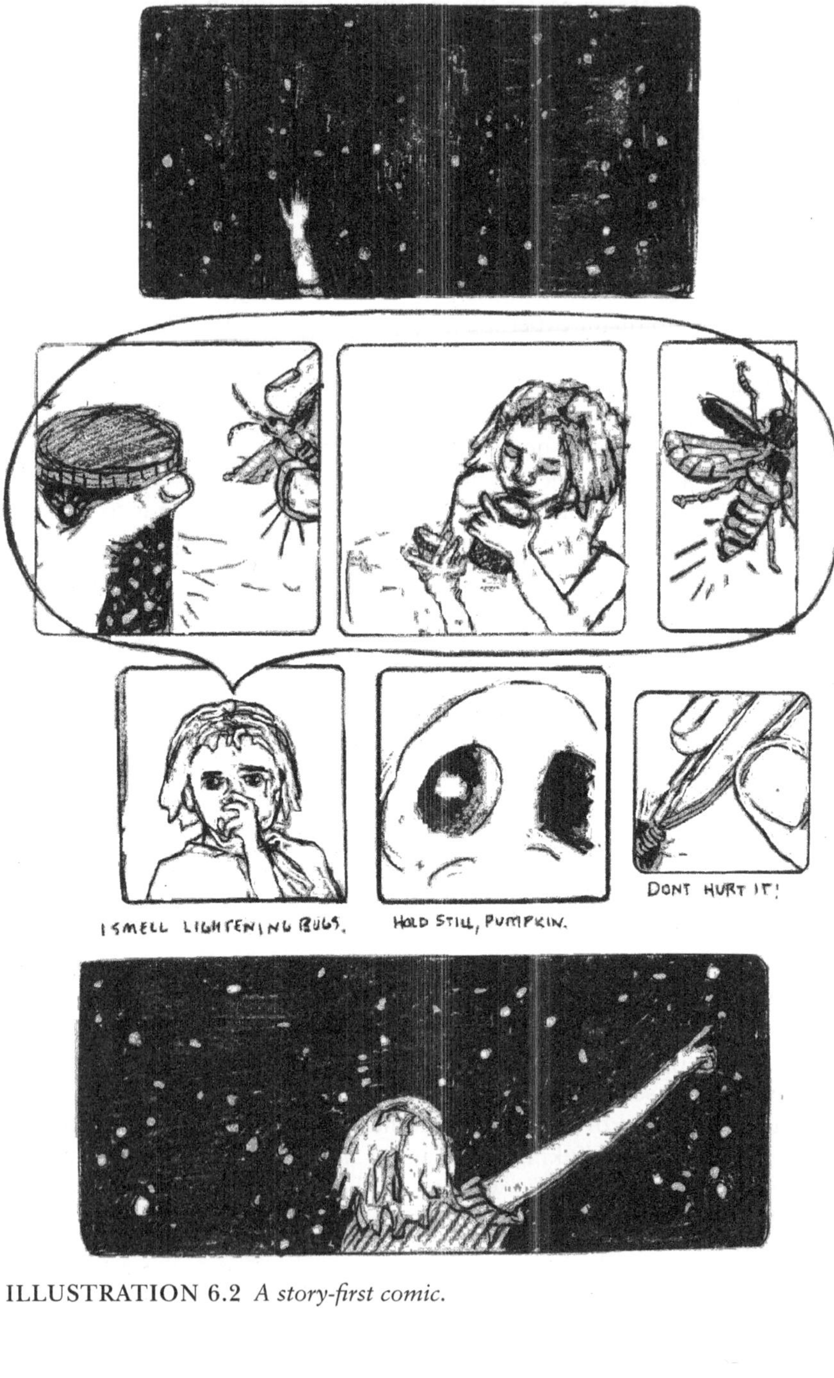

ILLUSTRATION 6.2 *A story-first comic.*

Panel 2: From left: Same hand holding jar of fireflies. From right: Forefinger and thumb grasping a firefly headed to jar.
Panel 3: Girl smelling or looking very closely into firefly jar.
Panel 4: A lit firefly.
Panel 5: Girl rubbing nose saying "I smell lightning bugs."
Panel 6: Close-up of nose with lit firefly blinking deep inside. Voice saying, "Hold still, Pumpkin."
Panel 7: Tweezers held by thumb and forefinger pinching out a firefly. Voice saying, "Don't hurt it."
Panels 2, 3 and 4 are memories/thoughts held in the little girl's head as she rubs her nose.

Note how the final comic differs from the script.

Illustration 6.3 shows how Leigh Ann worked through a similar process when she drew the Percy-inspired script from the previous chapters. She began by reading the script until she could see the characters and context in her head. Then she listed all the visuals: table, cigarette pack, glass, refrigerator, container of milk, woman, and man. The visual reference for the kitchen was her recollection of her own childhood kitchen. This changed as the drawing evolved due to choreographing when it came to the table and the sink and the refrigerator. She drew a kitchen floor plan to keep the drawing consistent. The characters appeared quickly. She knew that she wanted a couple in their mid to late 20s. Both the man and the woman are dressed in slightly rumpled clothing and have unkempt hair. This is informed by the fact that it is late evening and the couple seem pinched for money. The young man is purposely not hyper-masculine or intimidating. Instead she tried to make him slight in body and a bit of a hipster. Leigh Ann follows Ben Percy (author of the script outline from Chapter 2) on Twitter, and it amused her to give the young man a short-cropped beard and a flannel like Percy's. She drew the initial two-page design very quickly with a thick Sharpie in more or less randomly arranged panels. After assessing the deficits of the first drawing, she edited the panel sequence and made a careful pencil drawing. Lots of online research and real-life posing by her children helped to solidify the forms: people, dishes, refrigerator, etc. When the pencil drawing was satisfactory, she traced it to lighter paper on a lightbox.

ILLUSTRATION 6.3 *Script-first process.*

EXERCISE 6.2 *WRITING FIRST*

Write a story in paragraph form and then develop it into a one-page comic. Though the comic can be about anything, it may help to begin with something entirely new and so not related to any of your previous drawings. This will show you more fully what happens when words are the beginning point for a comic and the drawings develop only in response to verbal descriptions. For a more extreme version, ask someone else to write a paragraph for you instead, so that you can't visualize anything during the writing stage. Once you have a paragraph, you can write a script or start sketching images and layouts or combine the two however you like. Keep experimenting until you have a full one-page sketch that you like, then revise and redraw to complete it.

Layout First

Begin with the page arrangement and adapt the story content to suit it. A pre-determined layout of empty frames can even create content by guiding story choices. In a collaboration, an artist might select the shape and size of panels before knowing anything about the writer's story. Single authors might too. Newspapers require comic strips to remain within the horizontal gutters dividing them from other strips, columns, and advertisements directly beneath or above. This accounts for the norm of uniform rows of identical panels, which comic books initially reproduced even though artists controlled the entire page space.

Despite their non-artistic origins, many creators still prefer grids. Adrian Tomine's "Killing and Dying" follows a 5 × 4 grid, "Go Owls" a 4 × 3, and "Intruders" 3 × 3 (2015). Alan Moore and Dave Gibbons' *Watchmen* uses a 3 × 3 base layout, altered only by panel combination and symmetrical subdivisions that maintain the impression of an implied grid. The repetition and rigidity of the formal structure also creates metaphorical significance. Moore explores predetermination and nihilism. One of Tomine's characters is trapped in an abusive relationship with a partner who can't change. Irregular layouts can shape, imply and even determine story content too. A rigid character living a monotonous life might belong in a grid, while an unreliable or constantly traveling character might suggest more chaotic arrangements. Any formal choice can suggest meaning.

A layout-first page approach requires a frame-first approach for individual images. Begin with the shape of the frame and adapt the story content to it. That requires either shaping the image to match the frame or to contrast it, cropping or expanding surrounding material as needed. If a frame is wide, a skyscraper has to be drawn either from a panoramic distance that includes the rest of the cityscape or zoomed in so much that some of the building is out of frame. If a frame is tall, then a standing person viewed from a parallel perspective will fit more easily than a car—unless the car is viewed vertically from above. A panel may look like a window into another world when you're done drawing it, but its dimensions actually sculpt that world, determining the placement and cropping of all its elements, including the actions of the characters. If the frame is the literal frame of the page edges, then you made your choice when you selected your page and its dimensions. Unless the page is square, you can still choose between a tall or wide orientation. Most photographers and painters work frame-first.

Illustration 6.4 is a one-page comic that Leigh Ann developed by first drawing just the panel frames and then filling them in. Notice how the overlapping panels influenced the movement and cropping of the dogs. Some of the content was drawn from photographs, and some of it was recalled or invented as needed.

Layout-first can also guide script-writing. Illustration 6.5 shows the development of a page from "The One and Only," a fictious Silver Age comic included in Chris' novel-in-progress *The Patron Saint of Superheroes*. Note that:

1 Because the fictitious artist of the novel secretly signs all of her uncredited comic art with a St. John's cross, Chris began by adapting the cross to a layout.
2 He then applied that layout when writing a script that included a visual mock-up.
3 Artist Sean Michael Robinson used both the script and the mock-up when developing drafts.
4 After revisions, Sean finalized the page on a background suggesting an aged artboard.

EXERCISE 6.3 *DRAWING LAYOUT FIRST*

Sketch several layouts. Try blocking out panels with no pattern in mind. Then start with a very specific pattern in mind and draw it. Invent an especially unusual layout. Create a layout that follows some kind of internal logic for how the panels relate in size and shape. Look over all of your sketches. Which ones do you like most? Do any begin to suggest some kind of content that could fill the shapes? Pick one, redraw it, and start drawing the interiors of the panels. Experiment and restart as many times as you like, but keep letting the angles, shapes, and other qualities of the frames and their relationships guide the image content that emerges. Once you have all of the panels filled in a way that satisfies you, revise and redraw your one-page comic.

ILLUSTRATION 6.4 *A layout-first comic.*

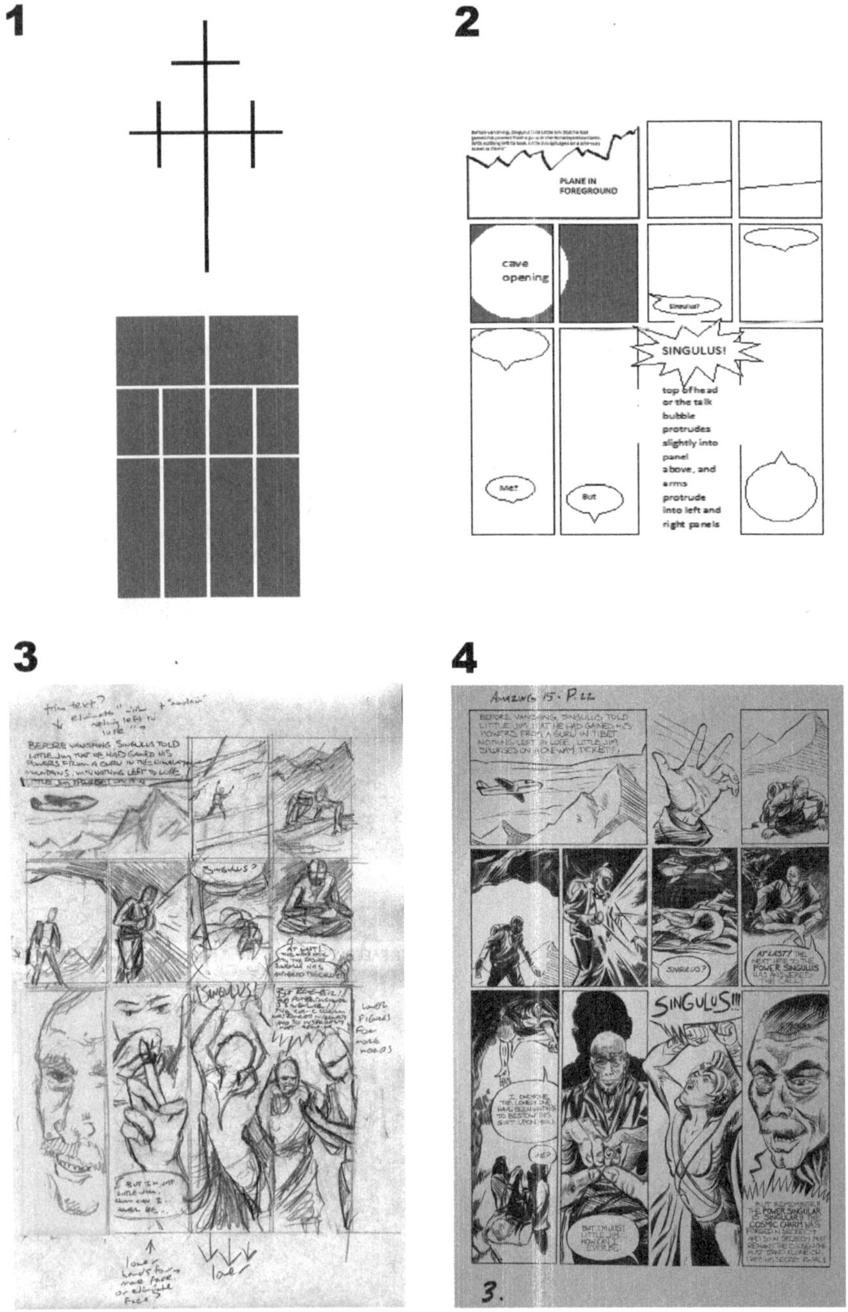

ILLUSTRATION 6.5 *A layout-first process.*

Canvas First

Perhaps the most effective approach is a combination of the first three, developing story, image, and layout simultaneously. Though the page is always a kind of canvas, canvas-first emphasizes the page as a whole, treating other parts of the creative process as elements that evolve to suit it. So while a creator may begin with plot, image, or arrangement ideas, they will change according to what works best on the page. Nothing is set in stone.

Illustration 6.6 shows our student Henry's canvas-first process for creating his one one-page comic "Homesick." Recall in Chapter 1, Henry developed his main character from a doodle, inventing his background and plot situation after revising him visually first. Some of the images in "Homesick" originated while Henry was drawing the character in multiple poses for homework.

1. He begins by brainstorming textual descriptions:

> "we have a center-framed GABE experiencing the drudgery of being reduced to a simple worldly person.
>
> "the daily toil and drudgery of a demon?
>
> "Stepping on the bodies of the damned, stabbing through the heads of non-believers"

Note the tiny sketch beneath the words: "Maybe begin with a lot of them," and then the creative epiphany: "Daily toil and drudgery of <u>human</u> life." His first row of four panels begin with Gabe hanging upside down, presumably sleeping as inspired by his bat wings, before enacting the "stabbing" from the descriptions. The next row shows Gabe sighing on a desk, an example of "human drudgery." The rest of the row is undrawn, with the word "flying" substituting for images, as he establishes a layout idea of separately spaced and enlarging panels, followed by lines indicating the start of a full-width panel and the words "big panorama panel." The next row begins the page over, revising the first draft row, adding "7:00" on a clock behind Gabe, suggesting that he has just woken up—though he is no longer hanging upside down. Notice how the sketchbook page begins the process by working in images, story ideas expressed in words, and layout designs all together.

2. Henry next sketches a full draft of the comic page. Row one is now a two-panel action of Gabe waking up as shown by a close-up of the clock followed by a close-up of his face. Row two consists of three one-panel actions of Gabe centered while performing individual acts of human drudgery: brushing his teeth, driving to work, sitting at a desk. The second half of the page enters his thoughts, with the largest panel labeled "Bosch World," indicating Henry's plan to develop Gabe's memories with images based on Hieronymus Bosch's *c.* 1500 painting *Hell.* The layout idea of

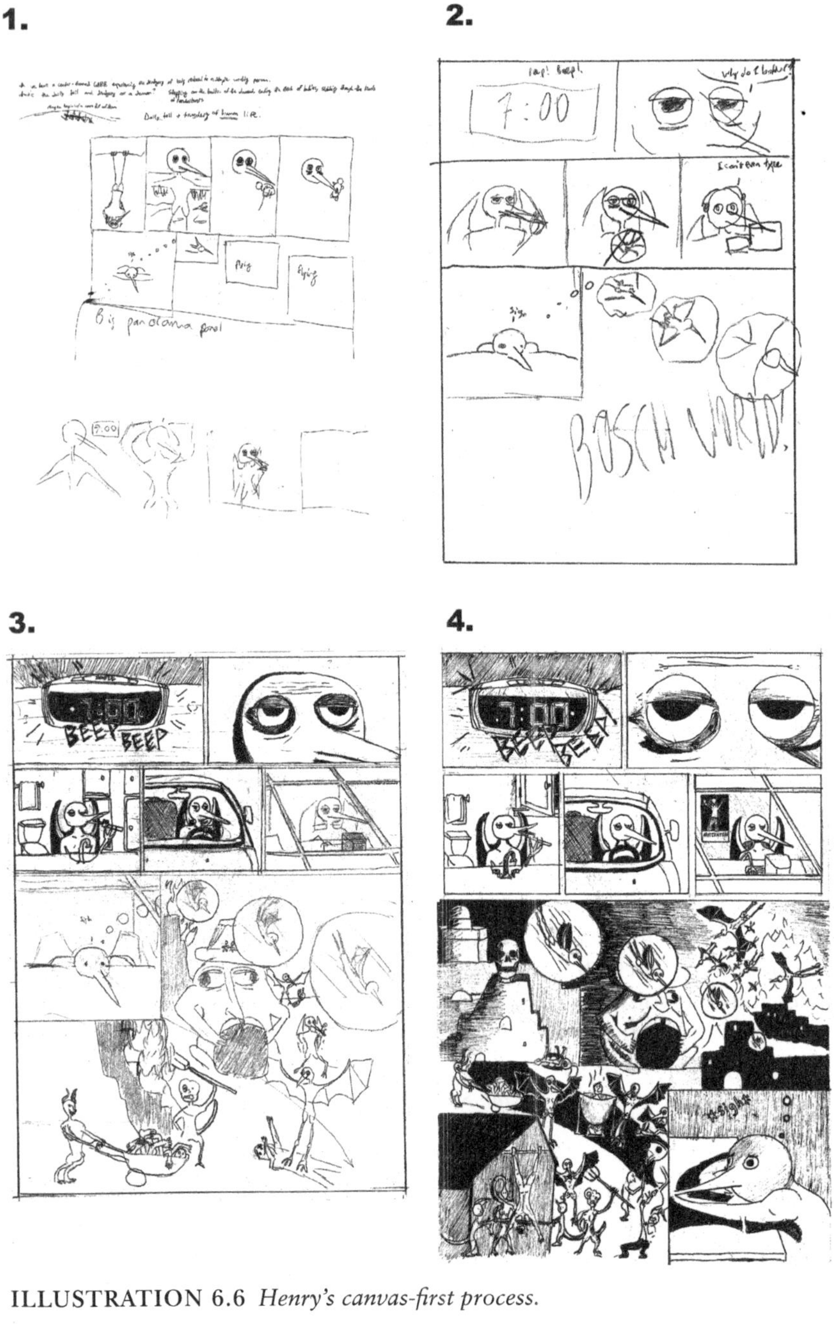

ILLUSTRATION 6.6 *Henry's canvas-first process.*

spaced and enlarging square panels has evolved into circular panels that emerge from Gabe's head like the circles of a thought balloon tail, with a sketch of Gabe flying inside each.

3. Henry refines the first three rows, giving Gabe's bathroom a toilet, towel, towel rack, cabinets, counter, and sink. The car in the second panel is now much more than simply the driver's wheel of the previous sketch. And in the third, Gabe's workplace includes constricting cubicles—though Henry has cut Gabe's statement, "I can't type." Henry has also begun arranging the Bosch-inspired details in the central panel.

4. The final draft includes further refined details: a tighter close-up of Gabe's eyes, so that the full strangeness of his anatomy isn't revealed till the second row. One of his bathroom cabinets is now ajar and his towel features a realistic crease. There's also a "Motivation" poster hanging behind his desk now. The chaos of the large Bosch panel is fully developed and suggestively unframed. Because this is a one-page comic, ending on Bosch produced a cliff-hanger effect, so Henry moved the daydreaming Gabe to the final position, with his thought circles now flying back inside his head, completing the page's action with his "sigh."

EXERCISE 6.4 *DRAWING CANVAS FIRST*

Create a one-page comic combining various elements of image, story, and layout simultaneously and however best suits you. Your sketchbook should be full of images and layouts and story ideas, so feel free to develop work you've already begun. Or begin something entirely or mostly new. Sometimes the key to a canvas-first approach is letting the material tell you how best to proceed. You can experiment, jotting some words down, sketching a quick image or cluster of panels, and then develop them incrementally, building upon whatever you discover from one area as you move to the next. Keep experimenting, testing, backing up, redrawing, and finalizing until you have a one-page sketch that you like. And then revise and redraw your complete page.

Page Schemes

Process approaches also apply to book-wide effects. Though you may arrive at an initial page layout by beginning with image- or story-first, once that layout develops you might decide to use it as the basis for later pages, switching to a layout-first approach. It's important to consider how you want to develop later pages, whether it's through a rigid, pre-set pattern; an organic, one-page-at-a-time aesthetic; or somewhere between.

While accents and phrasing occur within a single page, similar affects can be created across multiple pages. Groensteen describes how panels that occupy the same location on separate pages can "rhyme" (2007: 148). Because the layouts create a formal relationship between the images, they also connect their story content. The other accent techniques discussed in Chapter 4 can create rhymes too: images in circular panels in a book consisting otherwise of rectangular panels; images that share a distinctive tilt or frame design; images that break the Z-path norm to produce brief N-paths. The range is wide. By rhyming two images, you make your reader experience a connection between two story moments that would otherwise be formally unrelated.

Rhyming can also apply to layouts overall. Jessica Abel and Matt Madden note that grids provide "continuity to multiple-page stories," which is true of any repeating layout (2008; 71). A comic that repeats the same layout on every page produces no layout rhymes—or rather it produces unvarying rhymes that differentiate no pages. Alan Moore typically writes in a 3 × 3 grid, which is either overt or implied through the combination of panels. A comic that repeats no layouts also doesn't highlight and connect any pages through a rhyme scheme. In poetry a rhyme scheme refers to the pattern of end-word rhymes; a Shakespearean sonnet, for example, follows an ABAB CDCD EFEF GG pattern, and a Petrarchan ABBAABBA CDECDE. Comics that use layout schemes relate pages for similar work-wide effects, connecting the entire story content of each page.

The sixth chapter of Charles Burns' *Black Hole* (2005) includes twenty-seven pages. After an unpaired non-rectangular splash page, pages vary between row- and column-based layouts. Sixteen pages either use a 3 × 2 grid or imply it by combing panels, while another six feature 1 × 3 columns; the remaining four pages variously combine a regular row with a row of tall panels that echo the columns:

A

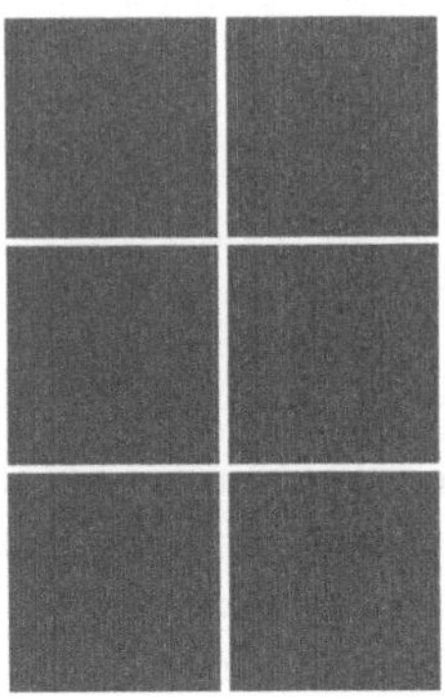

B

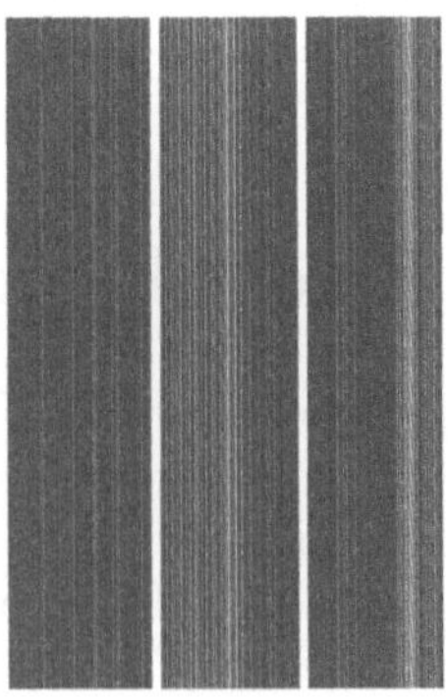

C

Divided into two-page spreads, the page scheme is:

AA BB BB AA BC BB BB CC BC BB BB AA BB

Since the 3 × 2 pages are most prominent, B is the base pattern, giving emphasis to the three A spreads and the three C pages. The scheme also connects the story content of the A and C pages. The A spreads are the most memory-focused, with flashback images interspersed into the current action. The C pages are transition points, highlighting the introduction of a new character and then a movement into that character's new space—each disrupting both the narrative and formal status quo. The scheme also reveals Burns' pattern of rhyming couplets, giving additional emphasis to the one break in the pattern, when in the fifth spread a row layout pairs with a combined layout—further highlighting the new character.

In Robert Kirkman and Tony Moore's *The Walking Dead* #1 (2010), over half of the pages are regular three-rows, establishing a dominant base pattern. The two full-page images rhyme the two formally largest moments in the narrative: the protagonist waking for the first time after his apocalypse-triggering injury, and the first, apocalypse-signifying depiction of zombies. The concluding pages also rhyme with page one, giving the issue implied 4 × 2 bookends. The half-page columns on pages eight and twenty-four produce the most striking rhyme, depicting the only two times that the protagonist kills a zombie. In both the zombie is beneath or below him, with its head lowest in the frame. An action-produced sound effect—"WHUMP!" and "BLAM!"—partially cover the hero both times. In the first panel, his zombie killing is accidental, as he tumbles down the stairs upside down. The second time the killing is intentional, and the hero's body is rigid and right side up—a visual and thematic reversal suggesting the change in his mental state. The two columns are formally unique, shaping their two narrative moments into N-paths and so highlighting a contrast that would be lost if the story were drawn in identically sized and shaped panels. The layouts don't simply transmit narrative. The rhyme portrays character development in a way additional to the words and images.

Illustration 6.7 shows the rhyme scheme for Maddie's ten-page comic: ABCDCDCDBA. Maddie began image-first, creating her main character from a class doodle that she then visually researched, revised, and redrew multiple times from multiple angles until she could render it easily for any story situation that might arise. She developed her first page by drawing her character in a page-width panel, which she then repeated for the other images, adjusting the number of panels to suit the page and using a single line for framing rather than the white space of a formal gutter. Because page one ended with her fish feeling alone, the rest of the story developed into a search for companions. She had initially thought that one of the animals he meets would return with him, and that a wise mentor figure would convince him to return, but both characters and plot points seemed unnecessary once she was drawing the actual comic.

Her page scheme developed from her character's first adventure away from home, which she drew in a three-row layout of full-width panels, except for the evenly divided middle row of the second page. When her character enters his second adventure, she used the same two-page template, rhyming the layouts and, more specifically, the center panel of the second page where in all three adventures the main character discovers that he can't be happy with his new group of friends. When he returns, she repeated the opening two page's layouts—but now in reverse order. Where on the second page the fish swims out into the full-page vastness of the ocean, on the penultimate page, he swims toward the viewer, with all of his ocean friends now visible behind him. And when he approaches his own fish community, it's in the same four-row arrangement as page one, ending now with his joining them.

Illustration 6.8 shows Emily's nine-page comic. Her approach is less regular than Maddie's, but she still uses page scheme effects. Page one establishes both the story-world space of the bookshelf and the formal space of the layout with a two-panel row at the top implying a three-row base for the following five pages. Page two then creates an internal, fantasy space of the cube's thoughts by using panels shaped like thought balloons over a black background and gutters. Sometimes each page's fantasy sequence begins in the second panel of row one, and sometimes it ends in the first panel of row two, but the page scheme always includes the complete middle row. Emily then breaks that norm with page eight—which includes no fantasy and switches from an implied 3 × 2 grid to an overt 5 × 3 of square panels that echo the shape of the cube. The new layout deepens the sense of the cube's immobility within the story-world—until the owner's hand reappears at the bottom of the page and then rolls the cube on the final page in an unframed sequence of embedded images showing the cube's actual movement. Without the repetition of the base layout in the first seven pages, the last two pages would have less formal significance and so their story content would have less significance too.

EXERCISE 6.5: *PLANNING PAGES*

Look at each of the four one-page comics you drafted for this chapter. Select one that you would like to continue in a multi-page comic, anywhere from two to two hundred pages. Sketch possible layouts for future pages:

1 Create a set layout for every page that never varies.
2 Create two layouts that switch back and forth according to the story situation.

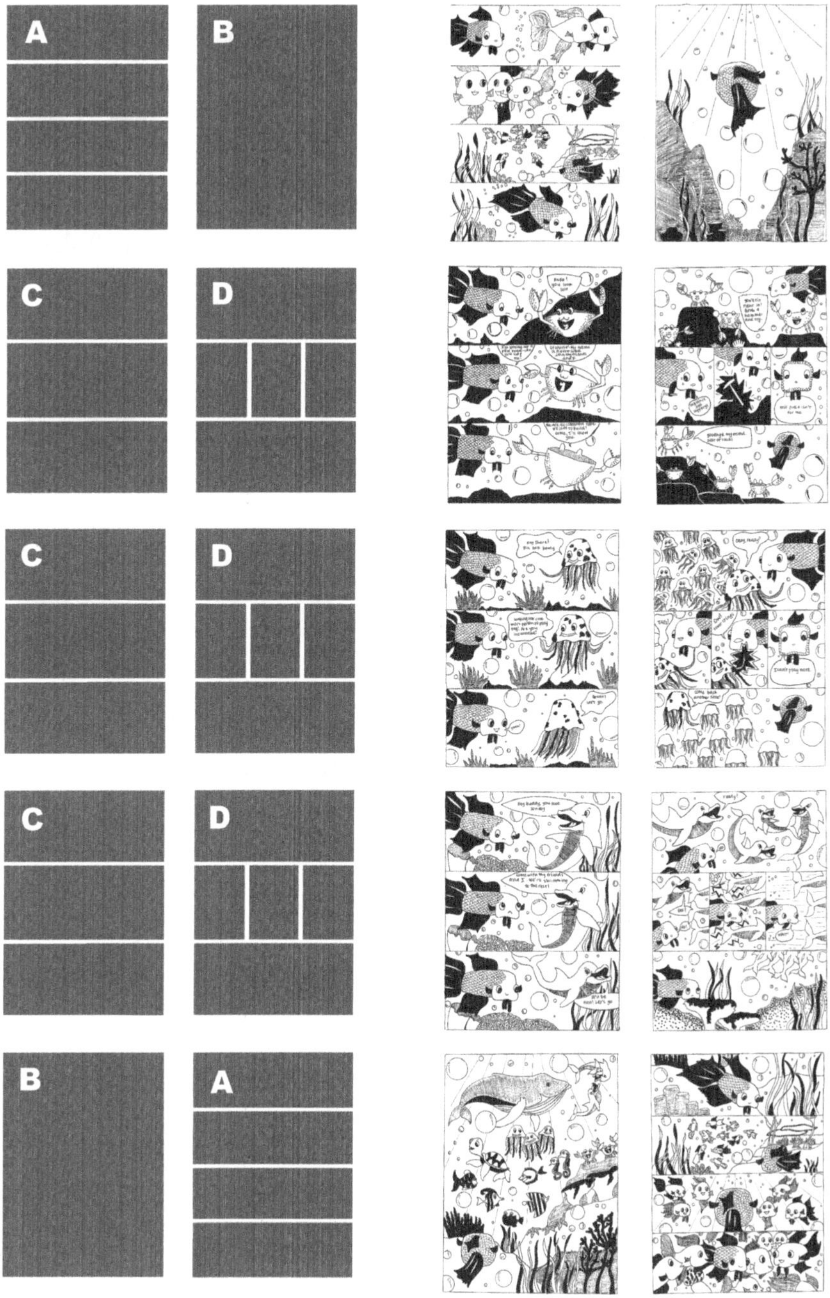

ILLUSTRATION 6.7 *Maddie's page scheme.*

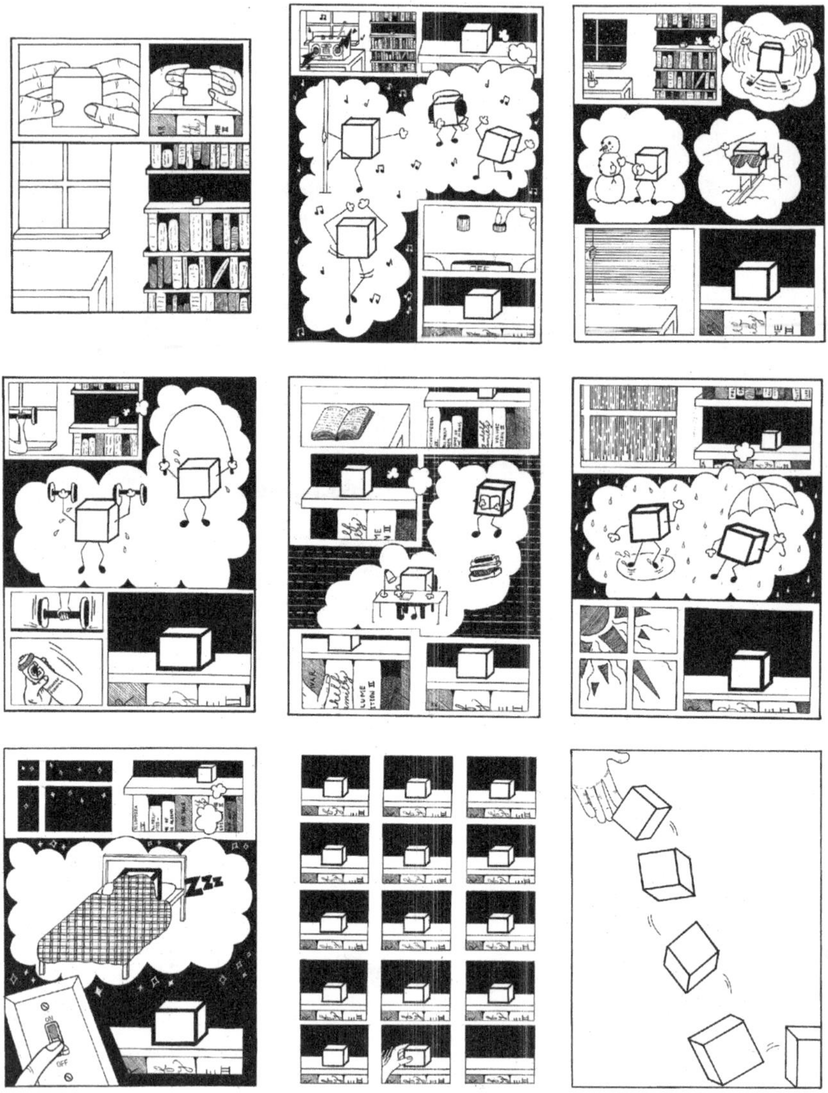

ILLUSTRATION 6.8 *Emily's nine-page comic.*

3 Create multiple layouts, each designed to parallel a story element. If the element repeats later in the story, repeat the layout then too. If the story element doesn't repeat, the layout is just used once.
4 Select your favorite page scheme approach and sketch the entire comic.

Sketchbook

We asked you to start using a sketchbook in Chapter 1. If you used if for every exercise, it should be pretty full by now. If you also used it for your own self-directed sketches, you may have moved onto a second by now. We hope a third, fourth, etc. are in your future too. The more you draw, the better. It also makes you create content that can evolve into your own comics. Having worked through this textbook, you know how to do that now. You probably also know a lot about your own style and your own process. Both of those will keep evolving, but you already have the first-hand know-how of a comics author.

For your final exercise, look through your sketchbook. What are your favorite moments? Mark those pages. They belong in one of your future comics. Look back at the character you created in Chapter 1. How has it evolved? What are your favorite story ideas that feature it? You already have everything you need to start creating your own graphic novel, including the process that best suits your own creativity. Follow it. If that means writing out a story description, write it now. If that means writing a script, start scripting. If that means page-by-page layouts, get started. Or if it means drawing a first image and seeing what happens next, get drawing. If it means all of the above, then jump in wherever you like.

Anthology

All drawing materials have their own characteristics, their own demeanor. The way you use a drawing material is technique, and there are many techniques for each material. Almost any material can be used with any other, and most drawing techniques can be used in conjunction. How an artist uses and combines materials or techniques defines her process, and the artists in our anthology represent a wide range of processes. Since we only have their final product, it's hard to know many specifics about their process, but experimentation with both materials and technique would have been key in developing it.

In our first comics class, we made the following materials available to our students: graphite pencils, ink, brushes, gouache watercolors, watercolor pencils, wax crayons, color markers, black markers, non-photo blue pencils, white plastic erasers, professional white correctional fluid, scanners, light tablets, color copiers, rulers, t-squares, triangles, architectural templates, heavy, non-acidic drawing paper, cheap drawing paper, comic boards, acid-free glue, clear tape. For our second class, we reduced the range by focusing only on black and white image-making (a focus we kept for this book too). We encouraged both classes to experiment with techniques: doodling, sketching from life, copying free-hand, tracing, photographing, cutting and pasting (using actual paper and glue), collaging drawings with other drawings, drawing over drawings, drawing digitally, shrinking and enlarging all or parts of a drawing on a copier—anything that might make students comfortable with their drawing tools and open the image-making process up so that the art flows.

Comics artists evolve very specific, ever-changing methods to get the final comic to paper and production. The works in this anthology encompass an astonishingly broad range of material and techniques, and, in fact, the breadth of media used in the comic world is virtually limitless. But one of the greatest joys of making comics is that they can be made using only a pencil, an eraser, a black marker, and white drawing paper.

Lynda Barry famously extols the ease of using the simplest materials: graphite pencils, wax crayons, and composition books. She uses graphite to make a line drawing, colors the interiors with crayon, and uses the prosaic lines of a composition book page as her background. Barry's pages in the anthology are inked, likely over a rough draft drawn with non-photo blue pencil. Estrada, Katin, Libicki, Lightman, Siciliano, and Ma also use graphite to extremely varying effect in their comics. Libicki's pencil drawings are sharp, densely valued and crisp with believable, fully realized shapes. Her drawing takes advantage of a sharp pencil's ability to carve planar shapes to make precise forms. Estrada's drawing process in *Alienation* is deceptively simple and accentuates the inchoate snail interaction in a twilight setting. She uses soft graphite, neutral values and photocopies it all in a muted blue scale (which is lost when reproduced in black and white in our anthology). Ma's *Leaf* reveals a carefully layered graphite application with lots of value variation but very little contrast, creating drawings that are still, mute, and oddly magical. Eventually graphite drawings need to be scanned, creating some challenges but also opportunities for digital manipulation. Though he uses ballpoint pen instead of graphite, Craig Thompson describes a similarly simple process when making *Blankets*. He made daily preliminary thumbnail sketches with a blue ballpoint pen on folded pages of typing paper. After he slowly amassed enough pages for a book, he refined the images and copied them.

Many artists still use the classic method of comic illustration: rough preliminary sketches that are refined and then inked and colored. Bechdel alternates between hand-drawing, photography and computer. She draws the initial rough sketches in an illustration program, photographs herself in corresponding poses, and then uses these photos to refine her initial drawings. All of her images are photo-sourced for realistic anatomy that she reduces to a minimal line. Other artists, such as Dhaliwal, work primarily in illustration programs, often mimicking non-computer materials and techniques.

If you're not working on or scanning images into a computer, a copy machine is another useful though clunky drawing tool. Whether you are shrinking or enlarging or combining multiple images, the copy machine allows for a fresh view. In *Micrographica,* French enlarges her images as if they've been magnified by a microscope; large and taken completely out of context, her images have very little connection to the world or the figure as a whole. This is an effect that could not be easily attained with a pen or pencil alone. The art for Comeau's quirky *Winter Cosmos* is surprisingly organic considering it is constructed by collaging vintage photographs, old posters, drawings, and his own posed photos and then using a copier to bring it all together. Max Ernst followed a similar collage process over a hundred years earlier.

Printmaking methods—etching, engraving, lithography, woodcut, linotype—are ideal for illustrating comics. All printmaking methods were invented to make printing multiples of the same image easy, making it a perfect tool for serial images. You have the ability to print the same image over and over again and to alter that image as it is printed. The detailed imagery in Hogarth's *Gin Alley* was acquired by drawing with a needle on a copper plate, while Valloton cuts his images into wood to make relief prints or woodcuts. Tobocman appears to use a linotype process. Thomas Ott instead uses scratchboard, scraping off black ink from the surface to reveal the white layer beneath.

It is even more difficult to determine the writing process behind finished comics. *March*, however, is a memoir of John Lewis as co-scripted with his press secretary Andrew Aydin and then drawn by Nate Powell. Though her own artist, Libicki also completes a script before drawing. For her memoir, Lightman appears to have selected images she made previously, interweaving them with narration and new images.

There are no rules when it comes to what you draw with and how you draw it. Some artists never even touch pencil to paper. Chris uses Microsoft Paint. The limitations of the program work to his advantage as he distorts and manipulates photographs and draws new content with his touch pad. Everyone develops their own evolving process. There's isn't one or even one best way. When making comics, anything goes. We hope *Creating Comics* has given you enough experience with materials and techniques that you have already begun to develop and refine your own process. How you apply it is up to you to discover next.

7

Anthology

Jessica Abel

ungh.
nnn... dizzy...
unnnh...
HUNH!
Jesus...

Jessica Abel

HHUUUUGH!!
H-HUUGHH

IN THE WINDOW OF THE UNDOCUMENTED STRIKERS OF MONTREUIL IS A PHOTOGRAPH. A PHOTOGRAPH OF THOMAS SANKARA. TO FIND OUT WHO THOMAS SANKARA IS, DON'T BOTHER LOOKING HIM UP IN LAROUSSE.

Yvan Alagbé

THERE IS NO ENTRY FOR HIM IN THAT STAR DICTIONARY OF THE LAGARDÈRE GROUP. HE MUST FALL UNDER THE HEADING "WITHOUT A SIGNIFICANT ENOUGH ROLE IN HISTORY."

AS FOR MONSIEUR BLAISE COMPAORÉ, HE HAS WON A SURE PLACE UNDER "GOOD FRIENDS OF FRANCE." FURTHERMORE, HE HAS THE GOOD TASTE NOT TO GO ABOUT IN MILITARY UNIFORM.

Yvan Alagbé

AND YET, DESPITE THE GOVERNORS, EMPERORS, AND WHITE-COLLAR KILLERS, IN THE WINDOW OF THE STRIKING TEMPS OF MONTREUIL, AS IN THE HEART OF AFRICA, THE MEMORY OF THOMAS SANKARA LIVES ON. THAT'S THE STORY, MISTER PRESIDENT. THAT'S HISTORY.

ERNIE POOK'S VAGUE CHILDHOOD MEMORIES
My yellow pillow
(© 1978 LYNDA BARRY)
My Uncle Jerry's Nose
The scariest thing in the world.
Ivan Burke (My brother Mike's scariest thing in the world)

Lynda Barry

under the bed
my favorite dream of my life.
THANKS ERNIE.
E
my mother's bra
ricky gonzalas
("I said COME HEAH EHNIE")

Alison Bechdel

I WAS A WRITER AND AN ARTIST!
KODAK KAROUSEL
RRRRRRRR
SKREEK!
WANDA WILLING THE CAT TO MOVE
WORDS CREPT INTO MY DRAWINGS OF LESBIANS.
ONE DAY, FOR SOME REASON, I ADDED NOT JUST A CAPTION BUT A TITLE AND A NUMBER.
DYKES TO WATCH OUT FOR, PLATE NO. 27
KER-CLUNK!
I HAD NOT ACTUALLY DRAWN TWENTY-SIX OTHER DYKES TO WATCH OUT FOR, BUT THE FAUX TEXTBOOK TONE INSPIRED ME. A CATALOG OF LESBIANS! I WOULD NAME THE UNNAMED. DEPICT THE UNDEPICTED!
AND BY FOLLOWING A METICULOUS INDUCTIVE METHODOLOGY, I WOULD DERIVE A UNIVERSAL LESBIAN ESSENCE FROM THESE PARTICULAR EXAMPLES.
flip
MY FIRST CARTOON WAS PUBLISHED IN THE 1983 LESBIAN PRIDE ISSUE OF THE LOCAL FEMINIST NEWSPAPER.
Twyla is appalled to learn that Irene is a morning person.
KA-CHUNK
READERS SEEMED TO LIKE IT, AND THIS EGGED ME ON.
BUT TO BE HONEST, IT WAS SO COMFORTING TO SEE MY QUEER LIFE REFLECTED BACK AT ME, I WOULD HAVE KEPT DRAWING THESE DYKES TO WATCH OUT FOR JUST FOR MYSELF.

Alison Bechdel

ASTONISHINGLY, THE GREAT POET AND ESSAYIST ANSWERED MY LETTER.
SHE SAID SHE WAS FAMILIAR WITH MY COMIC STRIP. AND FURTHERMORE...
by your letter. I've always admired the way your work tries to explode dyke essentialism & explore our real humanity. I wish you all the best in
EXPLODING ESSENTIALISM! EXPLORING OUR HUMANITY!
PERHAPS MY LITTLE EXPERIMENT WAS NOT A FAILURE AFTER ALL.
I HAD SET OUT TO NAME THE UNNAMED, TO DEPICT THE UNDEPICTED, TO MAKE LESBIANS VISIBLE. AND I HAD DONE IT!
OH, PLEASE, MO. YOU'RE SO PROVINCIAL. CAN'T YOU SEE I'M DISARTICULATING THE EPISTEMOLOGICAL FOUNDATION OF GENDER THROUGH DEFERRAL AND DECONSTRUCTION OF FIXED SEXUAL SIGNIFIERS?
OH.
WAIT A MINUTE...
WHAT TH'?
I FORGOT TO ACCOUNT FOR THE OBSERVER EFFECT!
I'VE DISRUPTED THE SPACE-TIME CONTINUUM.
LATE MODERN DTWOF
ROCOCO DTWOF
YOU CAN'T PIN THINGS DOWN WITHOUT CHANGING THEM, SOMEHOW.
SMEK
#@*a!
GOOD LORD. HOW MANY YOUNG WOMEN HAVE TOLD ME THESE WERE THE FIRST LESBIANS THEY EVER MET? THAT MY CARTOON CHARACTERS WERE--OH, I CAN HARDLY SAY THE WORDS--
DYKES TO WATCH OUT FOR AT THE ROTARY CLUB!
-CHOKE- ROLE MODELS!

I HAD COMMITTED A GRAVE ERROR IN REASONING, OF COURSE. AS ANY LOGICIAN WILL TELL YOU, INDUCING THE GENERAL FROM THE PARTICULAR DOESN'T REALLY HOLD WATER.
LET ALONE MILLIONS OF LESBIANS.
MY TIDY SCHEMA WENT ALL TO HELL IN THE NINETIES.
LESBIANS COULD BE REACTIONARY PROVOCATEURS.
AND COLONELS.
ARCH CONSERVA-TIVES AND NEOCONS COULD BE GAY.
OH, AND APPARENTLY NO ONE WAS ESSEN-TIALLY ANYTHING!
SQUEEEP!
ESSENTIALIST vs CONSTRUCTIONIST
GENDER TROUBLE JUDITH BUTLER
YANK!
IS THERE SOMETHING YOU'D LIKE TO TELL ME, SPARROW? ASIDE FROM THE FACT THAT ORGANZA IS BACK?
OH MY GOD! I BET MY MOM SENT THIS! EVER SINCE I CAME OUT TO HER ABOUT STUART, SHE THINKS IT MEANS I'M STRAIGHT. SHE CAN'T UNDER-STAND THAT I'M A BISEXUAL LESBIAN!
THWACK!
I COULD BARELY KEEP UP.
click
THIS WAS THE POINT AT WHICH A MORE SENSIBLE PERSON MIGHT HAVE INDEED GOTTEN A JOB.
PLAP PLAP PLAP!
BUT ONE DAY IN 1999, I RAN ACROSS THAT OLD REJECTION LETTER FROM ADRIENNE RICH.
I hope this is helpful. Don't be put off, or discouraged. Writing is a very long, demanding training, more hard work than luck. Strength to you.
In sisterhood,
K.D. LANG WEDGE
I CAN'T BELIEVE SHE TOOK THE TIME TO WRITE TO SOME PUNK KID. I'VE GOTTA THANK HER!
FLASHBACK SOUNDTRACK: RICKY MARTIN, SHE'S ALL I EVER HAD.
16 - COUNT 'EM - 16 MB of RAM!

ONCE YOU SPEAK THE UNSPEAKABLE...
...IT BECOMES SPOKEN!
CONVENTIONAL.
BORING!
HAVE I CHURNED OUT EPISODES OF THIS COMIC STRIP EVERY TWO WEEKS FOR DECADES MERELY TO PROVE THAT WE'RE THE SAME AS EVERYONE ELSE?!
HERE. YOU DECIDE. ESSENTIALLY THE SAME?
the ESSENTIAL Dykes to Watch Out For
OR ESSENTIALLY DIFFERENT?
25 =COUNT 'EM= 25 COPIES
ESSENTIAL DYKES TO WATCH OUT FOR
HOEDOWN MUFFIN, PUBLISHER
MAKE YOURSELVES COMFORTABLE. CLEARLY, I NEED TO RETHINK THIS THING.
BACK TO THE DRAWING BOARD.
ARCHIV
RUSTLE RUSTLE
MOST DISCONCERT-ING.
&$@#

Elizabeth Bick

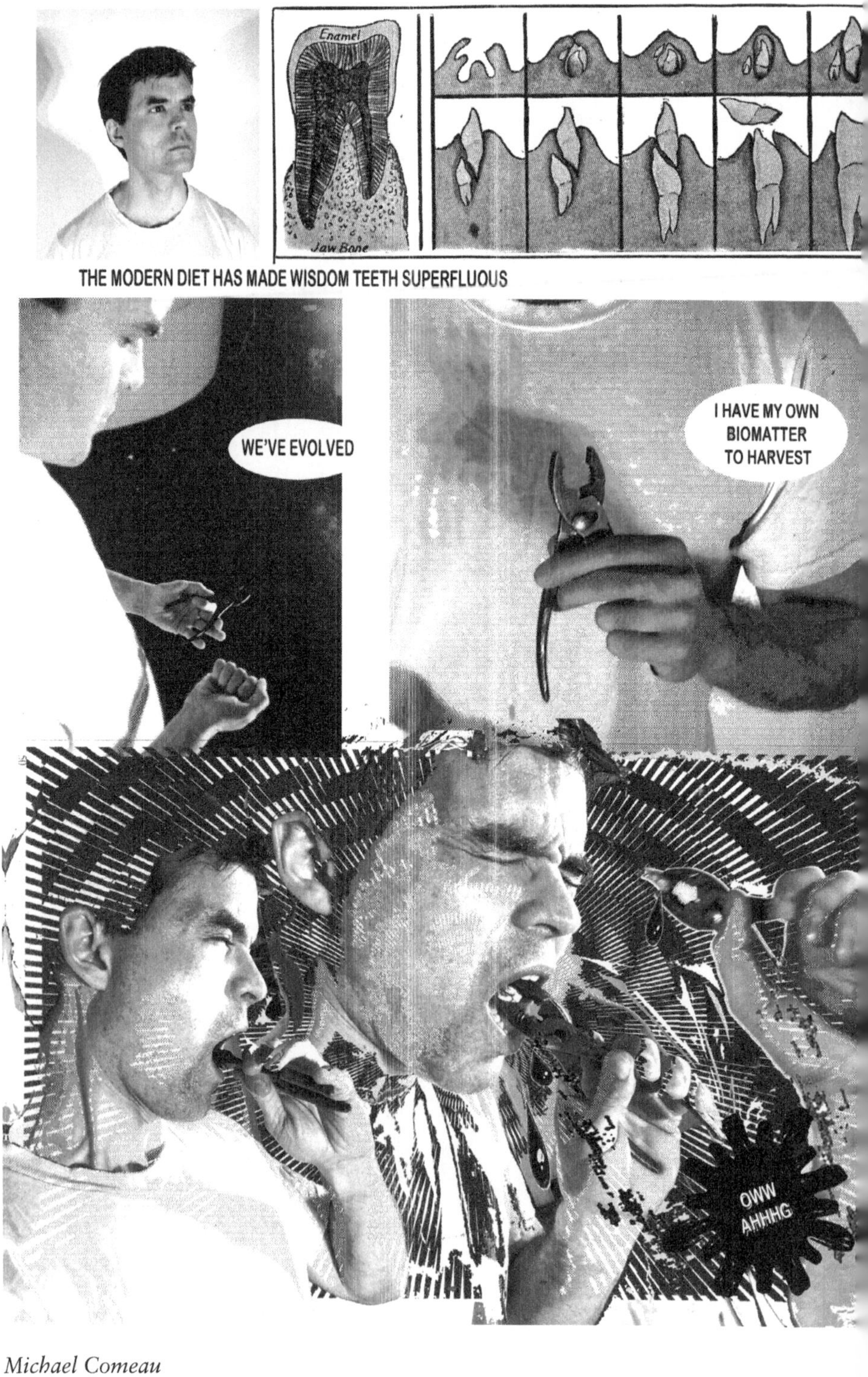

Michael Comeau

HUUHH
AAHH

Michael Comeau

Leela Corman

Something bad happened to Mrs. Gold today.
Yeah?
She fell outta the door bleeding!
Really?!
An' I had to go get a doctor, 'cept she wasn't a real one, she was for ladies.
And I dunno, but I think she bled out all the way, 'cause she was all white, and she wasn't sayin' nothin'.
Whoa!
And then she bled all the way out, right there in the street!
You girls wanna know what happened to Mrs. Gold?

Leela Corman

Did you see the baby in the blood?
No, just all over her tuchus!
Who's Bronia?
The Lady-doctor.
What's a Lady-doctor?
Sssnnrrrk...

Marcelo D'Salete

Marguerite Dabaie

present: I still find the comics SCARY, but I think I understand their importance now.
Everyone, meet HANTHALA. His back is always turned, he's dressed in RAGS, and he has VERY STRANGE HAIR.
Everyone, meet NAJI AL-ALI, Hanthala's creator. In Al-Ali's 30-year comic career, Hanthala's iconic backside was drawn into many of the works, serving as a silent witness to the comic's happenings.
ممنوع الوقوف
AND WHAT HAPPENINGS THEY WERE...

Marguerite Dabaie

AL-ALI was shot dead in 1987 by an "UNKNOWN ASSAILANT."
He had received over 100 death threats prior.
I started NOTICING his comics 1 year afterwards.
Ceepy... Just so... creepy...
THEY must have been reprints.
He gave INSIGHT into widely-held public opinion through these COMICS, all the more valuable considering how many people wanted him SILENCED.
It's a shame that he's gone.
The Palestinians need ANOTHER HANTHALA.

Eleanor Davis

I WANTED MORE FROM LIFE THAN THIS
LET'S HAVE A BABY.

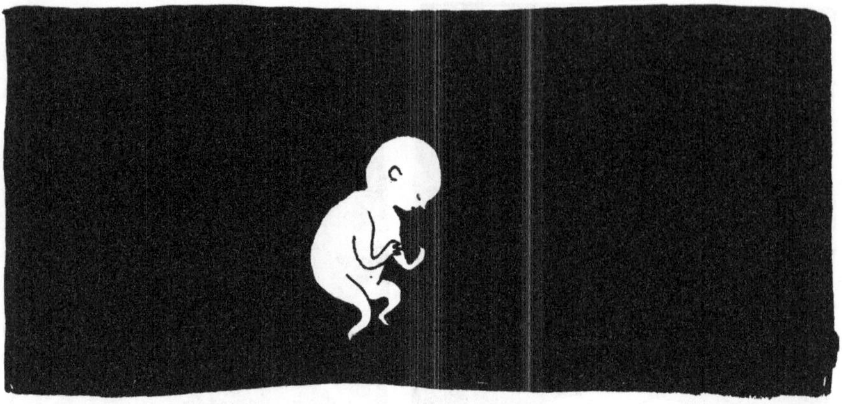

Eleanor Davis

END

Aminder Dhaliwal

MAYBE THE REASON IS BEYOND OUR UNDERSTANDING
I LIKE THAT. IT'S BEYOND US.
OR MAYBE HUMANKIND HAS A HABIT OF IDOLIZING THE UNKNOWN RATHER THAN ATTEMPTING TO UNDERSTAND IT.
EVERYTHING WAS MORE ETHEREAL WHEN WE WERE SWIMMING. I MISS IT

40

Julie Doucet

i THiNK YOU'LL NEED LOTS OF LESSONS! HEH HEH
m!
A BIT LATER....
SiNCE ALCOHOLiSME iS AMONG OUR MOST iMPORTANT PASTiME, iT DƎSERVES ATTEN--SSSHiON!
HEY WOW YOUR ƎNGLiSh iz GETTiNG BETTER!
LATER
FFRANK!! two MUCH MORe BERRZ HERe!
Medical science does not yet know the precise cause or causes of alcoholism. Authorities agree, however, that emotional difficulties—tension, worry, guilt and other dreaded feelings—are certainly connected with alcoholism.
...MUCH MORE LATER
OH JULiƎ NO MORE MONƎY anyMORE!
Then shall the dust return to the earth as it was; and the spirit shall....
BYE bYƎ FRANK!
NEXT MORNING...
BEEEUH! j'ME SOUVIENS PLUS DE RiEN!*
BELCH
BELCH
END TWO
BY JULiE DOUCET 1990
*"ARGHRGH i CAN'T REMEMBER ANYTHING..."

41

180

Julie Doucet

PLease STOP
SNAP
18
21
GO MAN GO
LET'S GO SHOPPiNG NOW!!!
J.D. 1993
MALL
END

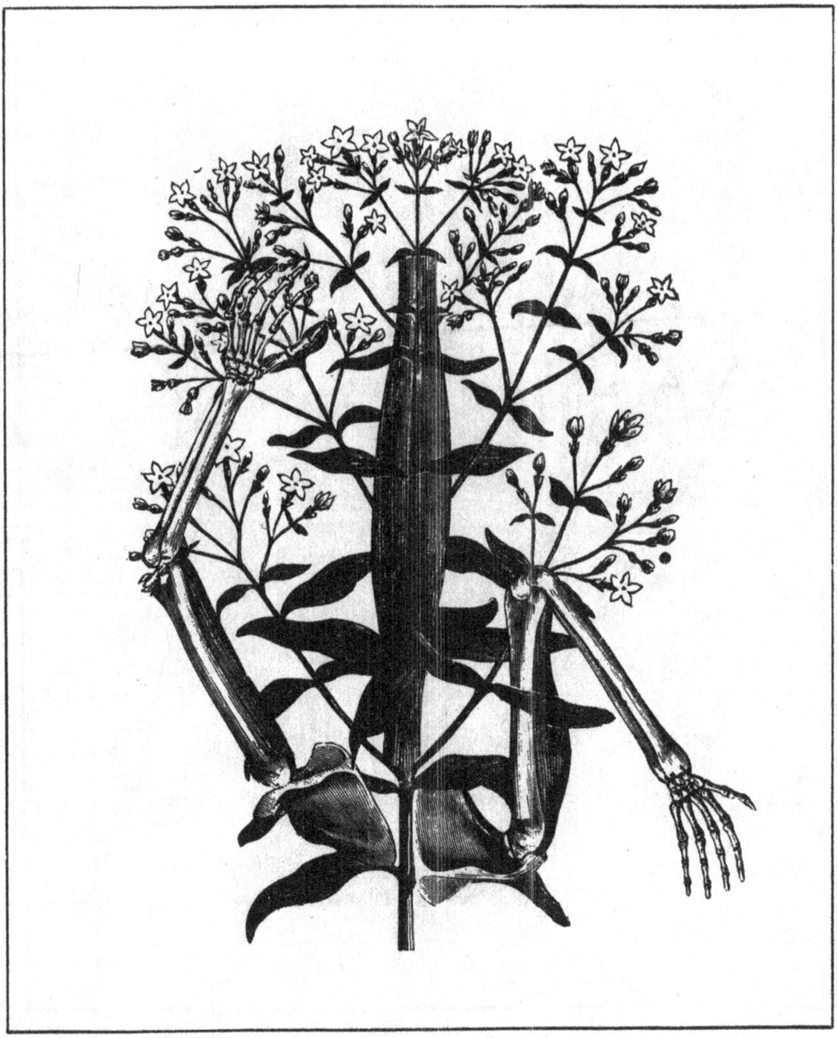

Max Ernst

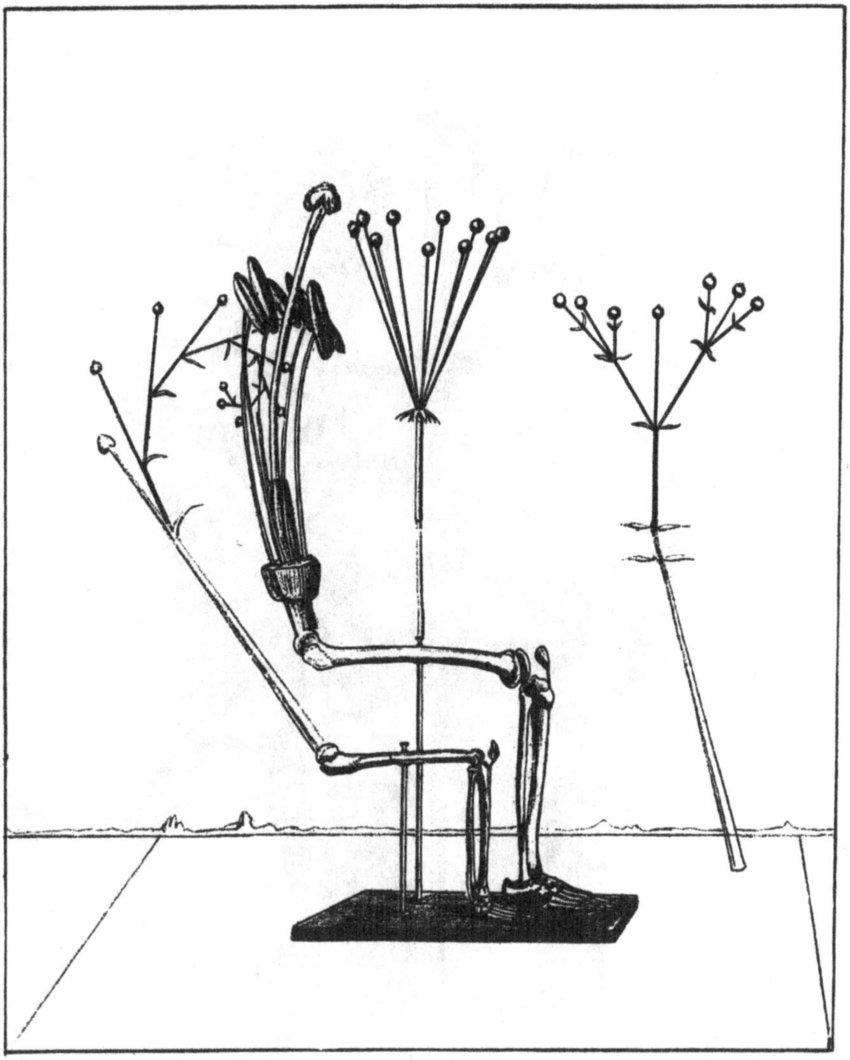

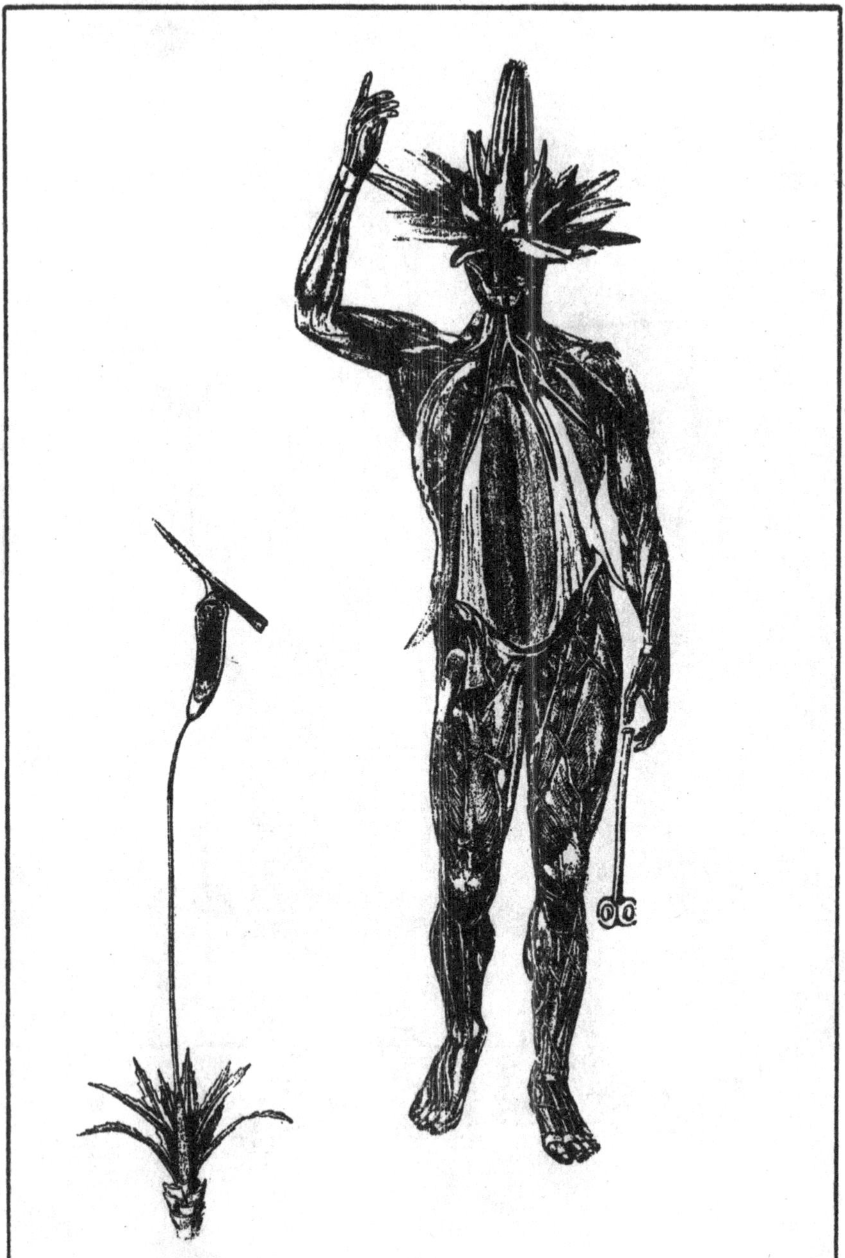

Max Ernst

Max Ernst

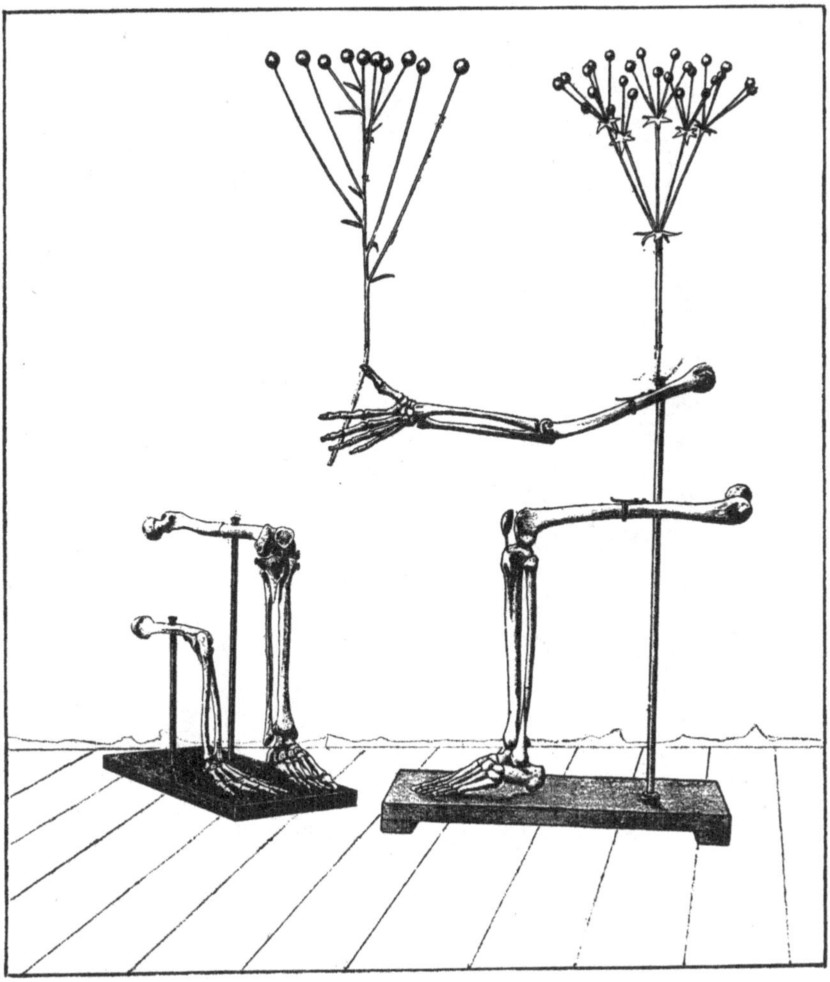

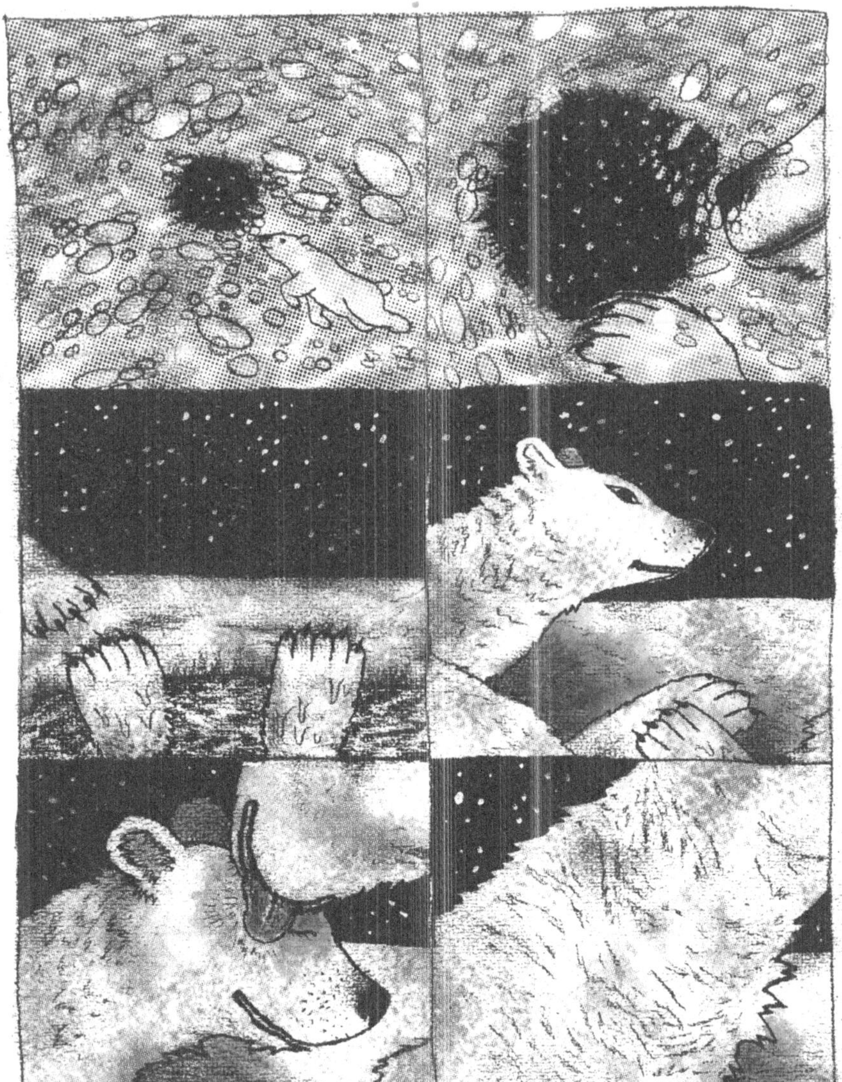

Inés Estrada

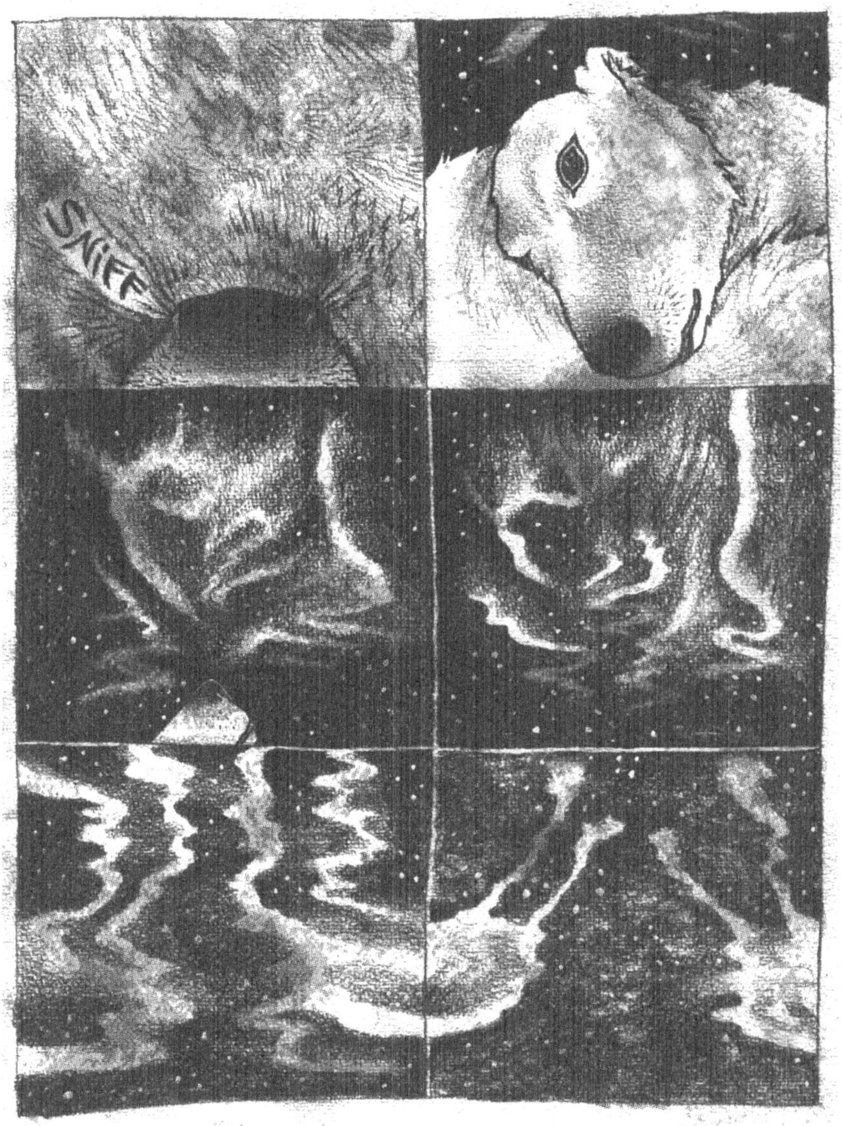
SNIFF

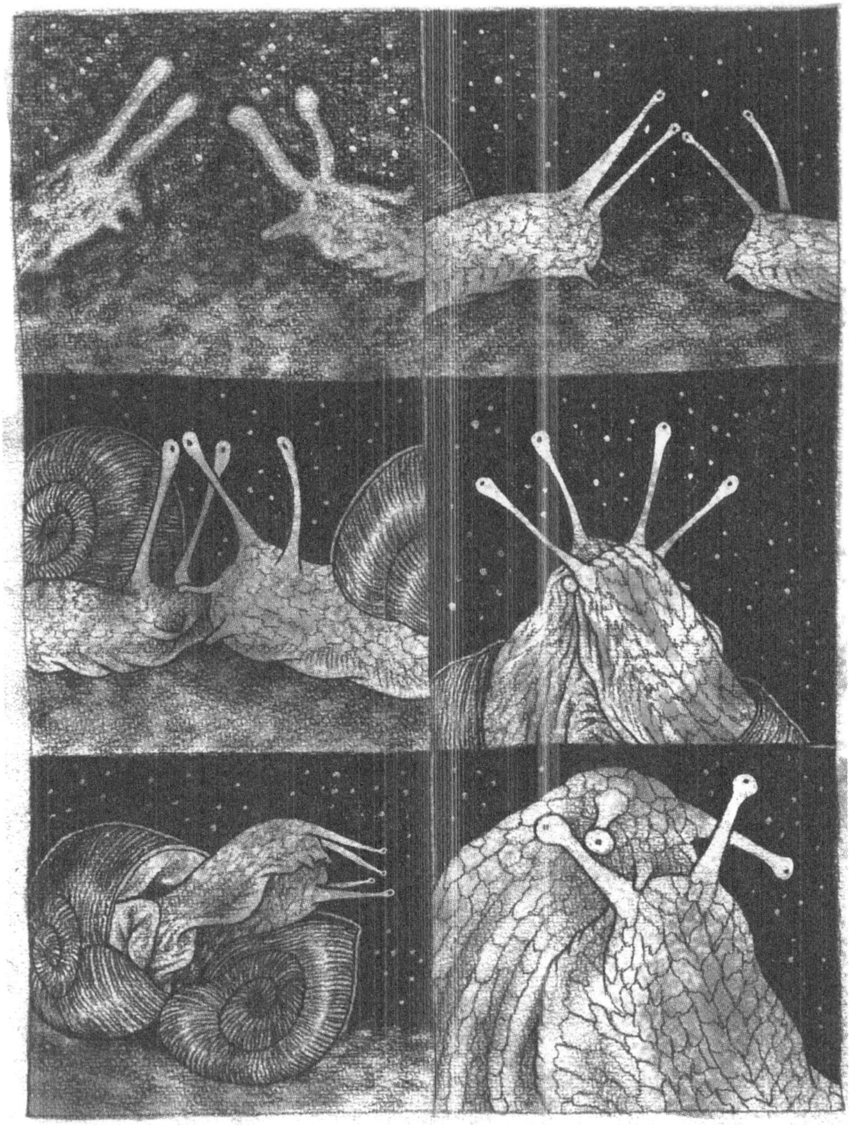

Inés Estrada

<--- Return to pages 86 – 87

KINDERGARTEN
I ATTEND A MONTESSORI SCHOOL RUN BY NUNS.
SISTER MATILDA IS THE MOST HOMEOPATHIC AND HEAVY-BREATHING OF THE NUNS.
SHE IS MY TEACHER.
DURING RECESS, THE NUNS SIT IN A CLUSTER ON THE LAWN—
REGALING EACH OTHER WITH STORIES ABOUT CHILDREN WHO STUCK THEIR HEADS OUT OF CAR WINDOWS—
—AND WERE DECAPITATED.
I SPEND RECESS UNDER A GIANT HEMLOCK—
HELLO
—COMMUNING WITH ROCKS AND PLANTS AND INSECTS. I SEE HUMANITY IN THESE THINGS. (NOT IN HUMANS.)
HOW BEAUTIFUL YOU ARE.
ONE DAY I TRY TO STOP THE BOYS FROM PULLING APART A BUTTERFLY THEY CAUGHT.
CLAP
SCRAMBLE
THE NUNS TELL ME TO LET THEM BE;
NO!!!
PULL ITS WINGS OFF!
"BOYS WILL BE BOYS."
EEW, THERE'S GOO INSIDE!

Liana Finck

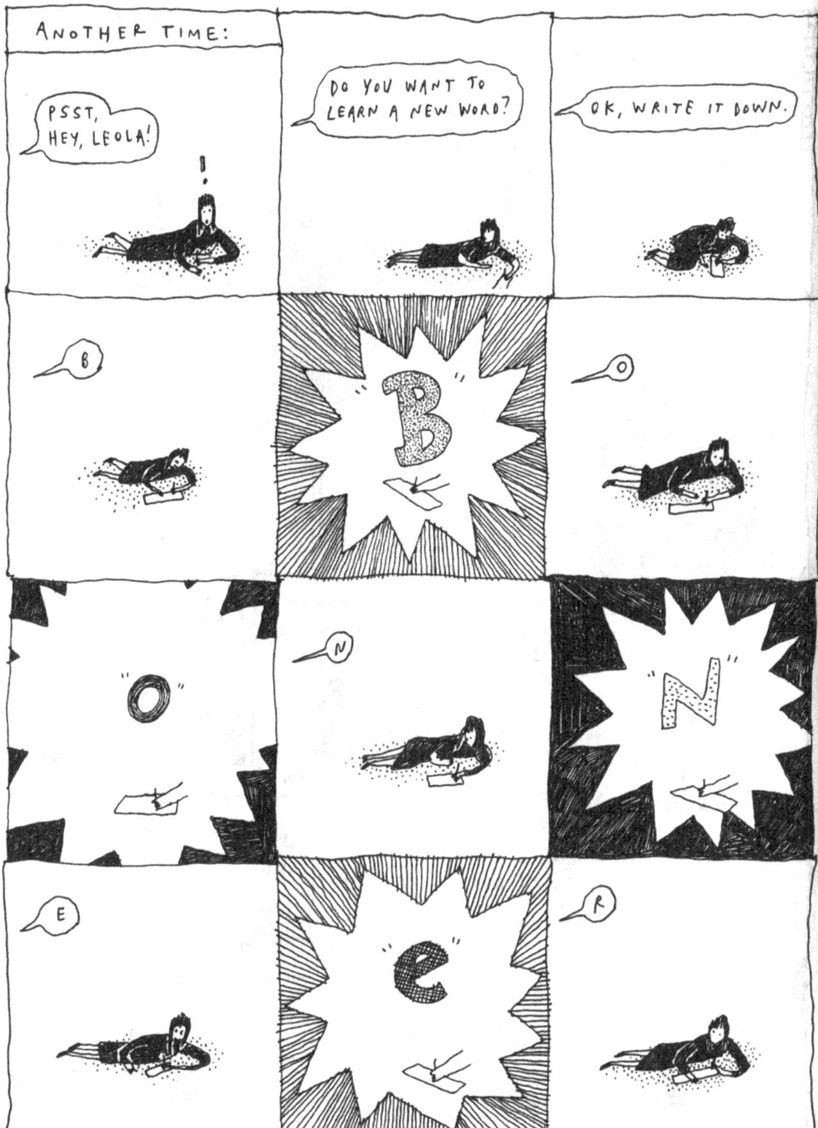
ANOTHER TIME:
PSST, HEY, LEOLA!
!
DO YOU WANT TO LEARN A NEW WORD?
OK, WRITE IT DOWN.
B
"B"
O
"O"
N
"N"
E
"e"
R

"R"
HA HA HA HA HA HA HA HA HA HA HA HA HA HA HA HA HA HA HA HA HA HA HA HA HA HA HA HA HA HA
GIVE ME THAT!
SISTER MATILDA! SISTER MATILDA! LOOK WHAT LEOLA DID!
SISTER MATILDA STOPS WHAT SHE IS DOING.
OH
BONER
SHE HEAVES UP OUT OF HER CHAIR;
OH, NO
HER EYES ARE FULL OF DISAPPOINTMENT.
I HIDE UNDER A BOOKSHELF.
ZOOM
THE FEELINGS OF SHOCK AND BETRAYAL GIVE WAY TO THIS DARK KNOWLEDGE.
PANT PANT PANT PANT
SOMETHING IS WRONG WITH ME.
THERE ARE CERTAIN LINES AND I AM BLIND TO THEM, I CROSS THEM.
[SOB]
FOR A PERSON LIKE ME IT WILL NEVER BE POSSIBLE TO BE CAREFUL ENOUGH—
NO!

Liana Finck

—TO BE QUIET ENOUGH.
NO!!

Reneé French

Reneé French

Reneé French

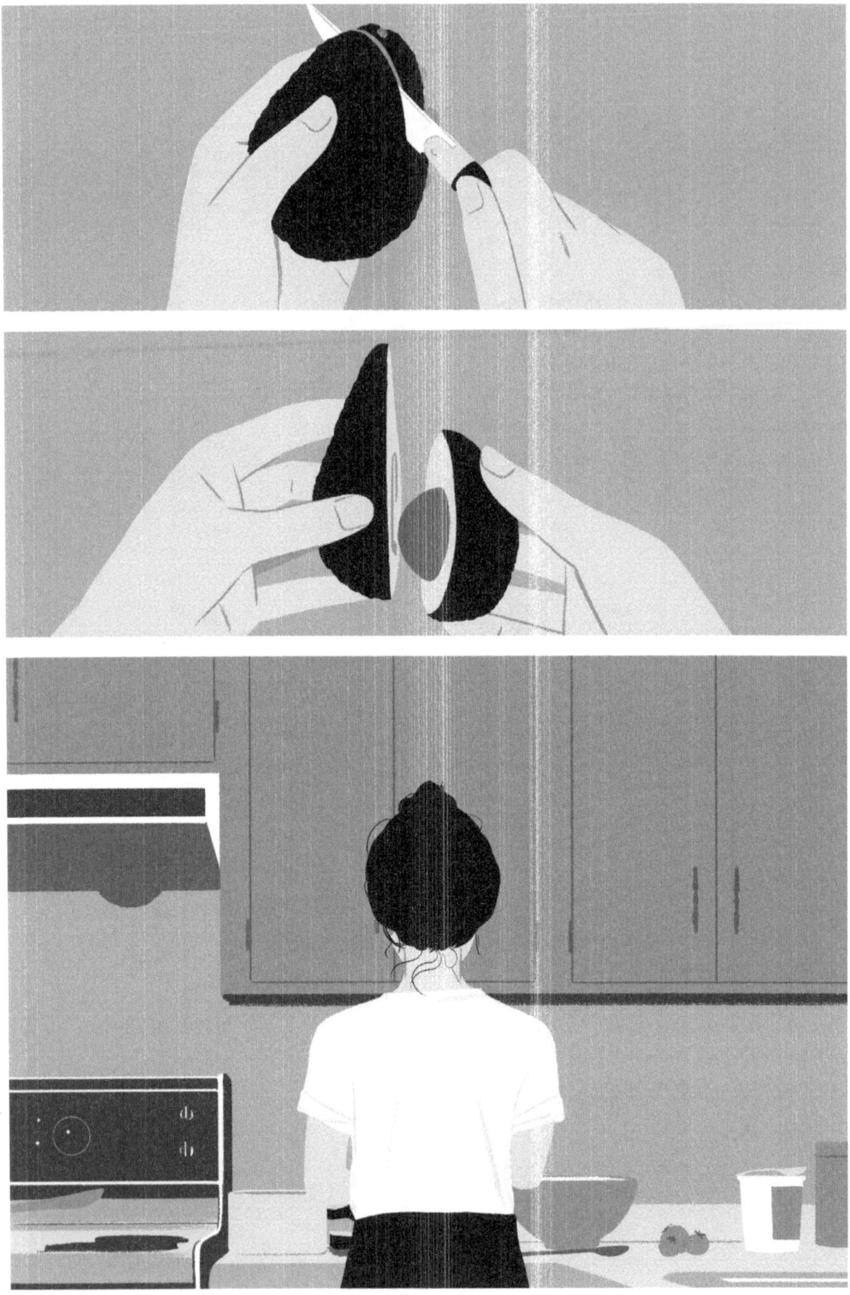

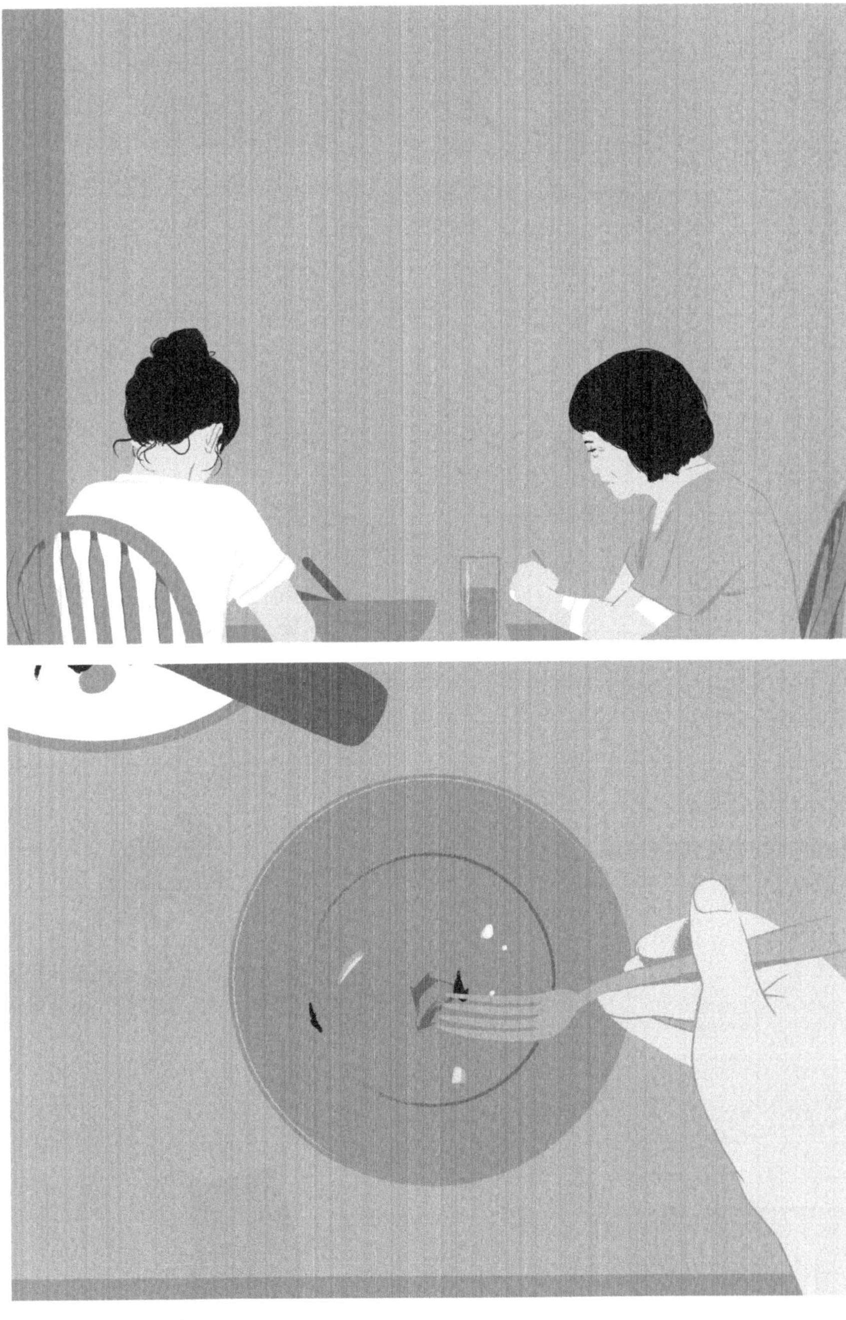

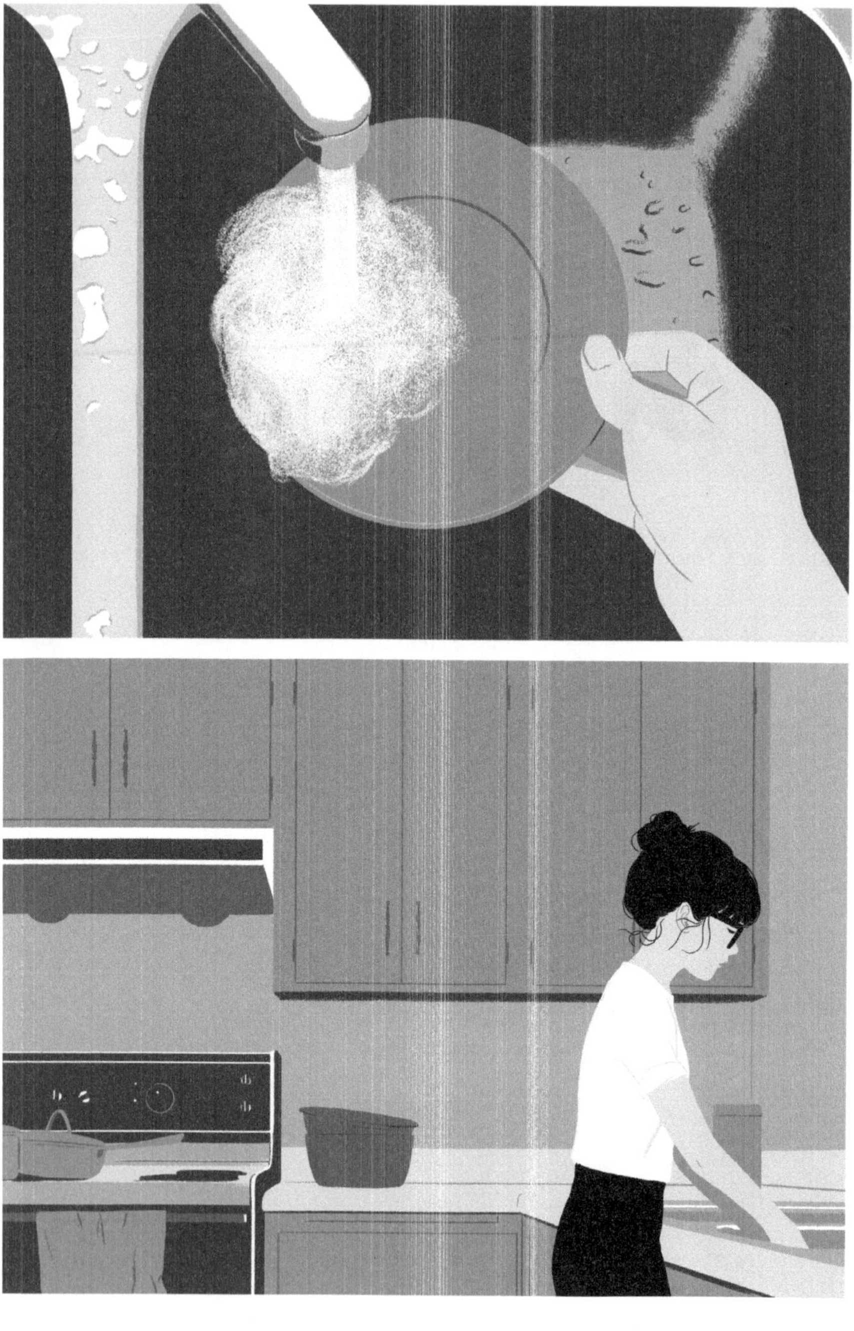

Did you look at these pictures of your little niece ? So cute !
Too bad they live so far away and we never see them .
When will I get grandkids from you ? Your little sister will have two soon .

She's doing so well in everything . When will you be successful ?
Oh, can you buy some more bandages the next time you go out ?

LOT C (SOME TIME LATER)

Under a canopy of branches in one of Lot C's grassy interstices, I took off my shirt, lay down, and closed my eyes. We were finished at last. Many a night we had dozed off together, in your truck, but only ever because we were on the same degree track at the community college.

You murmured over and over in my ear, "Have you heard of e-mail? Have you heard of e-mail?" Whether it was the mid-Nineties or some time later, your question lulled me to sleep. You e-mailed me a photo of a cat sleeping on your chest. I replied with an over-earnest personal anecdote. Some time later, you removed your sweater, and I immediately heard wheezing. "Seeking the elusive frisson," you wrote in an e-mail, before you said it in person, your hand under my sweater, resting on my chest. We were both breathing with great effort.

John Hankiewicz

I parked in Lot C and walked a long way, to Lot T, intending to stir you with a description of the snow flurries at the end of the pier at Gray's Beach, a thousand miles east. I stood in snow flurries at the edge of Lot T, looking for your truck.

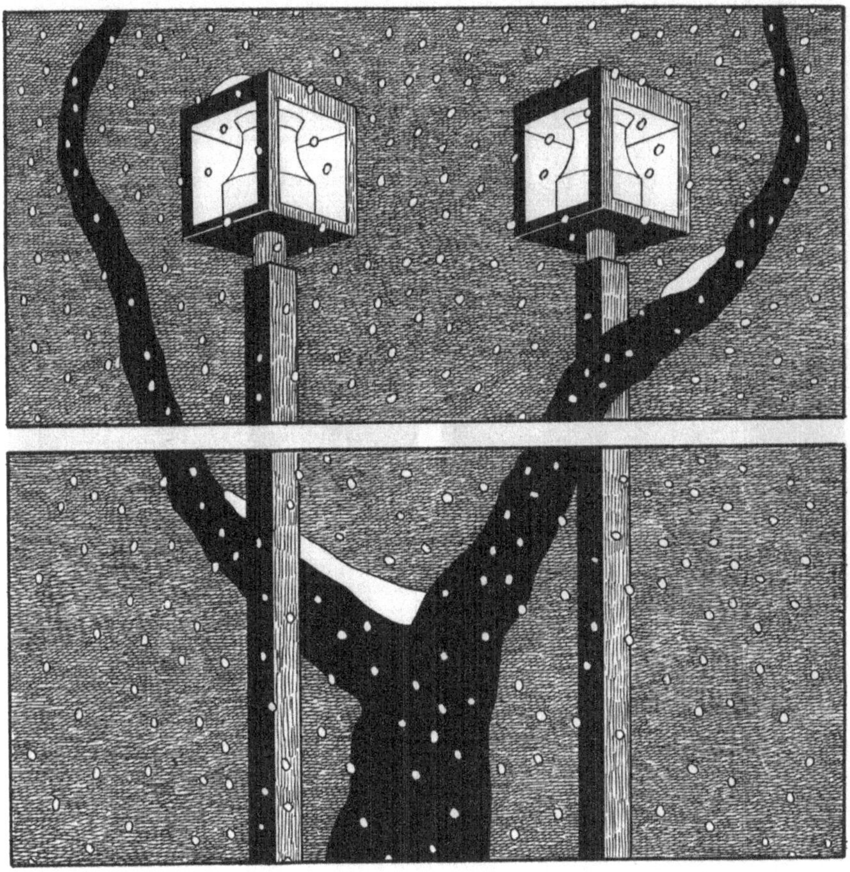

Even though we were on the same degree track at the community college, you were secretly undecided, supremely undecided. But beneath it all, determined. "I go back..." you whispered, and your voice trailed off. Then one of us continued: I go back to my high school all the time, to speak at assemblies and in extracurricular discussion groups, and on weekends to do landscaping. Simply put, I am in a position to initiate change. All you need to do is *return*, and you attain immeasurable influence.

You e-mailed me a cat photo. You forwarded me a joke. Against my better judgment, I sent you long descriptions of places I'd been. Some time later, I parked in Lot C, which had become a parody of itself since the mid-Nineties. I unzipped my windbreaker and rubbed the interstices of my ribcage. I felt a deep static in my left lung. I turned off the motor, and I suddenly heard your wheezing beside me, though you were still in your truck, en route.

They repaved all the lots, A through Z, then tore out large sections of the parking alphabet. Much of the time, Lot C was inaccessible, sometimes absent. It was repaved, repainted, torn out, restored. It was roped off for special events at the college. The first e-mail I ever sent was a question to a professor. You—you finished the degree track we were on, and returned, some time later, to teach. You were forever returning. I took your class.

John Hankiewicz

I put my ear to your left breast. It felt like another ear. In a hurry to prepare for your class, you promised to e-mail me. In class, you had a knack for making distinctions: "Friction versus frisson: only one of them is at all elusive." Some time later, in an e-mail, one of the seminal e-mails, you wrote, "What a good listener. . . ."

I drew my ear from your breast. You had made a full recovery. I couldn't hear anything. It was as late as we'd ever stayed awake together. And now your night class. Lot C was roped off for a special event. I was breathing hard, and you—what word did you use—

Jaime Hernandez

TRUE

Jaime Hernandez

FIN

William Hogarth

Gareth A. Hopkins and Erik Blagsvedt

mortal coffee sheep dance

Gareth A. Hopkins and Erik Blagsvedt

R. Kikuo Johnson

WILL DO.
HEY LOREN!
I'M KINDA IN A RUSH HERE, DAD.
WELL, SLOW DOWN A MINUTE. I HAVEN'T HAD A CHANCE TO TELL YOU HOW GREAT THE YARD LOOKS!
WHEN DID YOU FIND TIME TO MOW?
UMM... BOUT A WEEK AGO.
SURE DOESN'T LAST LONG, DOES IT?
JEEEZ
OUR POOR YARD...
...YOU'D THINK WE WERE SPRAYING MIRACLE-GROW ON THAT SUCKER.
IS THAT ALL?
GO ON.
BYE.
BYE.

R. Kikuo Johnson

FFSS
Narlboro

Mariam Katin

ONE QUIET MOONLIT NIGHT.
WHERE TO, NEIGHBORS, AT THIS LATE HOUR?
THERE ARE DEAD SOLDIERS ON THE FIELD. JUST LEFT BEHIND.
WE CAN USE SOME THINGS THEY GOT.
COME ON WITH US.
THOSE SURE DON'T NEED NOTHING NO MORE.

Mariam Katin

EXCELLENT PREWAR MAKE.
TAP TAP
YOU SAID YOU CAN SEW. THIS IS GOOD FABRIC.
JUST WASH OUT THE BLOOD AND THE DIRT. WITH SOME ALTERATION WE CAN USE IT. EARN YOUR KEEP.

John Lewis, Andrew Aydin, and Nate Powell

FORWARD!
what the--?!
EQUAL

John Lewis, Andrew Aydin, and Nate Powell

WHAT DO YOU WANT?
F'EEDOM.
HATE HIS BROTHER
IT WAS AN EMBARRASSMENT TO THE CITY.

Miriam Libicki

FRIDAY, 29 SEPTEMBER, ROSH HASHANAH* EVE
FOUR PALESTINIANS ARE KILLED AND SOME 200 WOUNDED BY SECURITY FORCES, WHILE 29 ISRAELI POLICEMEN ARE LIGHTLY WOUNDED BY STONE THROWERS ON AND AROUND THE TEMPLE MOUNT FOLLOWING FRIDAY PRAYERS AT THE AL-AQSA MOSQUE.
*jewish new year
ETHIOPIAN IMMIGRANT BORDER POLICE INSPECTOR YOSSI TABAJI IS SHOT DEAD BY A PALESTINIAN POLICEMAN NEAR KALKILYA.
SATURDAY, 30 SEPTEMBER, FIRST DAY ROSH HASHANAH
CLASHES ERUPT IN JUDEA, SAMARIA, AND GAZA.
FOURTEEN PALESTINIANS KILLED BY IDF SOLDIERS,
INCLUDING TWELVE-YEAR-OLD MOHAMMED ALDURA,
WHOSE DEATH IS CAUGHT ON VIDEOTAPE.

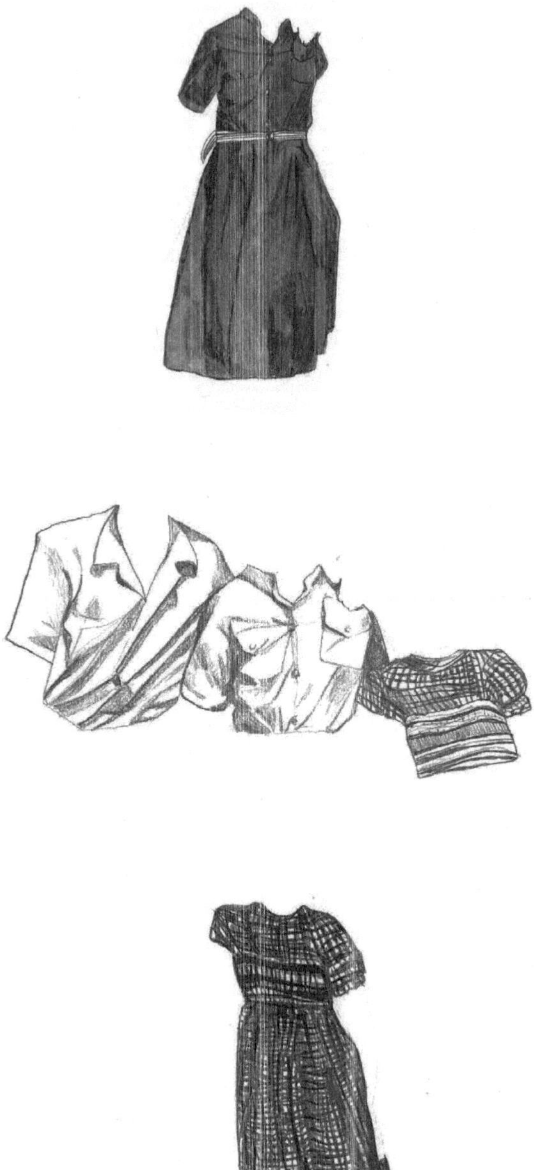

34

Sarah Lightman

Families are like glass.

You see yourself and reality through them.

Constructing yourself...

in an already established community.

Mummy said Daniel will never find a girl to marry…

who is as good as his sisters.

I don't think Daniel ever got over the shock of me learning Latin.

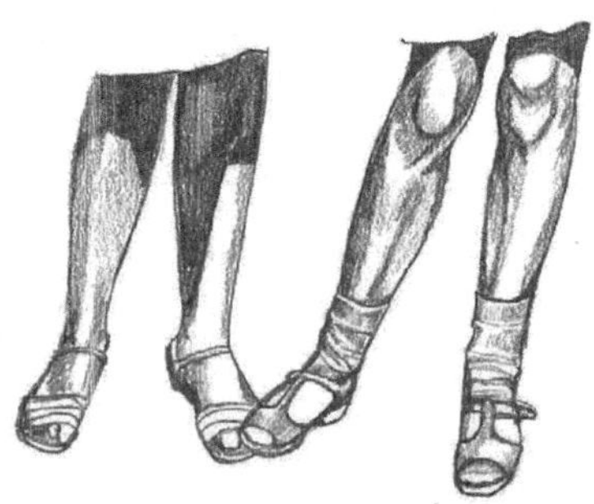

Wearing Esther's shoes didn't help me understand myself.

36

Sarah Lightman

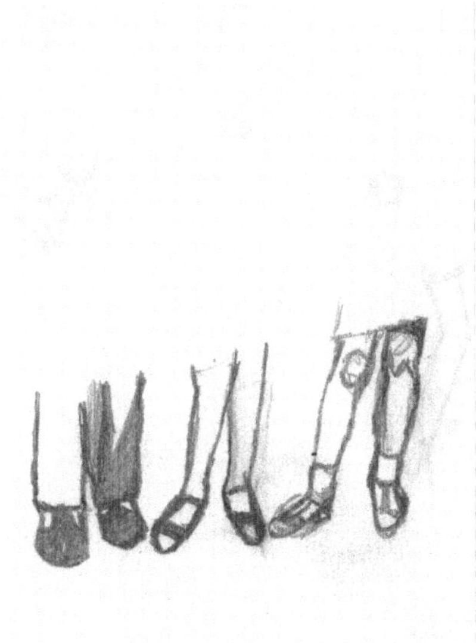

Moving out of home was supposed to define where I was propped up and to help me stand up on my own.

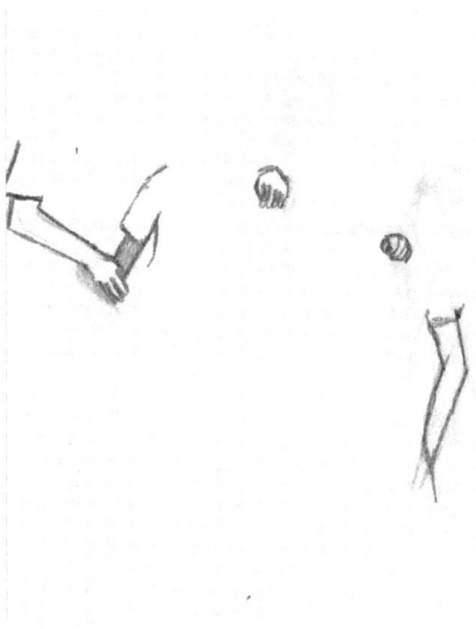

Perhaps all I did was recreate the world I left behind. Put us all together in the same room and nothing's changed.

I suppose I still needed propping up.

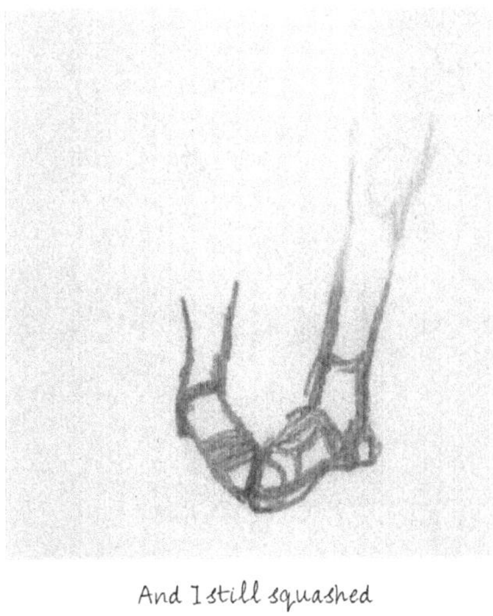

And I still squashed Esther a bit.

Daishu Ma

José Muñoz and Carlos Sampayo

G-NGANGANA
NGA-ANGNG
NGAAN
GANG
-NGANGAN-
.dreams.

Sylvia Nickerson

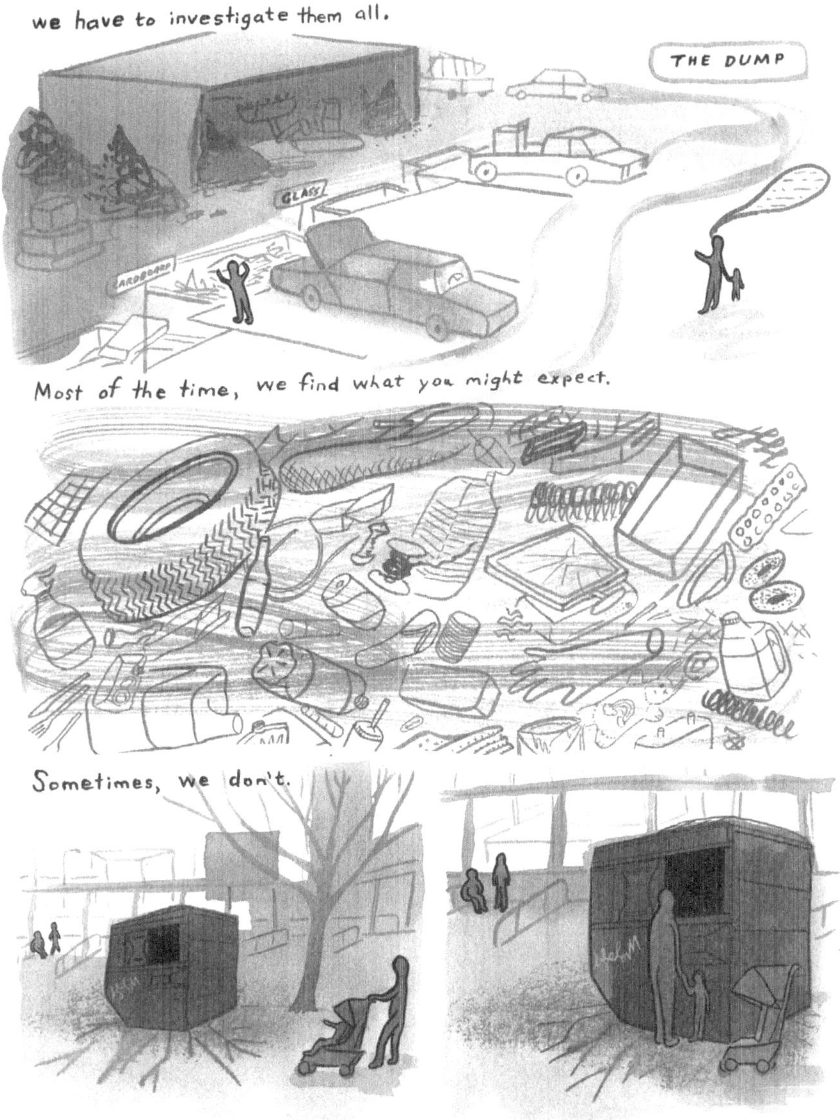
we have to investigate them all.
THE DUMP
GLASS
Most of the time, we find what you might expect.
Sometimes, we don't.

Sylvia Nickerson

He's fine.
Just sleeping.

Thomas Ott

DONT
WALK

Thomas Ott

Kristin Radtke

I feel like Didion at the beginning of "Goodbye to All That."
Didion didn't have to pee in a bucket in the garage.
I haven't been to the studio in three days.
I haven't written anything in four days.
We began resenting each other for the time we spent or wanted to spend together, and the ends of our words sharpened in a way that was unfamiliar to us both.

Keiler Roberts

The drive to the vet to put him to sleep was sunny with no traffic. He sat up calmly.
Scott was in New York.
The night before, we'd sat in the animal E.R. not knowing it was unfixable.
This is the best cat I've ever had.
I'm so sorry.
My next dog is going to be better than this one.
Oops. I'm sorry.
RED
The TV was revealing the 2004 presidential election results.

Marjane Satrapi

LIKE ALL MY PREDECESSORS I HAD MY HOLY BOOK.
THE FIRST THREE RULES CAME FROM ZARATHUSTRA. HE WAS THE FIRST PROPHET IN MY COUNTRY BEFORE THE ARAB INVASION.
YOU MUST BASE EVERYTHING ON THESE THREE RULES: BEHAVE WELL, SPEAK WELL, ACT WELL.
I ALSO WANTED US TO CELEBRATE THE TRADITIONAL ZARATHUSTRIAN HOLIDAYS. LIKE THE FIRE CEREMONY,
BEFORE THE PERSIAN NEW YEAR, NOROUZ, ON MARCH 21ST, THE FIRST DAY OF SPRING.
ONLY MY GRANDMOTHER KNEW ABOUT MY BOOK.
RULE NUMBER SIX: EVERY-BODY SHOULD HAVE A CAR.
RULE NUMBER SEVEN: ALL MAIDS SHOULD EAT AT THE TABLE WITH THE OTHERS.
RULE NUMBER EIGHT: NO OLD PER-SON SHOULD HAVE TO SUFFER.
IN THAT CASE, I'LL BE YOUR FIRST DISCIPLE.
REALLY?
BUT TELL ME HOW YOU'LL ARRANGE FOR OLD PEOPLE NOT TO SUFFER?
IT WILL SIMPLY BE FORBIDDEN.

Marjane Satrapi

NONETHELESS, MY PARENTS WERE PUZZLED.
SO TELL ME, MY CHILD, WHAT DO YOU WANT TO BE WHEN YOU GROW UP?
A PROPHET.
I WANT TO BE A DOCTOR.
THAT'S FINE MY LOVE. THAT'S FINE.
I FELT GUILTY TOWARDS GOD.
YOU WANT TO BE A DOCTOR? I THOUGHT THAT...
NO, NO, I WILL BE A PROPHET BUT THEY MUSTN'T KNOW.
I WANTED TO BE JUSTICE, LOVE AND THE WRATH OF GOD ALL IN ONE.

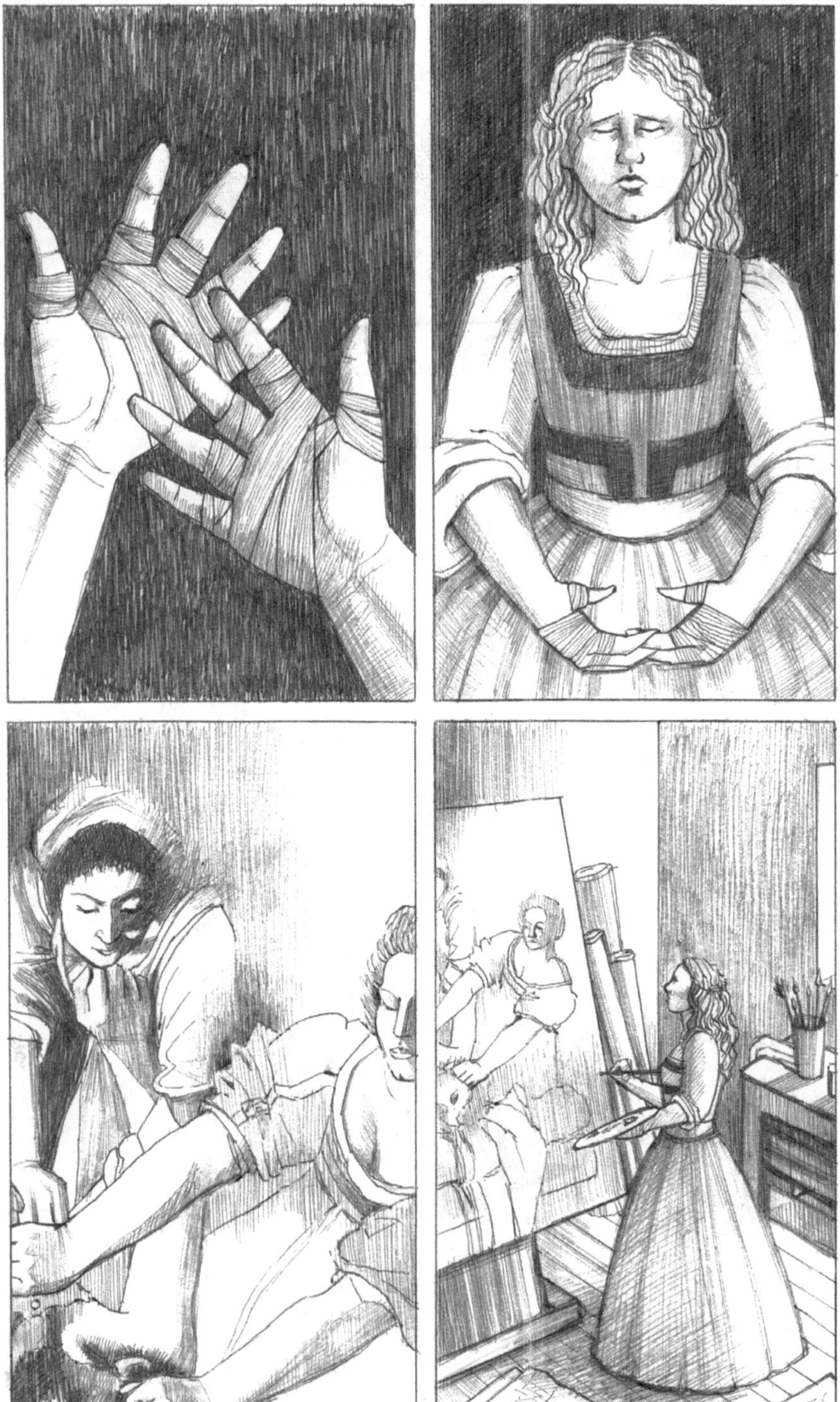

Gina Siciliano

A VIRGIN WAS A VALUABLE COMMODITY. IF A WOMAN WAS DISHONORED, THE HUSBAND OR FATHER WHO OWNED HER WAS DISHONORED.
RAPE WAS NOT CONSIDERED A VIOLATION OF THE BODY AND SPIRIT, BUT ONLY A DISRUPTION OF THE FAMILY NAME AND SOCIAL STATUS.
AND YET, IN THE FIFTEENTH CENTURY, THE FAMOUS MEDIEVAL WRITER CHRISTINE DE PIZAN WROTE THAT RAPE "CAUSES THE GREATEST POSSIBLE SUFFERING."
THROUGHOUT HISTORY, WOMEN HAVE INSTINCTIVELY RESISTED SEXUAL ASSAULT.
RAPE HAS ALWAYS WOUNDED WOMEN, PERPETUATING GRIEF AND SHAME.
TO PREVENT THE GRIEF FROM KILLING HER, THE SURVIVOR MUST SUMMON ALL OF HER STRENGTH AND POWER.

ONE.
QUARTERED.
THE HEAD WILL NOT SAY WHAT HE REALLY THINKS.
THE HEAD IS RULED BY OTHER THAN THE HEART.
STINKS
1995 SNIPEHUNT

Fiona Smyth

3
the definition of expression is narrowed.
L
U
K
ink
BOXED

4
GOODbYE
ADIEU TO THE HEAD.
HELLO
HELLO TO THE HEART.
Good bye
hello
HELLO
GOOD BYE
GOOD BYE
GOODBYE
Hello
FIONA SMYTH 1995

1996 SNIPEHUNT

Fiona Smyth

KAREN BLACK
FOXY
KATE DAWN
RIP

Jillian Tamaki

Craig Thompson

click

Seth Tobocman

BUT WHEN YOU ARE SLEEPING IN DOORWAYS WITH GLASS IN YOUR BAREFEET AND CRAWLING IN AND OUT OF YOUR FRIEND'S APARTMENT WINDOW AND YOU HAVEN'T CHANGED YOUR CLOTHES IN WEEKS
AND MOST PEOPLE
TAKE ONE LOOK AND STAY AWAY.
WILL ANY OF THEM TAKE YOU IN?
& BE PATIENT AND PUT UP WITH YOUR BULLSHIT UNTIL YOU GET YOUR SHIT TOGETHER.
OR WILL THEY DECIDE TO:

Seth Tobocman

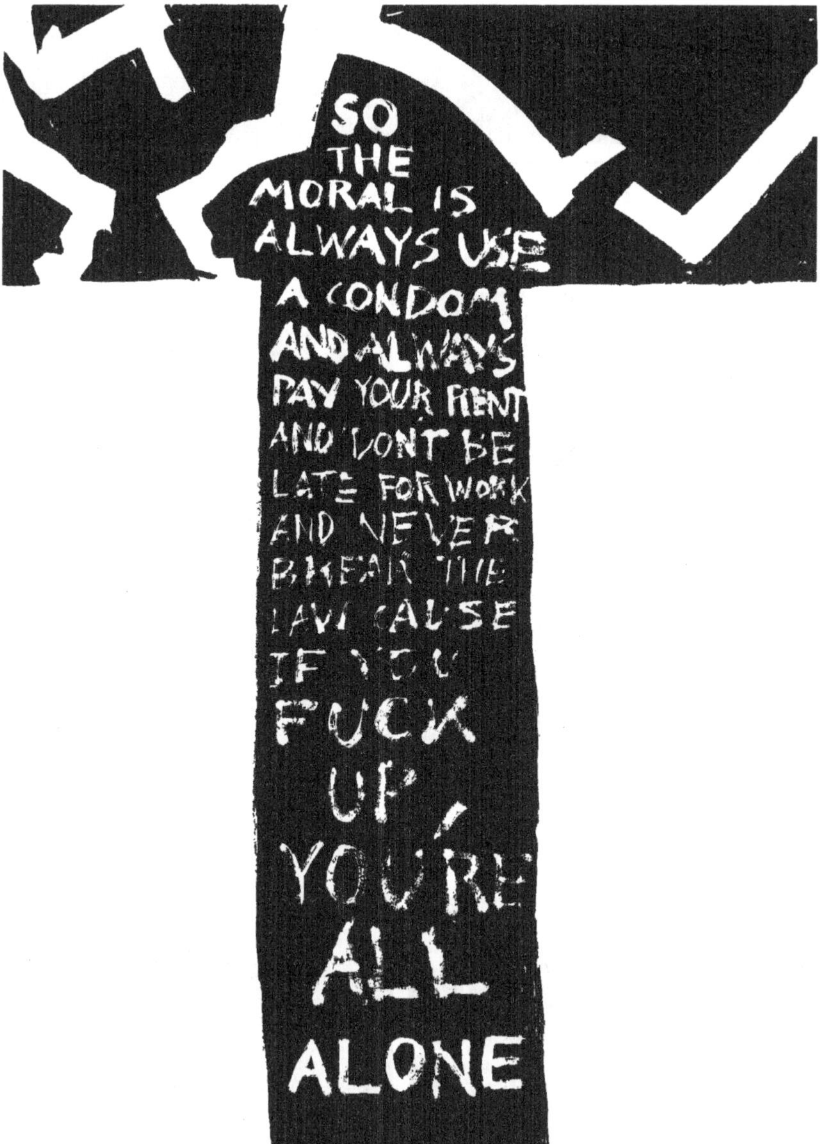
SO
THE
MORAL IS
ALWAYS USE
A CONDOM
AND ALWAYS
PAY YOUR RENT
AND DONT BE
LATE FOR WORK
AND NEVER
BREAK THE
LAW CAUSE
IF YOU
FUCK
UP
YOU'RE
ALL
ALONE

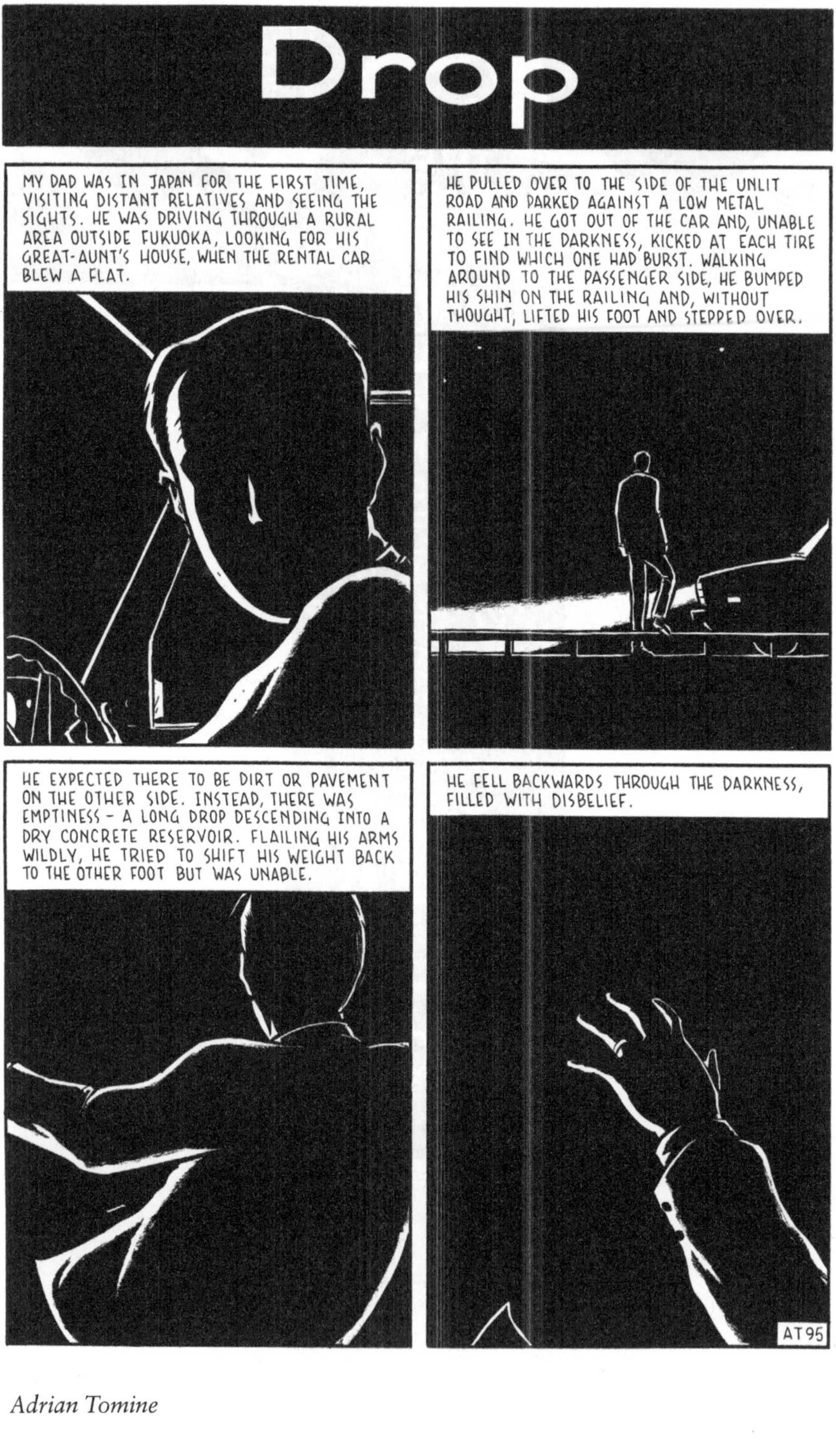

Adrian Tomine

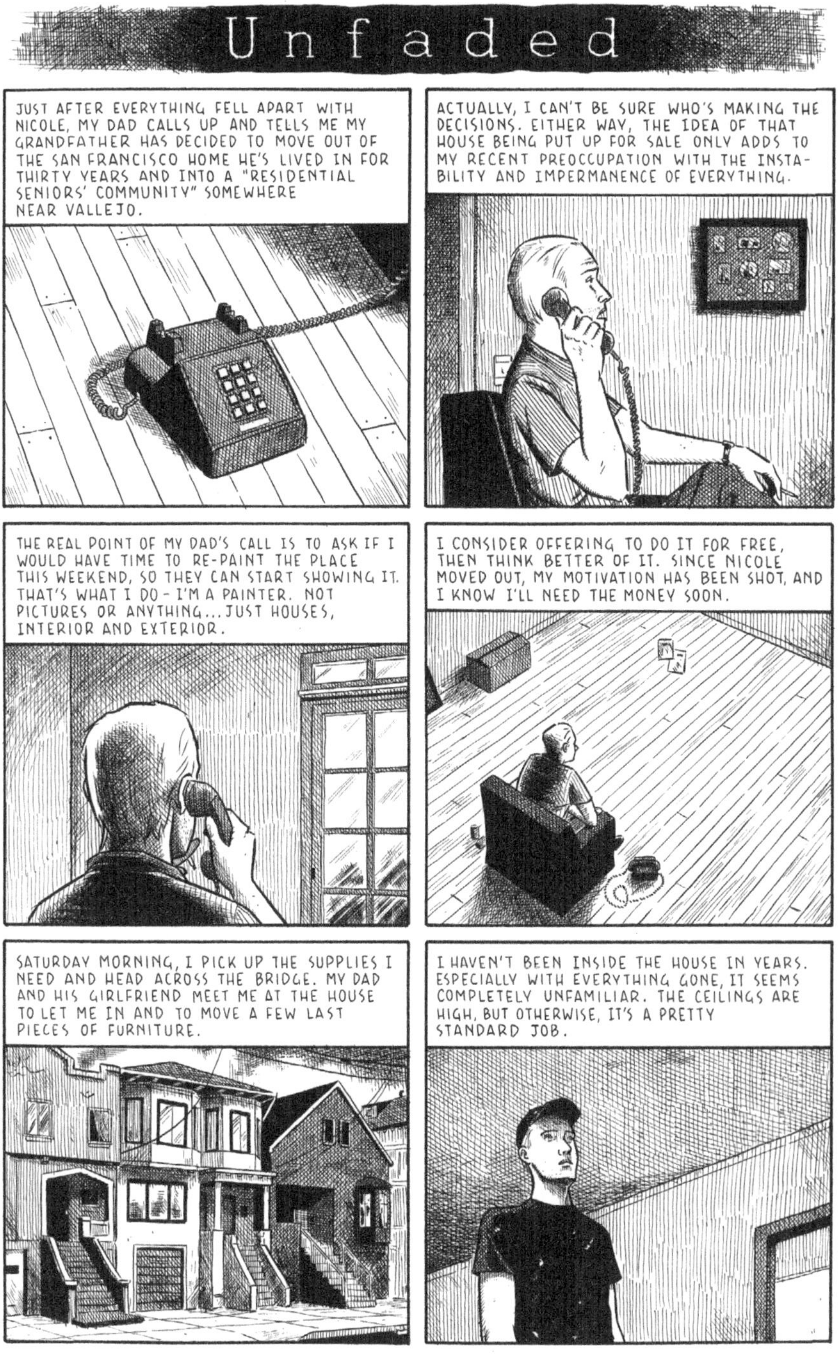
Unfaded
JUST AFTER EVERYTHING FELL APART WITH NICOLE, MY DAD CALLS UP AND TELLS ME MY GRANDFATHER HAS DECIDED TO MOVE OUT OF THE SAN FRANCISCO HOME HE'S LIVED IN FOR THIRTY YEARS AND INTO A "RESIDENTIAL SENIORS' COMMUNITY" SOMEWHERE NEAR VALLEJO.
ACTUALLY, I CAN'T BE SURE WHO'S MAKING THE DECISIONS. EITHER WAY, THE IDEA OF THAT HOUSE BEING PUT UP FOR SALE ONLY ADDS TO MY RECENT PREOCCUPATION WITH THE INSTABILITY AND IMPERMANENCE OF EVERYTHING.
THE REAL POINT OF MY DAD'S CALL IS TO ASK IF I WOULD HAVE TIME TO RE-PAINT THE PLACE THIS WEEKEND, SO THEY CAN START SHOWING IT. THAT'S WHAT I DO - I'M A PAINTER. NOT PICTURES OR ANYTHING... JUST HOUSES, INTERIOR AND EXTERIOR.
I CONSIDER OFFERING TO DO IT FOR FREE, THEN THINK BETTER OF IT. SINCE NICOLE MOVED OUT, MY MOTIVATION HAS BEEN SHOT, AND I KNOW I'LL NEED THE MONEY SOON.
SATURDAY MORNING, I PICK UP THE SUPPLIES I NEED AND HEAD ACROSS THE BRIDGE. MY DAD AND HIS GIRLFRIEND MEET ME AT THE HOUSE TO LET ME IN AND TO MOVE A FEW LAST PIECES OF FURNITURE.
I HAVEN'T BEEN INSIDE THE HOUSE IN YEARS. ESPECIALLY WITH EVERYTHING GONE, IT SEEMS COMPLETELY UNFAMILIAR. THE CEILINGS ARE HIGH, BUT OTHERWISE, IT'S A PRETTY STANDARD JOB.

Adrian Tomine

I STARE INTENTLY AT THE IMAGES, TREMBLING AND OVERWHELMED. I STUDY EACH ONE. I DON'T MOVE UNTIL I HEAR THE CLICK OF THE FRONT DOOR UNLOCKING.
HEY, DAD?
YEAH? WHAT'S THE MATTER?
I WAS JUST WONDERING... WHAT WAS IN HERE WHEN YOU GUYS CLEANED IT OUT? I DON'T THINK I WAS ALLOWED BACK HERE AS A KID...
WHAT WAS...
NOTHING, REALLY. JUST A BUNCH OF MY DAD'S OLD JUNK...
WE THREW MOST OF IT OUT.
FOR THE FIRST TIME IN AWHILE, I LAUGH OUT LOUD. IT ECHOES AROUND THE ROOM, AND I START PAINTING.
TOMINE

DON'T MAKE SACRIFICES
OUR KING WOULD LIKE YOU TO BE AN OFFICIAL FOR THE STATE.
SORRY...
DO YOU SEE THAT SACRIFICIAL COW OVER THERE? EVERY DAY IT EATS THE BEST FEED AND IS COVERED BY A BEAUTIFULLY EMBROIDERED BLANKET...
BUT WHEN THE DAY COMES FOR IT TO BE BROUGHT INTO THE TEMPLE AND LAID UPON THE SACRIFICIAL ALTAR, IT WILL BE TOO LATE FOR ITS SUDDEN WISH TO GO BACK TO THE PASTURE AND LIVE LIKE THE REST OF THE COWS.

C. C. Tsai

ZHUANGZI ON HIS DEATHBED
WHEN ZHUANGZI WAS ON HIS DEATHBED, HIS DISCIPLES GATHERED AROUND AND TALKED ABOUT HONORING HIM WITH AN ELABORATE FUNERAL.
WHY BOTHER? AFTER I DIE, JUST USE HEAVEN AND EARTH AS MY COFFIN; USE THE SUN AND MOON AS BURIAL JADES, THE STARS AS JEWELS, AND EVERYTHING ELSE AROUND ME AS RITUAL WARE. WHAT FUNERAL COULD BE BETTER THAN THAT?
BUT MASTER, THE CROWS AND VULTURES WILL GET YOU.
ABOVE GROUND, THE CROWS AND VULTURES WILL GET ME. BELOW GROUND, THE WORMS AND ANTS WILL GET ME. WHY DO YOU INSIST ON TAKING FOOD OUT OF THE MOUTHS OF CROWS AND VULTURES AND GIVING IT TO WORMS AND ANTS?
DEATH IS A NATURAL DISPERSION AND TRANSFORMATION OF THE BODY, SO WHY NOT LET NATURE HANDLE IT?

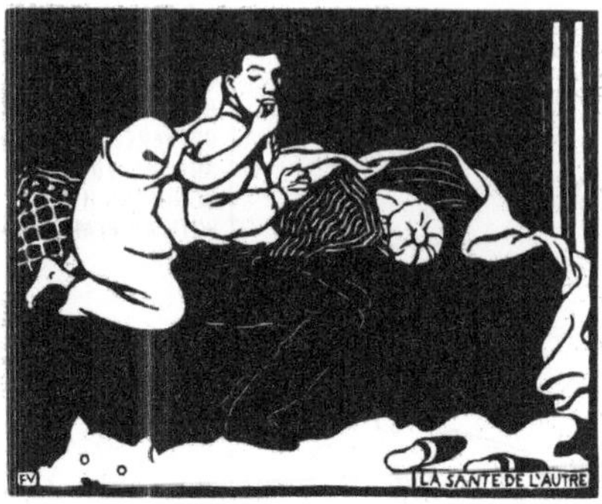

Felix Valloton

L'IRREPARABLE
FV

CINQ HEURES
FV

LA BELLE EPINGLE
FV

APPRETS DE VISITE
FV

FV
LA RAISON PROBANTE

WORKS CITED

Abel, Jessica (2008), *La Perdida*, New York: Pantheon.

Abel, Jessica, and Matt Madden (2008), *Drawing Worlds and Writing Pictures*, New York: First Second.

Alagbé, Yvan (2018), *Yellow Negroes and Other Imaginary Creatures*, New York: New York Review Comics.

Alphona, Adrian, and G. Willow Wilson (2014) *Ms. Marvel: No Normal*, New York: Marvel.

Barry, Lynda (2011), *Everything: Comics from around 1978–1981*, Montreal: Drawn & Quarterly.

Barry, Lynda (2014), *Syllabus,* Montreal: Drawn & Quarterly.

Barry, Lynda (2017), *One! Hundred! Demons!*, Montreal: Drawn & Quarterly.

Barry, Lynda (2019), *Making Comics,* Montreal: Drawn & Quarterly.

Beaty, Bart (2012), *Comics versus Art*, Toronto: University of Toronto Press.

Bechdel, Alison (2006), *Fun Home*. Boston: Mariner.

Bechdel, Alison (2008), *The Essential Dykes to Watch Out For,* New York: Houghton Mifflin.

Bendis, Brian Michael (2014), *Words for Pictures: The Art and Business of Writing Comics and Graphic Novels*, Berkeley: Watson-Guptill.

Bertram, John, and Yuri Leving, eds. (2013), *Lolita: The Story of a Cover Girl*, Blue Ash, Ohio: Print Books.

Brosgol, Vera (2011), *Anya's Ghost,* New York: Square Fish.

Brunetti, Ivan (2011), *Cartooning: Philosophy and Practice*, New Haven: Yale University Press.

Burns, Charles (2005), *Black Hole*, New York: Pantheon.

Busiek, Kurt, and Brent Anderson (1998), *Astro City*, Vol. 2, No. ½, January, New York: Homage Comics.

Cameron, Peter (2010), "The End of My Life in New York," *PEN/O. Henry Prize Stories 2010,* New York: Anchor.

Chast, Roz (2014), *Can't We Talk About Something More PLEASANT?*, New York: Bloomsbury.

Chute, Hillary, and Marianne DeKoven (2006), "Introduction: Graphic Narrative," *Modern Fiction Studies*, Vol. 52, No. 4, pp. 767–82

Cohn, Neil (2013), *The Visual Language of Comics*, London: Bloomsbury.

Cooke, Jon B. and George Khoury, eds. (2014), *Comic Book Creator: Swampmen*, 6, Raleigh, North Carolina: Tomorrows Publishing.

Comeau, Michael (2018), *Winter Cosmos*, Toronto: Koyama Press.

Corman, Leela (2012), *Unterzahkn,* New York: Schocken.

D'Salete, Marcelo (2019), *Angola Janga,* Seattle: Fantagraphics Books.

Dabaie, Marguerite (2018), *The Hookah Girl and Other True Stories*, Greenbelt, Maryland: Rosarium Publishing.

Davis, Eleanor (2014), *How to be Happy,* Seattle: Fantagraphics Books.

Daw, Dash (2010), *Body World*, New York: Pantheon.

Dean, Michael (2000), "The Image Story, Part One: Forming an Image," *The Comics Journal* No. 222 (April).

Delporte, Julie (2019), *This Woman's Work*, Montreal: Drawn & Quarterly.

Dhaliwal, Aminder (2018), *Woman World,* Montreal: Drawn & Quarterly.

Dixon, Kent, and Kevin Dixon (2018), *The Epic of Gilgamesh,* New York: Seven Stories Press.

Drasno, Nick (2018), *Sabrina*, Montreal: Drawn & Quarterly.

Egan, Jennifer (2011), *A Visit from the Goon Squad*, New York: Knopf.

Eisner, Will (2001), *Will Eisner's The Spirit Archives*, vol. 3, New York: DC.

Eisner, Will (2008), *Comics and Sequential Art: Principles and Practices from the Legendary Artist*. New York: Norton.

Eisner, Will (2008a), *Graphic Storytelling and Visual Narrative*. New York: Norton.

Ernst, Max (1976), *Une Semaine De Bonte: A Surrealistic Novel in Collage*, Mineola, New York: Dover Publications.

Estrada, Inés (2019), *Alienation*, Seattle: Fantagraphics Books.

Evans, Kate (2017), *Threads: From the Refugee Crisis*, London: Verso.

Feiffer, Jules (2003), *The Great Comic Book Heroes*, Seattle: Fantagraphics Books.

Finck, Liana (2018), *Passing for Human,* New York: Random House.

Fortress, Karl E. (1963), "The Comics as Non-Art," in David Manning White and Robert H. Abel (eds.), *The Funnies: An American Idiom*, New York: The Free Press.

Foster-Dimino, Sophia (2017), *Sex Fantasy,* Toronto: Koyama Press.

French, Renée (2007), *micrographica*, Marietta, Georgia: Top Shelf.

Frost, Elisabeth, and Dianne Kornberg (2015), *Bindle*, Los Angeles, California: Ricochet Editions.

Furmark, Anneli (2018), *Red Winter*, Montreal: Drawn & Quarterly.

GG (2017), *I'm Not Here*, Toronto: Koyama Press.

Garner, Dwight (2010), "The Curies, Seen Through an Artist's Eyes," *New York Times*, December 21. Available online: https://www.nytimes.com/2010/12/22/books/22book.html (accessed October 28, 2019).

Gertler, Nat, ed. (2002), *Panel One: Comic Book Scripts by Top Writers*, Thousand Oaks, California: About Comics.

Gillen, Kieron, and Jamie McKelvie (2013), *Phonograph: The Singles Club,* Berkeley, California: Image.

Goldstein, Sophie (2015), *The Oven*, Richmond, Virginia: AdHouse Books.

Groensteen, Thierry (2007), *The System of Comics*, trans. Bart Beaty and Nick Nguyen, Jackson: University Press of Mississippi.

Groensteen, Thierry (2013), *Comics and Narration*, trans. Ann Miller. Jackson: University Press of Mississippi.

Hankiewicz, John (2006), *Asthma*, Portland, OR: Sparkplug Books.

Hart, Christopher (2007), *Simplified Anatomy for the Comic Book Artist: How to Draw the New Streamlined Look of Action-Adventure Comics!*, New York: Watson-Guptill.

Hernandez, Jaime (1985), *Music for Mechanics*, Seattle: Fantagraphics Books.

Hopkins, Gareth A., and Erik Blagsvedt (2017), *Found Forest Floor,* 7tNbjV.

Illustration Class (2012), "Comics MFA? There is an alternative. . . No Joke," Illustration Concentration. Available online: https://illustrationconcentration.com/2012/12/20/comics-mfa-there-is-an-alternative-no-joke/ (accessed November 9, 2016).
Jacobs, Mira (2019), *Good Talk,* New York: One World.
Johnson, R. Kikuo (2005), *Night Fisher,* Seattle: Fantagraphics Books.
Kane, Bob, et al. (2006), *The Batman Chronicles*, vol. 1, New York: DC.
Katin, Miriam (2006), *We Are On Our Own*, Montreal: Drawn & Quarterly.
Kirkman, Robert, and Tony Moore (2003), *The Walking Dead, Volume I: Days Gone Bye,* Berkeley, California: Image.
Kornberg, Dianne, and Celia Bland (2014), *Madonna Comix*, Portland, OR: Media F8.
Lee, Hannah K. (2017), *Language Barrier*, Toronto: Koyama Press.
Lee, Stan, and John Buscema (1984), *How to Draw the Marvel Way*, New York: Simon & Schuster.
Lefèvre, Pascal (2009), "The Construction of Space in Comics," Jeet Heer and Kent Worcester (eds.), *A Comics Studies Reader*, Jackson: University of Mississippi Press.
Lewis, John, Andrew Aydin, and Nate Powell (2015), *March: Book 2,* Marietta, Georgia: Top Shelf.
Libicki, Miriam (2008), *Jobnik!,* Coquitlam, Canada: Real Gone Girls.
Libicki, Miriam (2016), *Toward a Hot Jew*, Seattle: Fantagraphics Books.
Lightman, Sarah (2019), *The Book of Sarah,* University Park, Pennsylvania: Pennsylvania State University Press.
Matisse, Henry (1985), *Jazz,* New York: George Braziller.
Ma, Daishu (2015), *Leaf,* Seattle: Fantagraphics Books.
Madden, Matt (2005), *99 Ways to Tell a Story: Exercises in Style*, New York: Chamberlain Bros.
Mag Uidhir, Christy (2014), "Comics and Collective Authorship," Aaron Meskin and Roy T. Cook (eds.), *The Art of Comics: A Philosophical Approach*, Oxford: Wiley Blackwell.
Mateu-Mestre, Marcos (2010), *Framed Ink: Drawing and Composition for Visual Storytelling,* Culver City, CA: Design Studio Press.
Mazzucchelli, David (2009), *Asterios Polyp*, New York: Pantheon.
McCloud, Scott (1993), *Understanding Comics: The Invisible Art*, New York: Kitchen Sink.
McCloud, Scott (2006), *Making Comics: Storytelling Secrets of Comics, Manga and Graphic Novels*, New York: Harper.
McFarlane, Todd, and Bob Wiacek (1988), cover art, *The Incredible Hulk,* No. 340, New York: Marvel.
McGuire, Richard (2014), *Here*, New York: Pantheon.
Mendelsund, Peter (2014), *What We See When We Read*, New York: Vintage.
Miller, Frank, and Bill Sienkiewicz (2012), *Elektra: Assassin*, New York: Marvel.
Mitchell, W. T. J. (1996), 'Word and Image', Robert S. Nelson and Richard Shiff (eds.), *Critical Terms for Art History*, Chicago: University of Chicago Press.
Mitchell, W. T. J. (2014), "Comics as Media: Afterword," *Critical Inquiry*, Vol. 40, No. 3, pp. 255–65.
Molotiu, Andrei (2009), *Abstract Comics*, Seattle: Fantagraphics Books.
Moon, Fábio, and Gabriel Bá (2011), *Daytripper,* New York: Vertigo.

Moore, Alan (2008), *Alan Moore's Writing for Comics*, Rantoul, Illinois: Avatar.
Moore, Alan, and Dave Gibbons (1987), *Watchmen*, New York: DC.
Morales, Robert, and Kyle Baker (2004), *Truth: Red, White and Black*, New York: Marvel.
Muñoz, José, and Carlos Sampayo (2017), *Alack Sinner,* San Diego: EuroComics.
Muth, Jon J. (1986), *Dracula: A Symphony in Moonlight and Nightmares,* New York: Marvel.
Muth, Jon J. (2008), *M*, New York: Abrams.
Nickerson, Sylvia (2019), *Creation*, Montreal: Drawn & Quarterly.
Nilsen, Anders (2015), *Poetry Is Useless,* Montreal: Drawn & Quarterly.
North, Sterling (1941), "The Antidote to Comics," *National Parent Teacher Magazine* (March), pp. 16–17.
O'Neil, Dennis (2001), *The DC Comics Guide to Writing Comics*, New York: DC.
Ott, Thomas (2010), *R.I.P.: Best of 1988–2004*, Seattle: Fantagraphics Books.
Percy, Benjamin (2016), "Superpowered Storytelling: What I've Learned from Writing Comics," *Poets & Writers*, Vol. 44, No. 4, pp. 25–8.
Pérez, George, et al. (2007), *Wonder Woman: The Greatest Stories Ever Told*, New York: DC.
Putnam, Hilary (1981), *Reason, Truth, and History*, New York: Cambridge University Press.
Pyle, Kevin (2012), *Take What You Can Carry*, New York: Square Fish.
Radtke, Kristen (2017) *Imagine Wanting Only This,* New York: Pantheon.
Redniss, Lauren (2015), *Radioactive: Marie & Pierre Curie: A Tale of Love and Fallout*, New York: Dey Street Books.
Roberts, Keiler (2018), *Chlorine Gardens,* Toronto: Koyama Press.
Rose, Lloyd (1986), "Comic Books for Grown-ups," *Atlantic Monthly*, Vol. 258, No. 2, pp. 77–80.
Rothman, Alexander (2015). "What is Comics Poetry?," *Indiana Review*. Available online: https://indianareview.org/2015/06/what-is-comics-poetry-by-alexander-rothman/ (accessed November 13, 2016).
Rucka, Greg, and J. H. Williams III (2010), *Batwoman: Elegy,* New York: DC.
Saenz, Mike (1988), *Crash,* New York: Marvel.
Sante, Luc (2015). "Richard McGuire's *Here*," *The New York Times*, October 12. Available online: http://www.nytimes.com/2015/10/18/books/review/richard-mcguires-here.html?_r=0 (accessed November 14, 2016).
Santoro, Frank (2019), *Pittsburgh*, New York: New York Review Comics.
Satrapi, Marjane (2003), *Persepolis,* New York: Pantheon.
Seth (2004). "An Interview with Seth," *Bookslut*. Available online: http://www.bookslut.com/features/2004_06_002650.php (accessed November 13, 2016).
Seth (2004), *It's a Good Life, If You Don't Weaken,* Montreal: Drawn & Quarterly.
Shapton, Leanne (2016), *Was She Pretty?,* Montreal: Drawn & Quarterly.
Siciliano, Gina (2019), *I Know What I Am: The Life and Times of Artemisia Gentileschi,* Seattle: Fantagraphics Books.
Sikoryak, Robert (2017), *Terms and Conditions,* Montreal: Drawn & Quarterly.
Small, David (2009), *Stitches*, New York: Norton.
Smolderen, Thierry (2014), *The Origins of Comics: From William Hogarth to Winsor McCay*, trans. Bart Beaty and Nick Ngyen, Jackson: University of Mississippi.

Smyth, Fiona (2018), *Somnambulance*, Toronto: Koyama Press.
Spiegelman, Art (1991), "A Problem of Taxonomy," *The New York Times*, December 29. Available online: http://www.nytimes.com/1991/12/29/books/l-a-problem-of-taxonomy-37092.html (accessed December 16, 2016).
Stelfreeze, Brian, and Ta-Nehisi Coates (2016), *Black Panther: A Nation Under Our Feet*, New York: Marvel.
Steranko, Jim (2013), *S.H.I.E.L.D by Steranko: The Complete Collection,* New York: Marvel.
Steranko, Jim (2014), *Marvel Masterworks: Captain America,* New York: Marvel.
Stone, Bianca (2016), *Poetry Comics,* Warrensburg, Missouri: Pleiades Press.
Tamaki, Jillian (2015), *SuperMutant Magic Academy*, Montreal: Drawn & Quarterly.
Tamaki, Jillian, and Mariko Tamaki (2014), *This One Summer,* New York: First Second.
Tamaki, Mariko, and Jillian Tamaki (2008), *Skim*, Toronto: Groundwood Books.
Thompson, Craig (2015), *Blankets,* Montreal: Drawn & Quarterly.
Tobocman, Seth (2009), *You Don't Have to Fuck People Over to Survive,* Oakland, California: AK Press.
Todorov, Tzvetan (1969), "Structural Analysis of Narrative," trans. Arnold Weinstein, *NOVEL: A Forum on Fiction*, Vol. 3, No. 1, pp. 70–6.
Tomine, Adrian (1997), *Sleepwalk and Other Stories*, Montreal: Drawn & Quarterly.
Tomine, Adrian (2015), *Killing and Dying*, Montreal: Drawn & Quarterly.
Tsai, C. C., and Zhuangzi (2019), *The Way of Nature*, Princeton, New Jersey: Princeton University Press.
Van Winckel, Nance (2016), *Book of No Ledge,* Warrensburg, Missouri: Pleiades Press.
Vlamos, James Frank (1941), "The Sad Case of the Funnies," *American Mercury*, (April), p. 411.
Vonnegut, Kurt (1999), *Bagombo Snuff Box*, New York: Putnam.
Waid, Mark, and Alex Ross (1997), *Kingdom Come*, New York: DC.
Walker, Mort (2000), *The Lexicon of Comicana*, Lincoln, Nebraska: Authors Guild.
Ware, Chris (1991) "I Guess," *Raw*, Vol. 2, No. 3. Available online: https://fromdusktilldrawnblog.wordpress.com/2016/09/18/i-guess-by-chris-ware-usa-1990/ (accessed October 8, 2019).
Warhol, Robyn (2011), "The Space Between: A Narrative Approach to Alison Bechdel's *Fun Home*," *College Literature*, Vol. 38, No. 3, pp. 1–20.
Wartenberg, Thomas E. (2012), "Wordy Pictures: Theorizing the Relationship between Image and Text in Comics," Aaron Meshkin and Roy T. Cook (eds.), *The Art of Comics: A Philosophical Approach*, Oxford: Wiley Blackwell.
Wein, Len, and Sal Buscema (2006), *Essential Defenders*, Vol. 2, New York: Marvel.
Wertham, Frederic (1954), *Seduction of the Innocent*, New York: Rinehart.
Wolk, Douglas (2007), *Reading Comics: How Graphic Novels Work and What They Mean*, Cambridge, MA: Da Capo Press.
Worcester, Kent, ed. (2016), *Silent Agitators: Cartoon Art from the Pages of* New Politics, New York: New Politics.

Wordsworth, William (1908), *The Poems of Williams Wordsworth*, London: Methuen.
Wrightson, Bernie, and Gaspar Saladino (1972), cover art, *Swamp Thing,* No. 1, New York: DC.
Yang, Gene Luen (2006), *American Born Chinese,* New York: Square Fish.

INDEX

Page numbers in **bold** refer to illustrations